W9-BZC-145

iPhone For Seniors

FOR

DUMMIES®

A Wiley Brand

4th Edition

iPhone For Seniors

FOR

DUMMIES®

A Wiley Brand

4th Edition

by Nancy Muir

FOR

DUMMIES®

A Wiley Brand

iPhone For Seniors For Dummies® 4th Edition

Published by: **John Wiley & Sons, Inc.,** 111 River Street, Hoboken, NJ 07030-5774, www.wiley.com

Copyright © 2015 by John Wiley & Sons, Inc., Hoboken, New Jersey

Published simultaneously in Canada

No part of this publication may be reproduced, stored in a retrieval system or transmitted in any form or by any means, electronic, mechanical, photocopying, recording, scanning or otherwise, except as permitted under Sections 107 or 108 of the 1976 United States Copyright Act, without the prior written permission of the Publisher. Requests to the Publisher for permission should be addressed to the Permissions Department, John Wiley & Sons, Inc., 111 River Street, Hoboken, NJ 07030, (201) 748-6011, fax (201) 748-6008, or online at http://www.wiley.com/go/permissions.

Trademarks: Wiley, For Dummies, the Dummies Man logo, Dummies.com, Making Everything Easier, and related trade dress are trademarks or registered trademarks of John Wiley & Sons, Inc. and may not be used without written permission. iPhone is a registered trademark of Apple, Inc. All other trademarks are the property of their respective owners. John Wiley & Sons, Inc. is not associated with any product or vendor mentioned in this book.

For general information on our other products and services, please contact our Customer Care Department within the U.S. at 877-762-2974, outside the U.S. at 317-572-3993, or fax 317-572-4002. For technical support, please visit www.wiley.com/techsupport.

Wiley publishes in a variety of print and electronic formats and by print-on-demand. Some material included with standard print versions of this book may not be included in e-books or in print-on-demand. If this book refers to media such as a CD or DVD that is not included in the version you purchased, you may download this material at http://booksupport.wiley.com. For more information about Wiley products, visit www.wiley.com.

Library of Congress Control Number: 2014945054

ISBN 978-1-118-94444-8 (pbk); ISBN 978-1-118-94445-5 (ebk); ISBN 978-1-118-94446-2 (ebk)

Manufactured in the United States of America

10 9 8 7 6 5 4 3 2 1

Contents at a Glance

Table of Contents

*I*f you bought this book (or are even thinking about buying it), you've probably already made the decision to buy an iPhone. The iPhone is designed to be easy to use, but still you can spend hours exploring the preinstalled apps, finding out how to change settings, and figuring out how to sync the device to your computer or through iCloud. I've invested those hours so that you don't have to — and I've added advice and tips for getting the most out of your iPhone.

This book helps you get going with the iPhone quickly and painlessly so that you can move directly to the fun part.

About This Book

This book is specifically written for mature people like you, folks who may be relatively new to using a smartphone and want to discover the basics of buying an iPhone 6 or 6 Plus, making and receiving phone calls, working with its preinstalled apps, and getting on the Internet. In writing this book, I've tried to consider the types of activities that might interest someone who is 50 years old or older and picking up an iPhone for the first time.

Conventions Used in This Book

This book uses certain conventions to help you find your way around, including

⟫ Text you type is shown in **bold**. Figure references, such as "see **Figure 1-1**," are also in bold, to help you find them.

⟫ Whenever I mention a website address, or *URL*, I put it in a different font, `like this`.

⟫ Figure callouts draw your attention to actions you need to perform. In some cases, points of interest in a figure may be indicated. The text tells you what to look for; the callout line makes it easy to find.

⟫ When I tell you to follow a series of actions, I string them together with arrows, like this: Settings⇨General⇨Device, which means to tap Settings, tap General, and then tap Device.

 Tip icons point out insights or helpful suggestions related to tasks in the step lists.

 New icons highlight features of iPhone 6s, iPhone 6 Plus, or iOS 8 that are new and exciting, in case you're moving up from earlier versions.

Foolish Assumptions

This book is organized by sets of tasks. These tasks start from the beginning, assuming that you've never laid your hands on an iPhone, and guide you through basic steps provided in nontechnical language.

This book covers going online using either a Wi-Fi or 3G/4G connection. I'm also assuming that you'll want to use the iBooks e-reader app, so I cover its features in Chapter 14, and that you might be interested in the new Health app, so I give you an overview of it in Chapter 20.

Why You Need This Book

The iPhone 6 and 6 Plus are cool and perfect for many seniors because they provide a simple, intuitive interface for making and receiving calls, and also for activities such as checking email and playing music. The less expensive iPhone 6 has just about all the features of the iPhone Plus, except that the iPhone 6 Plus is larger and its large screen offers some variety in what certain apps can fit on the screen. But why should you stumble around, trying to figure out their features? Following the simple, step-by-step approach used in this book, you can get up to speed with the iPhone right away as well as overcome any technophobia you might have.

How This Book Is Organized

This book is conveniently divided into several handy parts to help you find what you need:

➡ **Part I: Making the iPhone Work for You:** If you're about to buy your iPhone or are ready to get started with the basics of using it, this part is for you. These chapters highlight the newest features in iPhone 6, iPhone 6 Plus, and iOS 8 (the phones' latest operating system) and help you explore the different specifications, styles, and price ranges for all iPhone models. You find out how to set up your iPhone 6 or 6 Plus out of the box, including

- Opening an iCloud account to register and push content to all your Apple devices automatically.

- Opening an iTunes account to buy entertainment content and additional apps.

  These chapters also provide information for exploring the iPhone Home screen when you first turn the phone on, for using the Control Center and Notification Center features, and for working with useful accessibility features to help out if you have hearing or vision challenges, including the new Apple QuickType feature for the onscreen key-board. Finally, you explore the ability to pick up where you left off with the new Handoff feature.

➡ **Part II: Start Using Your iPhone:** In this part, you discover the basics of making and receiving calls — this is a phone, after all! You find out how to set up and manage your contacts, how to get the most out of some useful utility apps, and how to take advantage of iPhone's accessibility features for those who have vision, hearing, or motor skill challenges.

In this part, you're also introduced to Siri, the iPhone's useful feature that allows you to talk to your phone and have it respond by providing information and performing tasks for you. You also explore the exciting FaceTime feature, used for making video calls to other people and how to set up ringtones.

FaceTime works with people who use the iPhone 4, 4s or later; iPad 2 or later; an iPad mini; an iPod touch (fourth generation or later); or a Mac running OS X, 10.6.6 or later.

➠ You get acquainted with AirDrop, a feature compatible with iPhone 5 or later for sharing content with somebody nearby, and new multitasking features.

➠ Finally, you discover how integrated features for using Twitter, Facebook, and iMessage (the latter is accessed via the Messages instant-messaging app, which has several new features in iOS 8) help you to connect with others.

➠ **Part III: Taking the Leap Online:** Here, you find out how to connect to the Internet and use the built-in Safari browser and the stylish Tab view. You putter with the preinstalled Mail app that has some great email management features in its latest version, and set up your iPhone to access email from your existing email accounts. In this part, you also get to shop online at the iTunes Store for multimedia content, such as movies and music, and shop the App Store for additional iPhone apps. The new Family Sharing feature lets you allow up to six people in your family to purchase and share content using the same credit card.

➠ **Part IV: Having Fun and Consuming Media:** The iPhone has been touted by some as a great device for consuming media such as music (including the all new iTunes Radio), podcasts, and movies. Included with every iPhone are a Music app for playing music and the Videos app for watching video content. In addition, in this part, I explain how to use iBooks, the free e-reader app from Apple. You also explore playing games on your iPhone, which — trust me — is a lot of fun, and I help you experiment with the Maps app to find your favorite restaurant or bookstore with ease. You also discover the wonderful possibilities for using still and video cameras on iPhone, including sharing via photo streams and using new filters for taking photos. The latest Photos app provides collections for viewing your images by year or location where they were taken, and the ability to share them via the iCloud Photo Library. The improved camera features on iPhone 6 and 6 Plus offer slow motion for video and burst mode for capturing as much as 20 photos per second.

In this part, you also explore the Newsstand app for subscribing to and reading magazines, and the interesting new Health app that provides tools for tracking your activities and sharing information with your health provider.

➠ **Part V: Managing Your Life and Your iPhone:** For the organizational part of your brain, the iPhone makes available Calendar, Notification Center, Reminders, and Notes apps, all of which are covered in this part.

The Reminders app and Notification Center feature are also great for keeping you on schedule. Reminders is a great to-do list feature that allows you to enter tasks and details about them and can also display tasks from your online calendars. Notification Center lists all your alerts and reminders in one place.

Finally, I offer advice in this part about keeping your iPhone safe and troubleshooting common problems that you might encounter, including using the Find My iPhone feature to deal with a lost or stolen iPhone and using the new Touch ID fingerprint sensor. You can also use the iCloud service to back up your content or restore your iPhone.

Where to Go from Here

You can work through this book from beginning to end or simply open a chapter to solve a problem or acquire a specific new skill whenever you need it. The steps in every task quickly get you to where you want to go, without a lot of technical explanation.

Note: At the time I wrote this book, all the information it contained was accurate for the iPhone 4s, 5, 5s, and 5c, 6 and 6 Plus and version 8 of the iOS (operating system) used by the iPhone, and version 11 of iTunes. Apple is likely to introduce new iPhone models and new versions of iOS and iTunes between book editions. If you've bought a new iPhone and found that its hardware, user interface, or the version of iTunes on your computer looks a little different, be sure to check out what Apple has to say at www.apple.com/iphone. You'll no doubt find updates on the company's latest releases. When a change is very substantial, we may add an update or bonus information that you can download at this book's companion web site, www.dummies.com/go/iphoneforseniors.

Part I

Making the iPhone Work for You

Buying Your iPhone

You've read about it. You've seen on the news the lines at Apple Stores on the day a new version of the iPhone is released. You're so intrigued that you've decided to get your own iPhone to have a smartphone that offers much more than the ability to make and receive calls. iPhone also offers lots of fun apps such as games and exercise trackers; allows you to explore the online world; lets you read e-books, magazines, and periodicals; lets you organize your photos; and a lot more.

Trust me: You've made a good decision, because the iPhone redefines the mobile phone experience in an exciting way. It's also an absolutely perfect fit for many seniors.

In this chapter, you learn about the advantages of the iPhone, as well as where to buy this little gem and associated data plans from providers. After you have one in your hands, I help you explore what's in the box and get an overview of the little buttons and slots you'll encounter — luckily, the iPhone has very few of them.

Get ready to . . .

Discover What's New in iPhone 6 and 6 Plus, and iOS 8

Apple's iPhone gets its features from a combination of hardware and its software operating system (called *iOS*; the term is short for iPhone operating system. The most current operating system is iOS 8. It's helpful to understand which new features the iPhone 6 and 6 Plus phones and iOS 8 bring to the table (all of which are covered in more detail in this book). New features in iPhone 6 and 6 Plus include

➡ **Larger size:** Both new iPhone models are larger than previous models, while also being thinner. iPhone 6 measures 4.7" diagonally, while iPhone 6 Plus measures 5.5".

➡ **Improved display:** Apple claims that the new iPhone screens have higher contrast, brighter backlights, and a feature called dual domain pixels, which allows you to follow broader angle views of what's on your screen. In addition, the phones sport "ion-strengthened" cover glass. Their Retina HD (high definition) display is supposedly their brightest, crispest display ever.

➡ **An A8 chip:** This second-generation 64-bit chip contains 2 billion transistors, versus only 1 billion on its predecessor, the A7 chip. That means that the computer processing unit runs 25 percent faster while being 50 percent more energy efficient.

➡ **An M8 coprocessor:** This updated motion sensing coprocessor makes it possible for your iPhone to detect and monitor data that provides information about your motion. It's expected that this capability will enable lots of interesting new fitness apps, including the new Health app from Apple.

➤ **New gestures:** Because of the new, larger screens on iPhone 6 and 6 Plus, a "reachability" gesture allows you to press the Home button twice and have the display slide down, closer to your thumb for one-handed tapping. Also, bezel gestures allow you to start a gesture at the side of the glass display to move forward or backward.

➤ **Adjusted buttons:** The volume buttons have been elongated to make them easier to find. In addition, the Sleep/Wake button has been moved from the top to the side to make it easier to reach.

➤ **Support of Voice over LTE:** This feature improves the quality of calls, allowing simultaneous transmission of voice and data (translation: you'll hear the other person better than before). Improved noise reduction in the latest iPhones also helps you hear what's being said on calls.

➤ **An 8mp iSight camera:** The camera in iPhone 6 and 6 Plus offers features such as a True Tone Flash sensor that knows when flash is needed for a shot; Phase Detection Autofocus that is two times faster at automatically refocusing your camera; and improved stabilization, so you won't get those fuzzy shots as often.

➤ **Camera frames per second:** The camera offers video quality at 1080 pixels with 30 frames per second or 60 frames per second. The Slo-mo video feature allows you to take 240 frames per second.

➤ **Video improvements:** Features including Cinematic Video Stablization (this continually autofocuses while you're recording), improved face detection, new sensors, and a larger aperture make these iPhones the best ever at video recording.

➡ **Apple Pay:** With these new phones comes the ability to pay at selected retailers using the Apple Pay feature and Touch ID feature built into the Home button. You use credit cards stored at the iTunes Store and your fingerprint to make these transactions.

➡ **Improved battery life:** The iPhone 6 supports up to 24 hours of talk and up to 14 hours of video viewing. The 6 Plus can give you as many as 14 hours of talk and 11 hours of video.

 Throughout this book, I highlight features that are relevant only in using the iPhone 4s, 5s and/or iPhone 5c, as well as 6 and 6 Plus, so you can use the majority of this book no matter which version of the iPhone you own as long as you have iOS 8 installed.

Any iPhone device more recent than the iPhone 4s can make use of most features of iOS 8 if you update the operating system (discussed in detail in Chapter 2); this book is based on version 8 of iOS. This update to the operating system adds many new features, including

➡ **Family Sharing:** Apple has provided a new feature called Family Sharing with iOS 8. This feature allows up to six people to partake of purchased iTunes content on their separate devices. You can also create a Family calendar, which helps everybody in the family create and view upcoming family events,

➡ **Continuity:** This concept, being promoted with iOS 8, allows you to move from one iOS device to another to pick up where you left off using a feature called Handoff. For example, you might start to watch a TV show on your iPhone on the train but then pick up where you left off viewing the movie on your iPad when you get home. You can even hand off a document and start where you left off on another device.

➠ **The Health app:** Use this new app as a health information aggregator so that all your medical and fitness information can be stored and accessed in one place. As new apps and medical or fitness equipment are developed to work with this app, it will become even more valuable and allow you to interact with your physician more easily.

➠ **Improved Notification Center:** Notification Center is a centralized location for reviewing things like calendar appointments, messages, and weather. With iOS 8, you can interact with notifications from the Control Center — for example, by replying to a message listed there — and access Notification Center from the Lock screen (the screen that appears when your iPhone has essentially gone to sleep).

➠ **Mail improvements:** In iOS 8, you can access other email messages while composing a new message. You are prompted to add an event mentioned in an email to your Calendar app. You can also flag, mark, or delete email by simply dragging across the screen to access those commands.

➠ **QuickType for iPhone keyboard:** Now the iPhone onscreen keyboard uses predictive technology to suggest words as you type. The keyboard also notes whether you're typing an email or message and makes suggestions based on the tone of voice that each type of message calls for.

➠ **Improvements to the Photos app:** To help you organize your photos, in iOS 8 you can now use iCloud to share photos with others in your iCloud Photo Library. Photos or videos can also be shared among up to six devices using Family Sharing. There are also several improved tools for editing photos in iOS 8.

➠ **Shazam:** Shazam is a music identifier service built into iOS 8 that allows Siri to identify songs as they play.

➡ **Messaging:** The Messages app has some improvements. For example, you can organize messages into groups, name threads of messages, and remove people from conversations. You can also set up a Do Not Disturb feature for certain threads so that you're not interrupted by messages on those threads, and you can record and send voice messages. Finally, you can read or listen to messages from the Lock screen.

➡ **Siri Hands-Free:** If you are driving or otherwise occupied and want help from Siri, such as getting directions or to send a message, you can use a new feature to open Siri without touching your iPhone. With this feature enabled and the phone plugged into a power source, all you have to do is say "Hey, Siri," and your electronic personal assistant opens, ready to hear your wish, which is, of course, his or her command.

➡ **Instant hotspot:** You've been able to use your iPhone as a hotspot in the past, essentially using your iPhone connection to get other devices online. With iOS 8, this personal hotspot is improved; nearby devices such as a computer now automatically display the iPhone as an optional network that you can join to go online.

Choose the Right iPhone for You

iPhone 6, measuring 4.7" diagonally and 6.9 mm thick, is bigger and thinner than previous iPhones with their 4" screen (see **Figure 1-1**). iPhone 6 Plus is even bigger at 5.5" and only slightly thicker than iPhone 6, at 7.1 mm thick. You can get iPhone 6 or 6 Plus in gold, silver, or space gray. Because of its large screen, iPhone 6 Plus also supports new, expanded views of the Home screen and some apps when you hold it in a horizontal orientation. Other differences between iPhone models come primarily from the current iOS, iOS 8.

Figure 1-1

iPhone 6 and 6 Plus models have a few variations:

➠ Color of the phone (silver, gold, and space gray).

➠ Amount of built-in memory, ranging from 16GB to 128GB.

➠ Screen resolution (the higher the resolution, the crisper and brighter the phone display). The iPhone 6 provides 1334 x 750 resolution (more than 1 million pixels) and 6 Plus provides 1920 x 1080 (more than 2 million pixels).

Read on as I explain these variations in more detail in the following sections.

Table 1-1 gives you a quick comparison of iPhone 5s, 5c, 6, and 6 Plus. All costs are as of the time this book was written.

Table 1-1		iPhone Model Comparison	
Model	**Memory**	**Cost (with a Two-Year Contract)**	**Carriers**
5s	16, 32, and 64GB	$99 and $149 with contract	AT&T, Verizon, Sprint, contract free with T-Mobile
5c	16 and 32GB	Free with contract, unlocked through T-Mobile $549 and $649	AT&T, Verizon, Sprint, contract free with T-Mobile
6	16, 64, and 128GB	$199, $299, $399 with contract; $649, $749, and $849 unlocked (no contract)	AT&T, Verizon, Sprint, contract free with T-Mobile
6 Plus	16, 64, and 128GB	$299, $399, $499 with contract; $749, $849, and $949 unlocked.	AT&T, Verizon, Sprint, contract free with T-Mobile

Decide How Much Memory Is Enough

Memory is a measure of how much information — for example, movies, photos, and software applications (apps) — you can store on a computing device. Memory can also affect your iPhone's performance when handling tasks such as streaming favorite TV shows from the World Wide Web or downloading music.

 Streaming refers to playing video or music content from the web (or from other devices) rather than playing a file stored on your iPhone. You can enjoy a lot of material online without ever downloading its full content to your phone's memory — and given that every iPhone model has a relatively small amount of memory, that's not a bad idea. See Chapters 15 and 17 for more about getting your music and movies online.

Your memory options with an iPhone 6 and 6 Plus are 16, 64, or 18 gigabytes (GB). You must choose the right amount of memory because you can't open the unit and add memory, as you usually can with a desktop computer. However, Apple has thoughtfully provided iCloud, a service you can use to back up content to the Internet (you can read more about that in Chapter 3).

So how much memory is enough for your iPhone? Here's a rule of thumb: If you like lots of media, such as movies or TV shows, you might need 128GB. For most people who manage a reasonable number of photos, download some music, and watch heavy-duty media such as movies online, 64GB is probably sufficient. If you simply want to check email, browse the web, and write short notes to yourself, 16GB *might* be enough.

 Do you have a clue how big a gigabyte (GB) is? Consider this: Just about any computer you buy today comes with a minimum of 500GB of storage. Computers have to tackle larger tasks than iPhones do, so that number makes sense. The iPhone, which uses a technology called *flash memory* for data storage, is meant (to a great extent) to help you experience online media and email; it doesn't have to store much and in fact pulls lots of content from online. In the world of memory, 16GB for any kind of storage is puny if you keep lots of content and graphics on the device.

What's the price for larger memory? For the iPhone 6, a 16GB unit costs $199 with a two-year contract; 64GB jumps the price to $299; and 128GB adds another $100, setting you back a pricey $399. iPhone 6 Plus tops out at $499 for a 128GB model.

Understand What You Need to Use Your iPhone

Before you head off to buy your iPhone, you should know what other connections and accounts you'll need to work with it optimally.

At a bare minimum, to make standard cellular phone calls, you need to have a service plan with a cellular carrier such as AT&T, as well as a data plan that supports iPhone. The data plan allows you to exchange data over the Internet, such as emails and text messages.

You also need to be able to update the iPhone operating system and share media such as music among Apple devices. Though these things can be done without a phone carrier service plan, you have to plug your phone into your computer to update the iOS or update wirelessly over a network. You need to use a local Wi-Fi network to go online and make calls using an Internet service such as Skype. Given the cost and hi-tech nature of the iPhone, having to jury-rig these basic functions doesn't make much sense, so trust me: Get an account and data plan with your phone service provider.

You should open a free iCloud account, Apple's online storage and syncing service, to store and share content online. You can also use a computer to download photos, music, or applications from non-Apple online sources such as stores or sharing sites like your local library and transfer them to your iPhone through a process called *syncing*.

Apple has set up its iTunes software and the iCloud service to give you two ways to manage content for your iPhone — including apps, music, or photos you've downloaded — and specify how to sync your calendar and contact information.

There are a lot of tech terms to absorb here (iCloud, iTunes, syncing, and so on). Don't worry: Chapter 3 covers those settings in more detail.

Know Where to Buy Your iPhone

You can't buy an iPhone from every major retail store. You can buy an iPhone at the brick-and-mortar or online Apple Store and from the mobile phone providers AT&T, Sprint, T-Mobile, and Verizon. You can also find an iPhone at major retailers such as Best Buy and Walmart, through whom you have to buy a two-year service contract for the phone carrier of your choice. You can also find iPhones at several online retailers such as Amazon.com and Newegg.com, and through smaller, local service providers, which you can find by visiting `http://support. apple.com/kb/HT1937?viewlocale=en_US&locale=en_US`.

 Apple offers unlocked iPhones. Essentially, these phones aren't tied into a particular provider, so you can use them with any of the four iPhone cellular service providers. Though you save a lot by avoiding a service commitment, these phones without accompanying phone plans can be pretty pricey. That said, there's a trend for providers offering cheaper plans and installment payments on the hardware.

Explore What's in the Box

When you fork over your hard-earned money for your iPhone, you'll be left holding one box about the size of a deck of tarot cards. Here's a rundown of what you'll find when you take off the shrink-wrap and open the box:

➡ **iPhone:** Your iPhone is covered in a thick, plastic-sleeve thingie that you can take off and toss (unless you think there's a chance you'll return the phone, in which case you might want to keep all packaging for 14 days — Apple's standard return period).

➡ **Apple EarPods with Remote and Mic:** Plug the EarPods into your iPhone 6 or 6 Plus for a free headset experience.

➡ **Documentation (and I use the term loosely):**
Notice, under the iPhone itself, a small, white enve-
lope about the size of a half-dozen index cards.
Open it and you'll find:

- *A tiny pamphlet:* This pamphlet, named *Important
  Product Information Guide,* is essentially small print
  (that you mostly don't need to read) from folks
  like the FCC.

- *A label sheet:* This sheet has two white Apple logos
  on it. (I'm not sure what they're for, but my husband and I use one sticker to differentiate my
  iPhone from his.)

- *A small foldout card:* This card provides panels containing photos of the major features of iPhone 6
  or 6 Plus and information about where to find out
  more. (Prior to 4s, you got only a single card with
  a photo of the phone and callouts to major features; 4s documentation expanded exponen-
  tially . . . which isn't saying much!)

➡ **Lightning to USB Cable:** Use this cable (see
Figure 1-2) to connect the iPhone to your computer, or use it with the last item in the box, the
USB power adapter. If you own an iPhone 4s or
earlier, you have the Dock Connector to USB Cable,
a larger, bulkier, 30-pin connector.

➡ **Apple USB power adapter:** The power adapter (refer
to **Figure 1-2**) attaches to the Lightning to USB Cable
so that you can plug it into the wall and charge the
battery.

➡ **SIM Eject Tool:** This tool, which you can use to eject
a SIM card from any phone that uses this technology,
is provided with iPhones in some areas.

Lightning to USB Cable   Apple USB power adapter

Figure 1-2

That's it. That's all there is in the box. It's kind of a study in Zen-like simplicity.

 Try searching for iPhone accessories online. You'll find iPhone cases ranging from leather to silicone; car chargers; and screen guards to protect your phone's screen.

Take a First Look at the Gadget

The little card contained in the documentation (see the preceding section) gives you a picture of the iPhone with callouts to the buttons you'll find on it. In this section, I give you a bit more information about those buttons and other physical features of the iPhone 6 and 6 Plus. **Figure 1-3** shows you where each of these items is located.

Volume buttons

Ring/Silent switch

FaceTime camera

Receiver/front microphone

iSight Camera

Rear microphone

True Tone Flash

Status bar

Sleep/Wake button

SIM card tray

Multi-Touch Display

Home button/Touch ID sensor

Lightning connector

Headset jack

Speaker   Bottom microphone

Figure 1-3

Here's the rundown on what the various hardware features are and what they do:

➠ **(The all-important) Home button:** On the iPhone, you can press this button to go back to the Home screen to find just about anything. The Home screen(s) displays all your installed and preinstalled apps and gives you access to your iPhone settings. No matter where you are or what you're doing, press the Home button and you're back at home base. You can also press the Home button twice to pull up a scrolling list of apps so that you can quickly move from one to another (Apple refers to this capability as multitasking). If you press and hold the Home button, you open Siri, the iPhone voice assistant. Finally, with iPhone 5s and later, the Home button contains a fingerprint reader used with the Touch ID feature.

➠ **Sleep/Wake button:** You can use this button (whose functionality I cover in more detail in Chapter 2) to power up your iPhone, put it in Sleep mode, wake it up, or power it down.

➠ **Lightning connector:** Plug in the Lightning connector at one end of the Lightning to USB Cable that came with your iPhone to charge your battery or sync your iPhone with your computer (which you find out more about in Chapter 3).

➠ **FaceTime/iSight Cameras:** iPhone 4 and later models offer a FaceTime camera (on the front of the phone) and an iSight camera (on the back of the phone) that you can use to make video calls and shoot photos or video. Make note of the location of the iSight camera on the back of the phone — you need to be careful not to put your thumb over it when taking shots. (I have several very nice photos of my thumb already.)

⟫ **Ring/Silent switch:** Slide this little switch to mute or unmute the sound on your iPhone.

⟫ **(A tiny, mighty) Speaker:** One nice surprise when I first got my iPhone was hearing what a nice little sound system it has and how much sound can come from this tiny speaker. The speaker is located on the bottom edge of the phone, below the Home button.

⟫ **Volume buttons:** Tap the volume up button for more volume and the volume down button for less. You can use the volume up button as a camera shutter button when the camera is activated.

⟫ **Headset jack and microphones:** If you want to listen to your music in private, you can plug in the EarPods (which give you bidirectional sound) or 3.5mm minijack headphones. Three microphones (one on the front of the phone — this is also the Receiver — and one on the bottom of the phone, as well as one on the back of the phone) make it possible to speak into your iPhone to deliver commands or content. This feature allows you to do things such as make phone calls using the Internet, use video calling services such as Skype, or work with other apps that accept audio input such as the Siri built-in assistant.

⟫ **Receiver:** The mesh on the top front of the device that you hear through.

⟫ **SIM card tray:** The little slot for placing your phone carrier's SIM card, which allows your phone to connect to the carrier and stores data such as contacts in memory. Note that iPhones have a smaller SIM card (called a nano-card) than several other phones.

⟫ **True Tone flash:** The flash device for the built-in rear-facing camera.

Looking Over the Home Screen

Chapter 2

I won't kid you: You have a slight learning curve ahead of you if you're coming from a more basic cellphone (but if you own another smartphone, you've got a head start). For example, your previous phone might not have had a Multi-Touch screen and onscreen keyboard.

The good news is that getting anything done on the iPhone is simple, once you know the ropes. In fact, using your fingers to do things is a very intuitive way to communicate with your computing device, which is just what iPhone is.

In this chapter, you turn on your iPhone, register it, and then take your first look at the Home screen. You also practice using the onscreen keyboard, see how to interact with the touchscreen in various ways, get pointers on working with cameras, and get an overview of built-in applications (apps).

Have a soft cloth handy, like the one you might use to clean your eyeglasses. Although the iPhone's screen has been treated to repel oils, you're about to deposit a ton of fingerprints on your iPhone — one downside of a touchscreen device.

See What You Need to Use iPhone

You need to be able, at a minimum, to connect to the Internet to take advantage of most iPhone features, which you can do using a Wi-Fi network (a network that you set up in your own home or access in a public place such as a library) or a 3G/4G connection from your cellular provider. You might want to have a computer so that you can connect your iPhone to it to download photos, videos, music, or applications and transfer them to or from your iPhone through a process called *syncing* (see Chapter 3 for more about syncing). An Apple service called iCloud syncs content from all your Apple iOS devices (such as the iPhone or iPad), so anything you buy on your iPad that can be run on an iPhone, for example, will automatically be pushed to your iPhone. In addition, you can sync without connecting a cable to a computer using a wireless Wi-Fi connection to your computer.

Your phone will probably arrive registered and activated, or if you buy it in a store, the person helping you can handle that procedure.

For an iPhone 6 and 6 Plus, Apple's *iPhone User Guide* recommends that you have

⟹ A Mac or PC with a USB 2.0 or later port and one of these operating systems:

  • Mac OS X Lion version 10.6.8 or later

  • Windows 8, 7, Vista, or XP Home or Professional with Service Pack 3 or later.

⟹ iTunes 11.4 or later, available at www.itunes.com/download

⟹ An Apple ID

⟹ Internet access

Apple has set up its iTunes software to help you manage content for your iPhone — which includes the movies, music, or photos you've downloaded — and specify from where to transfer your calendar and contact information. Chapter 3 covers these settings in more detail.

Turn On iPhone for the First Time

1. The first time you turn on your iPhone, it will probably have been activated and registered by your phone carrier or Apple (if you buy it from Apple).

2. Press and hold the On/Off button on the top of the upper-right side of your iPhone until the Apple logo appears. In another moment, a series of screens appears, asking you to enter a password if you have an Apple ID; if you don't have one, you can follow the instructions to create one.

3. Next, follow the series of prompts to make choices about your language and location, using iCloud, connecting with a network, and so on.

Set Up and Register iPhone

1. Now you're ready to connect your iPhone to your computer to register it and make some settings using iTunes. iTunes is free software from Apple that allows you to manage and sync content between your computer and iPhone. Plug the Lightning to USB Cable that comes with your device into your iPhone.

2. Plug the other, larger end of the cable into a USB port on a computer. Both your computer and the iPhone think for a few moments while they exchange data.

3. Sign in with your Apple ID in the dialog that appears on your computer screen, and then accept Apple's terms and

conditions. Follow the simple onscreen instructions in subsequent screens to register your iPhone and so make a few settings. (You can change these settings later; these steps are covered in Chapter 3.) When you're done, your iPhone Home screen appears, and you're in business.

4. Unplug the Lightning to USB Cable.

If you buy your iPhone at an Apple Store, an employee will register it for you, and you can skip this whole process.

You can choose to have certain items transferred to your iPhone from your computer when you sync, including music, videos, downloaded apps, contacts, audiobooks, calendars, e-books, podcasts, and browser bookmarks. You can also transfer to your computer any content you download directly to your iPhone using iTunes, the App Store, or non-Apple stores. See Chapters 12 and 13 for more about these features.

Meet the Multi-Touch Screen

When the iPhone Home screen appears (see **Figure 2-1**), you see a pretty background and two sets of icons. One set appears in the Dock, along the bottom of the screen. The *Dock* contains the Phone, Mail, Safari, and Music app icons by default, though you can swap out one app for another. The Dock appears on every Home screen. Other icons appear above the Dock and are closer to the top of the screen. (I cover all these icons in the "Take Inventory of Preinstalled Apps" task, later in this chapter.) Different icons appear in this area on each Home screen. You can add new apps to populate as many as 10 additional Home screens for a total of 11 Home screens. You can also nest apps in folders, which theoretically gives you the possibility of storing limitless apps on your iPhone. You are, in fact, limited — but only by your phone's memory.

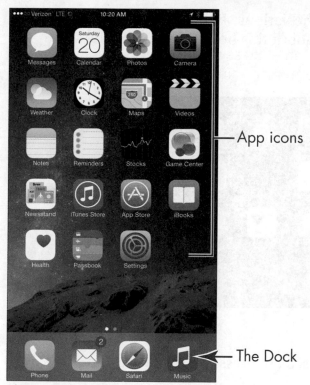

App icons

The Dock

Figure 2-1

 Treat the iPhone screen carefully. It's made of glass and will smudge when you touch it (and will shatter if you throw it at the wall or drop it on concrete).

If you have an iPhone 6 Plus model and you hold it horizontally, the Home screen will appear with some differences (see **Figure 2-2**).

The iPhone uses *touchscreen technology:* When you swipe your finger across the screen or tap it, you're providing input to the device just as you do to a computer using a mouse or keyboard. You hear more about the touchscreen in the next task, but for now, go ahead and play with it for a few minutes — really, you can't hurt anything. Use the pads of your fingertips (not your fingernails) and follow these steps:

1. Tap the Settings icon. The various settings (which you read more about throughout this book) appear, as shown in **Figure 2-3**.

Figure 2-2

2. To return to the Home screen, press the Home button.

3. Swipe a finger or two from right to left on the Home screen. This action moves you to the next Home screen. Note that the little dots at the bottom of the screen, above the Dock icons, indicate which Home screen is displayed.

4. To experience the screen rotation feature, hold the iPhone firmly while turning it sideways. The screen flips to the horizontal orientation. To flip the screen back, just turn the device so that it's oriented like a pad of paper again. (Note that some apps force iPhone to stay in one orientation or the other.)

●●●○○ Verizon 🔊　　　10:14 AM　　　　　 🔊 ■）

Settings

✈	Airplane Mode	⬭
🛜	Wi-Fi	Boysen ›
❋	Bluetooth	On ›
⦿	Cellular	›
◉	Personal Hotspot	Off ›
▣	Notifications	›
▣	Control Center	›
☾	Do Not Disturb	›
⚙	General	›
ᴀA	Display & Brightness	›
✿	Wallpaper	›
◁»	Sounds	›
⬚	Touch ID & Passcode	›

Figure 2-3

5. Drag your finger down from the very top edge of the screen to reveal the Notification Center (covered in Chapter 22); drag up from the very bottom edge of the Home screen to hide Notification Center, and then drag up to display Control Central (discussed later in this chapter).

6. To close either Notification Center or Control Central, drag the arrow at the bottom (Notification Center) or top (Control Central) of the display.

 You can customize the Home screen by changing its *wallpaper* (background picture) and brightness. You can read about making these changes in Chapter 7.

Say Goodbye to Endless Phone Menus; Say Hello to Tap and Swipe

You can use several methods for getting around and getting things done in iPhone using its Multi-Touch screen, including

➡ **Tap once.** To open an application on the Home screen, choose a field such as a search box, choose an item in a list, use an arrow to move back or forward one screen, or follow an online link, tap the item once with your finger.

➡ **Tap twice.** Use this method to enlarge or reduce the display of a web page (see Chapter 10 for more about using the *Safari* web browser) or to zoom in or out in the Maps app.

➡ **Pinch.** As an alternative to the tap-twice method, you can pinch your fingers together or move them apart on the screen (see **Figure 2-4**) when you're looking at photos, maps, web pages, or email messages to quickly reduce or enlarge them, respectively. This method allows you to grow or contract the screen to a variety of sizes rather than a fixed size, as with the double-tap method.

 You can use the three-finger tap to zoom your screen to be even larger or use multitasking gestures to swipe with four or five fingers (see the "Learn Multitasking Basics" task, later in this chapter). This method is handy if you have vision challenges. Go to Chapter 7 to discover how to turn on this feature using Accessibility settings.

➡ **Drag to scroll (known as *swiping*).** When you press your finger to the screen and drag to the right or left, the screen moves (see **Figure 2-5**). Swiping to the left on the Home screen, for example, moves you to the

next Home screen. Swiping down while reading an online newspaper moves you down the page; swiping up moves you back up the page.

Figure 2-4

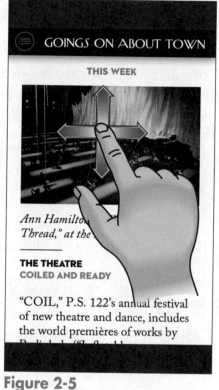

Figure 2-5

➡ **Flick.** To scroll more quickly on a page, quickly flick your finger on the screen in the direction you want to move.

➡ **Tap the Status bar.** To move quickly to the top of a list, web page, or email message, tap the Status bar at the top of the iPhone screen.

➡ **Press and hold.** If you're using Notes or Mail or any other application that lets you select text, or if you're on a web page, pressing and holding text selects a word and displays editing tools that you can use to select, cut, or copy and paste the text.

Notice that when you rock your phone backward or forward, the background moves as well, a feature called parallax. You can disable this feature if it makes you seasick. From the Home screen, tap Settings➪General➪Accessibility and then tap and turn off the Reduce Motion setting.

 With iPhone 6 and 6 Plus come a few new ways to interact with the display. Reachability involves a double-touch on the Home button, which makes the screen slide down so that it's closer to your thumb, making it easier to tap items onscreen with the fingers of one hand. In addition, you can use bezel gestures, which involves sliding left to right on the glass to go backward and sliding right to left to go forward.

Try these methods now by following these steps:

1. Tap the Safari button in the Dock at the bottom of any iPhone Home screen to display the web browser.

2. Tap a link to move to another page.

3. Double-tap the page to enlarge it; then pinch your fingers together on the screen to reduce its size.

4. Drag one finger around the page to scroll.

5. Flick your finger quickly on the page to scroll more quickly.

6. Press and hold your finger on a word that isn't a link (links are usually blue and take you to another location on the web). The word is selected, and the Copy/Define tool is displayed, as shown in **Figure 2-6**. (You can use this tool to get a definition of a word or copy it.)

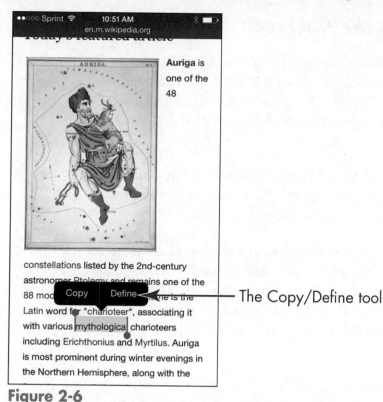

The Copy/Define tool

Figure 2-6

7. Press and hold your finger on a link or an image. A menu appears with commands that you select to open the link or picture, open it in a new page, add it to your Reading List (see Chapter 10), or copy it. If you press and hold an image, the menu also offers the Save Image command. Tap Cancel to close the menu without making a selection.

8. Position your fingers slightly apart on the screen and then pinch your fingers together to reduce the page; next, with your fingers already pinched together, place them on the screen and then move them apart to enlarge the page.

9. Press the Home button to go back to the Home screen.

Display and Use the Onscreen Keyboard

1. The built-in iPhone keyboard appears whenever you're in a text-entry location, such as a search field or an email message form. Tap the Notes icon on the Home screen to open this easy-to-use notepad and try the onscreen keyboard.

2. Tap the note page or if you've already created some notes, tap one to display the page and then tap anywhere on the note; the onscreen keyboard appears.

3. Type a few words using the keyboard, as shown in **Figure** 2-7. To make the keyboard display as wide as possible, rotate your iPhone to landscape (horizontal) orientation (note that if you've locked the screen orientation in Control Center, you have to unlock it to do this).

4. If you make a mistake while using the keyboard — and you will, especially when you first use it — tap the Delete key (it's near the bottom corner, with the little *x* on it) to delete text to the left of the insertion point.

5. To create a new paragraph, tap the Return button, just as you would do on a computer keyboard.

6. To type numbers and symbols, tap the number key (labeled 123) on the left side of the spacebar (refer to **Figure 2-7**). The characters on the keyboard change (see **Figure 2-8**). If you type a number and then tap the spacebar, the keyboard returns to the letter keyboard automatically. To return to the letter keyboard at any time, simply tap the key labeled ABC on the left side of the spacebar.

Figure 2-7   **Figure 2-8**

7. Use the Shift button (it's a thick, upward-facing arrow in the lower-left corner of the keyboard) just as you would on a regular keyboard to type uppercase letters. Tapping one of these buttons once causes just the next letter you type to be capitalized.

8. Double-tap the Shift key to turn on the Caps Lock feature so that all letters you type are capitalized until you turn the feature off. Tap the Shift key once to turn off Caps Lock. (You can control whether this feature is available in iPhone Settings under the General category by tapping Keyboard.)

9. To type a variation on a symbol or letter (for example, to see alternative presentations for the letter *A* when you press the A button on the keyboard), hold down the key; a set of alternative letters/symbols appears (see **Figure 2-9**). Note that this trick works with only certain letters and symbols.

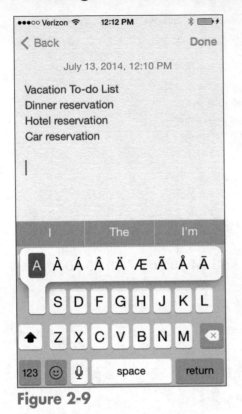

Figure 2-9

10. Tap the smiley-faced emoticon button to display the emoji keyboard containing symbols that you can insert, including numerical, symbol, and arrow keys, as well as a row of symbol sets along the bottom of the screen. Tapping one of these displays a portfolio of icons from smiley faces to pumpkins, hearts, cats, and more.

11. Press the Home button to return to the Home screen.

12. If you own an iPhone 6 Plus, turn it into horizontal orientation. Tap Notes and then tap in a note to display the onscreen keyboard, which now takes advantage of the wider screen and includes some extra keys such as Cut, Copy, and Paste (see **Figure 2-10**).

Cut   Copy   Paste

Figure 2-10

 To type a period and space, just double-tap the spacebar.

 Note that a small globe symbol will appear instead of the emoticon button on the keyboard if you've enabled multilanguage functionality in iPhone settings.

If you want to add punctuation, such as a comma, and then return immediately to the letter keyboard, simply tap the 123 key and then drag up to the punctuation you want to use.

 A new feature in iOS 8, QuickType, provides suggestions above the keyboard as you type. You can turn this feature off or on by tapping and holding the Emoji or International icon to display a menu. Tap the Predictive item on this menu to turn the feature off or on.

Flick to Search

1. The Spotlight Search feature in iPhone helps you find suggestions from the web, Music, iTunes, and the App Store as well as suggestions for nearby locations and more. Swipe down on any Home screen (but not from the very top or bottom of the screen) to reveal the Search feature (see **Figure 2-11**).

Figure 2-11

2. Begin entering a search term. In the example in **Figure 2-12,** after I typed the letters *lov,* the search results displayed some messages and some music I had downloaded. As you continue to type a search term, the results narrow to match it.

3. Scroll down and tap Search Web or Search Wikipedia to check results from those sources.

4. Tap an item in the search results to open it in its appropriate app or player.

Figure 2-12

Update the Operating System to iOS 8

1. This book is based on the latest version of the iPhone operating system at the time: iOS 8. To be sure that you have the latest and greatest features, update your iPhone to the latest iOS now (and do so periodically to receive minor upgrades to iOS 8). If you have set up an iCloud account on your iPhone, you'll receive an alert and can choose to install the update or not, or you can update manually by tapping Settings⇨General⇨Software Update.

2. To update your iPhone using a physical connection, plug the Lightning end (the smaller end) of the Lightning to USB Cable into your iPhone and plug the USB end into your computer; or if you've set up wireless syncing, be within range of the Wi-Fi network that your computer is using.

3. Open iTunes, click your iPhone (near the upper-right corner of the iTunes window or in the Devices list along the left, if it's displayed) and then click the Summary tab if it isn't already displayed (see **Figure 2-13**).

Click the Summary tab

Figure 2-13

4. Read the note next to the Check for Update button to see whether your iOS is up-to-date. If it isn't, click the Check for Update button. iTunes checks to find the latest iOS version and walks you through the updating procedure.

Learn Multitasking Basics

1. *Multitasking* lets you easily switch from one app to another without closing the first one and returning to the Home screen. With iOS 8, this is now accomplished by previewing all open apps and jumping from one to another; you quit an app by simply swiping upward. First, open an app.

2. Press the Home button twice.

3. On the Running Apps list that appears (see **Figure 2-14**), flick to scroll to the left or right to locate another app that you want to switch to.

Figure 2-14

4. Tap an app to open it.

 Press the Home button to remove the Running Apps list from the Home screen and return to the app that you were working in.

Examine the iPhone Cameras

iPhones have front- and back-facing cameras. You can use the cameras to take still photos (covered in more detail in Chapter 16) or shoot videos (covered in Chapter 17).

For now, take a quick look at your camera by tapping the Camera app icon on the Home screen. The app opens, as shown in **Figure 2-15.**

Timed Photo

Figure 2-15

You can use the controls on the screen to

➟ Switch between the front and rear cameras

➟ Change from still-camera to video-camera operation by using the slider at the bottom of the screen

➟ Take a picture or start recording a video

 ➟ Choose a 3- or 10-second delay with the new Timed Photos button

➡ Turn HDR (high dynamic range for better contrast) on or off

➡ Tap the Flash button to set flash to On, Off, or Auto

➡ Open previously captured images or videos

When you view a photo or video, you can use an iPhone sharing feature to send the image via AirDrop (iPhone 5 and later only), Message, or Mail. You can also share through iCloud Photo Sharing, a tweet, Facebook, or Flickr. More things that you can do with images are to print them, use a still photo as wallpaper (that is, as your Home or Lock screen background image) or assign it to represent a contact, and run a slideshow. See Chapters 16 and 17 for more detail about using the iPhone cameras.

Lock Screen Rotation

Sometimes you don't want your screen orientation to flip around when you move your phone around. Use these steps to lock the iPhone into portrait orientation:

1. Swipe up from the bottom of any screen to open Control Center.

2. Tap the Lock Screen button; it's the button in the top-right corner of Control Center.

3. Swipe down from the top of Control Center to hide it.

Explore the Status Bar

Across the top of the iPhone screen is the *Status bar* (see **Figure 2-16**). Tiny icons in this area can provide useful information, such as the time, battery level, and wireless-connection status. **Table 2-1** lists some of the most common items you find on the Status bar.

← Status bar

Figure 2-16

Table 2-1		Common Status Bar Icons
Icon	**Name**	**What It Indicates**
	Wi-Fi	You're connected to a Wi-Fi network.
	Activity	A task is in progress — a web page is loading, for example.
12:36 PM	Time	You guessed it: You see the time.
	Screen Rotation Lock	The screen is locked in portrait orientation and doesn't rotate when you turn the iPhone.
	Play	A media element (such as a song or video) is playing.
	Battery Life	This shows the charge percentage remaining in the battery. The indicator changes to a lightning bolt when the battery is charging.

If you have GPS, 3G, 4G cellular, or Bluetooth service or a connection to a virtual private network (VPN), a corresponding symbol appears on the Status bar whenever a feature is active. (If you can't even conceive of what a virtual private network is, my advice is not to worry about it.)

Take Inventory of Preinstalled Apps

The iPhone comes with certain functionality and applications — or *apps*, for short — built in. When you look at the Home screen, you see icons for each app. This task gives you an overview of what each app does. (You can find out more about every one of them as you read different chapters in this book.) The following icons appear in the Dock at the bottom of every Home screen (refer to **Figure 2-1**), from left to right:

→ **Phone:** Use this app to make and receive phone calls, view a log of recent calls, create a list of favorite contacts, access your voice mail, and view Contacts.

→ **Mail:** You use this application to access email accounts that you have set up in iPhone. Your email is then displayed without your having to browse to the site or sign in. You can use tools to move among a few preset mail folders, read and reply to email, and download attached photos to your iPhone. Read more about email accounts in Chapter 11.

→ **Safari:** You use the Safari web browser (see **Figure 2-17**) to navigate on the Internet, create and save bookmarks of favorite sites, and add web clips to your Home screen so that you can quickly visit favorite sites from there. You may have used this web browser (or another, such as Internet Explorer) on your desktop computer.

Figure 2-17

➠ **Music:** *Music* is the name of your media player. Though its main function is to play music, you can use it to play audio podcasts and audiobooks as well.

Apps with icons above the Dock on the Home screen include

➠ **Messages:** For those who love to instant message, the Messages app comes to the rescue. The Messages app has been in iPhone for quite some time. Now you can engage in live text- and image-based conversations with others via their phones or other devices that use email. In iOS 8, you can also send video or audio messages.

➠ **Calendar:** Use this handy onscreen daybook to set up appointments and send alerts to remind you about them.

➡ **Photos:** The Photos app in iPhone (see **Figure 2-18**) helps you organize pictures in folders, send photos via email, use a photo as your iPhone wallpaper, and assign pictures to contact records. You can also run slideshows of your photos, open albums, pinch or unpinch to shrink or expand photos, and scroll photos with a simple swipe. Your iPhone can use the Photo Sharing feature to share photos among your friends. Since iOS 7, Photos displays images by collections including Years and Moments.

➡ **Camera:** As you may have read earlier in this chapter, the Camera app is control central for the still and video cameras built into the iPhone.

➡ **Weather:** Get the latest weather for your location and others instantly with this handy app (see **Figure 2-19**). You can easily add other locations to check for weather where you're going or where you've been.

➡ **Clock:** This app allows you to display clocks from around the world, set alarms, and use timer and stopwatch features.

➡ **Maps:** With this iPhone mapping app, you can view classic maps or aerial views of addresses and find directions from one place to another whether traveling by car, foot, or public transportation (though this last requires that a third-party app be installed). You can even get your directions read out loud via a spoken narration feature.

➡ **Videos:** This media player is similar to Music but specializes in playing videos and offers a few features specific to this type of media, such as chapter breakdowns and information about a movie's plot and cast.

Figure 2-18

Figure 2-19

⟩ **Notes:** Enter text or cut and paste text from a website into this simple notepad app. You can't do much except save notes or email them — the app has no features for formatting text or inserting objects. You'll find Notes handy, though, for simple notes on the fly.

⟩ **Reminders:** This is a useful app that centralizes all your calendar entries and alerts to keep you on schedule, as well as allowing you to create to-do lists.

⟩ **Stocks:** See in one place, anytime you like, the latest information about stock exchanges and individual stocks as well as trending information.

➠ **Game Center:** This app helps you browse games in the App Store and play them with other people online. You can add friends and track your scores. See Chapter 18 for more about Game Center.

➠ **Newsstand:** Similar to an e-reader for books, Newsstand is a handy place to gather your subscriptions to magazines, newspapers, and other periodicals.

➠ **iTunes Store:** Tapping this icon takes you to the iTunes store, where you can shop 'til you drop (or until your iPhone battery runs out of juice) for music, movies, TV shows, and audiobooks and then download them directly to your iPhone. (See Chapter 12 for more about how iTunes works.)

➠ **App Store:** Here you can buy and download applications that do everything from enabling you to play games to building business presentations. You can also subscribe to periodicals for use with the Newsstand app. Some of these are even free!

Passbook: This feature lets you store a virtual wallet of plane or concert tickets, coupons, and more and use them with a swipe of your iPhone across a point of transaction device.

➠ **Compass:** Know where you are and where you're going with this handy app that uses location services to orient you to all directions based on your current location.

 Wrapped up in the Extras folder are some other handy tools: Contacts and Calculator. The Extras folder is on the second Home screen by default.

⟹ **Settings:** Settings is the central location on the iPhone where you can specify settings for various functions and do administrative tasks such as set up email accounts or create a password.

⟹ **Voice Memos:** Make handy, on-the-fly recordings to remind yourself of your brilliant ideas or to-do list.

⟹ **FaceTime:** Use FaceTime to place phone calls using video of the sender and receiver to have a more personal conversation.

⟹ **Podcasts:** Before iOS 8, you had to download the free Podcast app, but now it's built into your iOS iPhone. Use this app to listen to recorded informational programs.

⟹ **Health:** This is an exciting new app built into iOS 8 that you can use to record various health and exercise statistics and even send them to your doctor. See Chapter 20 for more about the Health app.

⟹ **iBooks:** The iBooks app is now bundled with the iPhone out of the box. Because the iPhone has been touted as being a good small screen *e-reader* — a device that enables you to read books on an electronic device, similar to the Amazon Kindle Fire HD — you should definitely check this one out. To work with the iBooks e-reader application itself, go to Chapter 14.)

 Several apps that used to cost you are free as of iOS 7. These include iMovie and iPhoto, as well as the Pages, Keynote, and Numbers apps of the iWork suite.

Discover Control Center

1. Control Center is a one-stop screen for common features and settings such as connecting to a network, increasing screen brightness or volume, and using the Calculator or Camera. To display Control Center, swipe up from the bottom of the screen.

2. In the screen that appears, tap a button or tap and drag a slider to access or adjust a setting (see **Figure** 2-20).

3. Swipe the top of Control Center down to hide it.

Figure 2-20

Lock iPhone, Turn It Off, or Unlock It

Earlier in this chapter, I mention how simple it is to turn on the power to your iPhone. Now it's time to put it to *sleep* (a state in which the screen goes black, though you can quickly wake up the iPhone) or turn off the power to give your new toy a rest. Here are the procedures you use to put the phone to sleep or turn it off:

➟ **Sleep:** Press the Sleep/Wake button on the top of the right side of the phone. The iPhone goes to sleep. The screen goes black and is locked.

➟ **Power Off:** From any app or Home screen press and hold the Sleep/Wake button until the Slide to Power Off bar appears at the top of the screen, and then swipe the bar. You've just turned off your iPhone.

➟ **Force Off:** If the iPhone becomes unresponsive, hold the Power and Home buttons simultaneously until the phone shuts itself off.

To wake the phone back up from Sleep mode, do the following:

➟ **Press the Home button and swipe the onscreen arrow on the Slide to Unlock bar (see Figure 2-21).** The iPhone unlocks.

 The iPhone automatically enters Sleep mode after a few minutes of inactivity. You can change the time interval at which it sleeps by adjusting the Auto-Lock feature in Settings. See this book's companion Cheat Sheet at www.dummies.com/cheatsheet/ iphoneforseniors to review tables of various settings.

Figure 2-21

Note that you can use the Camera icon at the bottom right of the Lock screen to use the camera without waking up the iPhone from Sleep mode. Also, if you were playing music before putting iPhone to sleep, you will see music controls on the Lock screen and your music will play from there.

Getting Going

Your first step in getting to work with the iPhone is to make sure that its battery is charged. Next, if you want to find free or paid content for your iPhone from Apple, from movies to music to e-books to audiobooks, you'll need to have an iTunes account.

You can also use the wireless sync feature to exchange content between your computer and iPhone over a wireless network. After you have an iTunes account and the latest iTunes software on your computer, you can also connect your iPhone to your computer and sync them to exchange content between them (especially useful for syncing videos or music you've obtained from somebody other than Apple to the iPhone).

If you prefer, you can take advantage of the iCloud service from Apple to store and push all kinds of content and data to all your Apple devices — wirelessly. New with iOS 8 comes the capability to pick up where you left off from one device to another through a feature called Handoff. Also, edits that you make to documents in iCloud are reflected in all iOS devices and Macs running OS X Yosemite or later.

Chapter 3

Get ready to . . .

Charge the Battery

1. My iPhone showed up in the box fully charged, and let's hope yours did, too. Because all batteries run down eventually, one of your first priorities is to know how to recharge your iPhone battery. Gather your iPhone and its Lightning to USB Cable (iPhone 5 and later; if you have an earlier model, you have the Dock cable) and the Apple USB power adapter.

2. Gently plug the Lightning connector end (the smaller of the two connectors) of the Lightning to USB Cable into the iPhone.

 Note that if you have a hard case for your iPhone, you should remove the phone from it if you're charging it over several hours because these cases retain heat, which is bad for the phone and the case.

3. Plug the USB end of the Lightning to USB Cable into the Apple USB power adapter (see **Figure 3-1**).

4. Plug the adapter into an electric outlet.

 Connector cables from earlier versions of iPhone or other Apple devices such as iPad or iPod don't work with your iPhone 5 or later. Adapters are available, however, from Apple.

Attach this end...   to the power adapter.

Then plug this end...   into the iPhone.

Figure 3-1

Download iTunes to Your Computer

1. If you're using a Mac, you already have iTunes installed, but to be sure that you have the latest version (at the time of this writing, it's version 11.4), open iTunes and choose Check for Updates. For Windows users, you should download the iTunes application to your computer so that you have the option of using it to *sync* (transfer) downloaded content to your iPhone. Go to www.apple.com/itunes using your computer's browser. (In these steps, I use Internet Explorer as an example browser.)

2. Click the Download iTunes link in the top-right corner of the iTunes Home page (see **Figure 3-2**). On the screen that opens, click the Download Now button.

Click this link.

Figure 3-2

3. In the dialog that appears, or using the Internet Explorer 10 download bar if you use that version (see **Figure 3-3**), click Run. The iTunes application downloads.

Do you want to run or save **iTunes64Setup.exe** (86.7 MB) from **secure-appldnld.apple.com**?

This type of file could harm your computer.   Run   Save ▼   Cancel

Click Run

Figure 3-3

4. When the download is complete, another dialog appears, asking whether you want to run the software. Click Run, and the iTunes Installer appears (see **Figure 3-4**).

Figure 3-4

5. Click Next.

6. Click the I Accept the Terms of the License Agreement check box in the following dialog and click Next.

7. Review the installation options, click to deselect the ones you don't want to use, and then click the Install button, as shown in **Figure 3-5**. A dialog appears, showing the installation progress.

Figure 3-5

8. When a dialog appears and tells you that the installation is complete, click Finish. You have to restart your computer for the configuration settings that were made during the installation to take effect.

 As of this writing, iTunes 11.3 is the latest version and includes a paid feature called iTunes Match that allows you to store all your music, even music that you've copied from DVDs, in the cloud and push it to all your Apple devices using iCloud. See Chapter 15 for more about music and iPhone.

Open an iTunes Account for Music, Movies, and More

1. To be able to buy or download free items from iTunes or the App Store on your computer or iPhone, you must open an iTunes account. First, open the iTunes app (you had to download it to your computer in the preceding task if you're running Windows). You can open iTunes by typing **iTunes** on your computer's Start screen in Windows. If you're on a Mac, click the iTunes item in the Mac Dock or Launchpad.

2. Click the iTunes Store button to open the Store; then click the Sign In button on the screen that appears (see **Figure** 3-6).

3. In the dialog that appears (see **Figure** 3-7), click the Create Apple ID button, and in the next screen that appears, click Continue.

4. On the following screen, click to select the I Have Read and Agree to the These Terms and Conditions check box and then click the Agree button.

Click this button

Figure 3-6

Figure 3-7

5. In the Provide Apple ID Details screen that follows (see **Figure** 3-8), fill in the information fields, click the last two check boxes to deselect them if you don't want to receive email from Apple, and then click the Continue button.

Figure 3-8

6. On the Provide a Payment Method screen that appears (see **Figure 3-9**), enter your payment information and click the Create Apple ID button.

Figure 3-9

7. A screen appears, confirming that your account has been created. Click the Done button to return to the iTunes Store.

 If you prefer not to leave your credit card info with Apple, one option is to buy an iTunes gift card and provide that as your payment information. You can replenish the card periodically through the Apple Store.

Make iPhone Settings Using iTunes

1. Open your iTunes software. (On a Windows 8 or 8.1 computer, begin to type iTunes on the Start screen and then click iTunes in the search results; on a Mac, click the iTunes icon in the Dock or Launchpad; if you still have iTunes open in the iTunes Store from the previous task, just click the Library button.)

2. Connect your iPhone to your computer using the Lightning to USB Cable; your phone is listed near the upper-right corner in the Devices list, as shown in **Figure 3-10**. (If you display the Sidebar, you'll find your iPhone listed there, instead.) At this point, you may need to tap Trust on your iPhone so that it will trust this computer.

3. Click your iPhone, and a series of tabs displays. The tabs offer information about your iPhone and settings to determine how to download music, movies, or podcasts, for example. (You can see the choices on the Summary tab in **Figure 3-11**.) The settings relate to the kind of content you want to download and whether you want to download it automatically (when you sync) or manually. See **Table 3-1** for an overview of the settings that are available on each tab.

Click your phone . . .

. . . to display this series of tabs.

Figure 3-10

Figure 3-11

4. Make all settings for the types of content you plan to obtain on your computer. **Table 3-1** provides information about settings on the different tabs. Note that if you've downloaded content through apps like iTunes and Podcast, you may see additional tabs.

Do go through these settings to choose what content you want to sync, because your iPhone has limited memory. It's usually best not to sync memory-intensive items like videos automatically.

Table 3-1	iPhone Settings in iTunes
Tab Name	*What You Can Do with the Settings on the Tab*
Summary	Perform updates to the iPhone software and set general backup and syncing options.
Info	Specify which information to sync: Contacts and Calendars for Windows users, Email accounts, Bookmarks, and/or Notes. Perform an advanced replacement of info on the phone with info from the computer.
Apps	Sync with iPhone the apps you've downloaded to your computer, and manage the location of those apps and folders, as well as associate data files with your various apps. Choose whether to automatically install new apps.
Music	Choose which music to download to your iPhone when you sync.
Movies	Specify whether to automatically download movies and which movies to sync.
TV Shows	Choose shows and episodes to sync automatically.
Photos	Choose the applications or folders from which you want to download photos or albums.
Books	Choose books and PDF files to sync to your iPhone.
On This iPhone (Windows computers only)	Select music on the iPhone to copy to iTunes.

Sync the iPhone to Your Computer Using iTunes

1. After you specify which content to download in iTunes (see the preceding task), you can use the Lightning to USB Cable to connect your iPhone and computer at any time and sync files, contacts, calendar settings, and more. After iTunes is downloaded to your computer and your iTunes account is set up, plug the data connection cord into your iPhone (using the smaller connector).

2. Plug the other end of the cord into a USB port on your computer.

3. iTunes opens and shows an item for your iPhone near the upper-right corner (refer to **Figure 3-10**). Click the Sync button in the lower-right corner and your iPhone screen shows the phrase *Syncing [Your Phone's Name] iPhone.*

4. When the syncing is complete, the Lock screen returns on the iPhone. Disconnect the cable. Any media you chose to transfer in your iTunes settings and any new photos in albums or folders on your computer that you've specified for syncing have been transferred to your iPhone.

Sync Wirelessly

You can also use the iTunes Wi-Fi Sync setting to allow cordless syncing if you're within range of a Wi-Fi network that has a computer connected to it with iTunes installed and open. There are a few steps you have to take with your iPhone connected to your computer before you can perform a wireless sync with iTunes:

1. Open iTunes and connect your iPhone to your computer using the Lightning to USB Cable.

2. Click your phone name (refer to **Figure 3-10**), click the Summary tab, and then scroll down and click the check box labeled Sync with this iPhone over Wi-Fi.

3. Disconnect your iPhone from your computer.

After you complete the preceding steps, you'll be able to wirelessly sync your iPhone with your computer. To do so, follow these steps:

1. To initiate a wireless sync, on the iPhone, tap Settings⇨ General⇨iTunes Wi-Fi Sync.

2. In the settings that appear, tap Sync Now to sync with a computer connected to the same Wi-Fi network. (If you need to connect your iPhone to a network, tap Settings⇨Wi-Fi and then tap a network to join.)

 If you have your iPhone set up to sync wirelessly to your Mac or PC and both are within range of the same Wi-Fi network, iPhone will appear in your iTunes Devices list. This setup allows you to sync and manage syncing from within iTunes. Also be aware that your iPhone will automatically sync with iTunes once a day if both are on the same Wi-Fi network, iTunes is running, and your iPhone is plugged in.

Understand iCloud

There's an alternative to syncing content by using iTunes. iCloud is a service offered by Apple that allows you to back up most of your content to online storage. (Some content, however, such as videos, isn't backed up, so consider doing an occasional backup of content to your computer, as well.) That content is then pushed automatically to all your Apple devices through a wireless connection. All you need to do is get an iCloud account, which is free, and make settings on your devices and in iTunes for which types of content you want pushed to each device. After you've done that, content that you create or purchase on one device — such as music, apps, and TV shows, as well as documents created in Apple's iWork apps, photos, and so on — is synced among your devices automatically.

See Chapter 12 for more about using the new Family Sharing feature to share content that you buy online and more with family members through iCloud.

When you get an iCloud account, you get 5GB of free storage. Content that you purchase from Apple (such as apps, books, music, iTunes

Match content, Photo Sharing contents, and TV shows) isn't counted against your storage. If you want additional storage, you can buy an upgrade from one of your devices. Having 10GB costs $20 per year; 20GB is $40 per year; and 50GB is $100 per year. Most people will do just fine with the free 5GB of storage.

To upgrade your storage, go to iCloud in Settings, tap Storage & Backup, and then tap Buy More Storage. Tap the amount you need and then tap Buy.

 You can make settings for backing up your content to iCloud in Settings, under the iCloud section of General settings. Here you can choose to have content backed up automatically or to back up content manually. See Chapter 24 for more about this topic.

 If you pay $24.99 a year for the iTunes Match service, you can sync up to 25,000 songs in your iTunes library to your devices, which may be a less expensive way to go than paying for added iCloud storage. Tap Match in iTunes or visit www.apple.com/itunes/itunes-match for more information.

Get an iCloud Account

Before you can use iCloud, you need an iCloud account. By default, Apple assumes that you want to use the Apple ID you probably already have for an iTunes account; however, you can create a separate iCloud ID if you want. You can turn on iCloud when first setting up your iPhone, or use Settings to sign up using your Apple ID.

1. When first setting up your phone after upgrading to iOS 8, in the sequence of screens that appear, you'll see the one in **Figure 3-12.** Tap Use iCloud.

2. In the next dialog, tap Backup to iCloud. Your account is now set up based on the Apple ID that you entered earlier in the setup sequence.

Tap this option

Figure 3-12

Here are the steps to set up iCloud on your iPhone if you didn't do so when first setting up iPhone:

1. Tap Settings and then tap Mail, Contacts, Calendars; next, under Accounts, tap iCloud.

2. Tap iCloud Drive and then tap the On/Off switch to turn on iCloud Drive (see **Figure 3-13**).

3. A message appears, letting you know that your iPhone will no longer back up to your computer when you sync with a cable or over Wi-Fi; tap OK.

4. An alert may appear, asking whether you want to allow iCloud to use the location of your iPhone. Tap OK to use iCloud and features such as Find My iPhone. Your account is now set up.

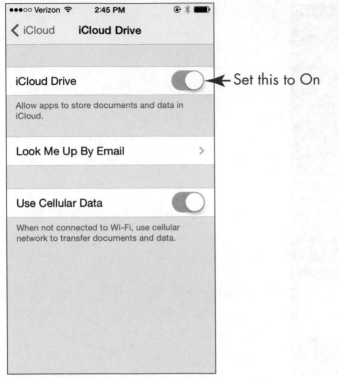

Set this to On

Figure 3-13

Make iCloud Sync Settings

1. When you have an iCloud account up and running (see the previous task), you have to specify which type of content should be synced with your iPhone via iCloud. To do so, tap Settings and then tap iCloud.

2. In the iCloud settings shown in **Figure 3-14,** tap the On/ Off switch for any item that's turned off that you want to turn on (or vice versa). You can sync Photos, Mail, Contacts, Calendars, Reminders, Safari, Notes, Passbook, and Keychain (an app that stores all your passwords and even credit card numbers across all Apple devices).

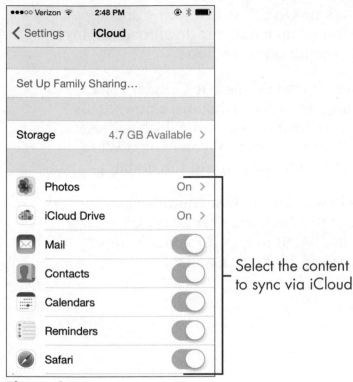

Select the content
to sync via iCloud

Figure 3-14

 If you want to allow iCloud to provide a service for locating a lost or stolen iPhone, tap the On/Off switch in the Find My iPhone field to activate it. This service helps you locate, send a message to, or delete content from your iPhone if it falls into other hands.

3. To enable automatic downloads of iTunes-purchased music, apps, and books, return to the main Settings screen by tapping the Settings button in the top-left corner of the screen (refer to **Figure 3-14**), and then tap iTunes & App Store.

4. Scroll down and tap the On/Off switch for Music, Apps, Books, or Updates to set up automatic downloads of any of this content to your iPhone via iCloud.

 You might want to turn off the Use Cellular Data option in Settings to avoid having these downloads occur over your cellular connection, which can use up your data allowance. Wait till you're on a Wi-Fi connection to have iPhone perform the updates.

 If you need help with any of these features, you can always go to http://manuals.info.apple.com/ MANUALS/1000/MA1565/en_US/iphone_user_ guide.pdf to view the Apple manual.

Part II
Start Using Your iPhone

Visit www.dummies.com/extras/iphoneforseniors for ideas about the many ways to use Siri, with sample commands for interacting with various apps.

Making and Receiving Calls

Chapter 4

If you're the type who wants a cellphone only to make and receive calls, you probably didn't buy an iPhone. Still, making and receiving calls is one of the primary functions of any phone, smart or not.

In this chapter, you discover all the basics of placing calls, receiving calls, and using available tools during a call to mute sound, turn on the speakerphone, and more. You also explore new features that help you manage how to respond to a call that you can't take at the moment, and how to change your ringtone.

Use the Keypad to Place a Call

1. Dialing a call with a keypad is an obvious first skill for you to acquire, and it's dead simple. On any Home screen, tap Phone in the Dock, and the app opens; tap the keypad button at the bottom of the screen, and the keypad appears (see **Figure** 4-1). (Note that if anything other than the keypad appears, you can just tap the Keypad button at the bottom of the screen to display the keypad.)

2. Enter the number you want to call by tapping the number buttons; as you do, the number appears above the keypad.

3. If you enter a number incorrectly, use the Delete button that appears on the keypad after you've begun to enter a number (a backward-pointing arrow with an X in it) to clear numbers one at a time.

4. Tap Call. The call is placed and tools appear, as shown in **Figure 4-2**.

Keypad

Figure 4-1   **Figure 4-2**

 When you enter a phone number, before you place the call, you can tap Add to Contacts (the + symbol to the left of the phone number) to add the person to your Contacts app. You can create a new contact or add the phone number to an existing contact using this feature.

If you're on a call that requires you to punch in numbers or symbols such as a pound sign, tap the Keypad button on the tools that appear during a call to display the keypad. See more about using calling tools in the "Use Tools During a Call" task, later in this chapter.

End a Call

In the following tasks, I tell you several other ways to place calls; however, I don't want to leave you on your first call without a way out. When you're on a phone call, the Call button changes to a red End button (see **Figure 4-3**). Tap End, and the call is disconnected.

— Tap here to disconnect

Figure 4-3

Place a Call Using Contacts

1. If you've created a contact and included a phone number in that contact record, you can use the Contacts app to place a call. Tap the Phone icon in any Home screen dock.

2. Tap the Contacts button at the bottom of the screen.

3. In the Contacts list that appears (see **Figure** 4-4), scroll up or down to locate the contact you need or tap a letter along the right side to jump to that section of the list.

4. Tap the contact to display his or her record. In the record that appears (see **Figure** 4-5), tap the phone number field. The call is placed.

Contacts button   Tap the phone number

Figure 4-4   **Figure 4-5**

If you locate a contact and the record doesn't include a phone number, you can add it at this point by tapping the Edit button, entering the number, and then tapping Done. Place your call following Step 4 in the preceding steps.

Return a Recent Call

1. If you want to dial a number from a call you've recently made or received, you can use the Recents call list, which you get to by tapping Phone in the Dock on any Home screen.

2. Tap the Recents button at the bottom of the screen. A list of recent calls that you've both made and received appears (see **Figure** 4-6). Missed calls appear in red.

3. If you want to view only the calls you've missed, tap the Missed tab at the top of the screen.

4. Tap the Info icon (a small *i*) to the right of any item to view information about calls to or from this person or establishment (see **Figure** 4-7).

5. Tap the Recents button to return to the Recents list, and then tap any call record to place a call to that number.

 Note that with iOS 8, you can access folks you've recently contacted using the Multitasking feature. Double-tap your Home button and the Multitasking screen appears with recent contacts listed in a row at the top of the screen. Tap on one and you can then connect by tapping mobile, message, or FaceTime.

Recents button

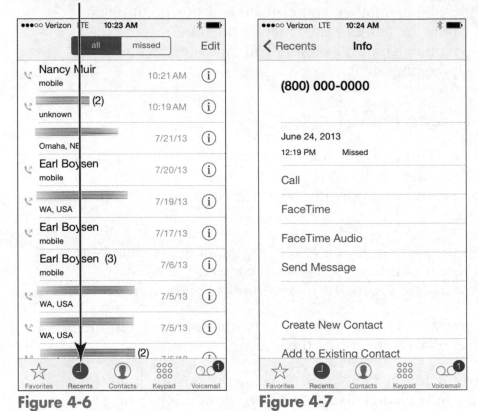

Figure 4-6   Figure 4-7

Use Favorites

1. You can save up to 50 contacts to Favorites in the Phone app so that you can quickly make calls to your A-list folks or businesses. Tap Phone on any Home screen.

2. Tap the Favorites button at the bottom of the screen.

3. In the Favorites screen that displays (see **Figure** 4-8), tap the Add button.

4. Your Contacts list appears and contact records that contain a phone number are bolded. Locate a contact that you want to make a Favorite and tap it. In the contact record, tap a phone number. Next, in the menu that appears, select Voice Call, FaceTime Audio, or FaceTime, depending on which type of call you prefer to make to this person most of the time (see **Figure** 4-9). The Favorites list reappears with your new favorite contact on it.

Figure 4-8   Figure 4-9

5. To place a call to a Favorite, display the Phone app, tap Favorites, and then tap a person on the list to place a call.

 If you decide to place a FaceTime call to a Favorite that you've created using the Voice Call setting, just tap the Information icon that appears to the right of the favorite's listing and tap the FaceTime call button in the contact record that appears. You can also create two contacts for the same person, one with a cellphone and one with a land phone, for instance, and place one or both in Favorites. See Chapter 9 for more about making FaceTime calls.

Receive a Call

There's one step to receiving a call. When a call comes in to you, the screen shown in **Figure 4-10** appears. Swipe Slide to Answer to pick up the call, or Message to send a preset text message that you can select in Settings under Phone, Respond with Text without picking up. Tap Remind Me to have iPhone send you a reminder to return the call without answering it. If you don't tap either button, the call goes to your voice mail after a few rings.

Figure 4-10

 There's another quick way to send a call to voice mail or decline it: Press the Sleep/Wake button on the top of your phone to send a call to voice mail or press the same button twice to decline the call.

With iOS 8's Handoff feature, if your iPhone is near an iPad or Mac computer (2012 model or later) and a call comes in, you can connect to the call via Bluetooth from any of the three devices by clicking or swiping the call notification. All devices have to be signed into the same iCloud account and have enabled Bluetooth and Handoff under Settings.

Use Tools During a Call

When you're on a call, whether you initiated it or received it, a set of tools, shown in **Figure 4-11**, is displayed.

Here's what these six buttons allow you to do, starting with the top-left corner:

➡ **Mute:** Silences the phone call so that the caller can't hear you, though you can hear the caller. The Mute button background turns white, as shown in **Figure 4-12,** when a call is muted. Tap again to unmute the call.

➡ **Keypad:** Displays the numeric keypad.

➡ **Speaker:** Turns the speakerphone feature on and off. If you are near a Bluetooth device and have Bluetooth turned on in your iPhone Settings, you will see a list of sources (such as a car Bluetooth connection for hands-free calls) and you can choose the one you want to use.

➡ **Add Call:** Displays Contacts so that you can add a caller to a conference call.

➡ **FaceTime:** Begins a video call with somebody who has an iPhone 4, 4S, or 5, iPod touch (4th generation or later), iPad 2 or third-generation or later, an iPad mini, or a Mac running OS X 10.7 or later.

➡ **Contacts:** Displays a list of contacts.

Figure 4-11 **Figure 4-12**

Turn On Do Not Disturb

1. Do Not Disturb is a feature that has iPhone silence incoming calls when iPhone is locked, displaying only a moon-shaped icon to let you know that a call is coming in. To turn the feature on, tap Settings.

2. Tap Do Not Disturb and then tap the On/Off switch labeled Manual to turn the feature on.

 When you turn on the Do Not Disturb feature, be aware that calls from Favorites are automatically allowed through by default, though you can change that setting by tapping the Allow Calls From option in Settings.

Set Up Exceptions for Do Not Disturb

1. If there are people whose calls you want to receive even when the Do Not Disturb feature is turned on, you can set up that capability. You can also set up a feature that allows a second call from the same number made within three minutes of the first to ring through. The theory with this feature is that two calls within a few minutes of each other might suggest an emergency situation that you'll want to respond to. With the Do Not Disturb feature turned on (see the previous task), tap Settings.

2. Tap Do Not Disturb, and on the Do Not Disturb screen, tap the Repeated Calls On/Off switch (see **Figure 4-13**).

Figure 4-13

If you want to schedule Do Not Disturb to be active only during a certain time period, such as your lunch hour, tap the Scheduled feature, shown in **Figure 4-13**, and then set a time range.

Reply to a Call via Text or Set a Reminder to Call Back

1. You can reply with a text message to callers whose calls you can't answer. You can also set up a reminder to call the person back later. When a call comes in that you want to deal with in one or both of these ways, swipe up on the screen.

2. Tap Message.

3. Tap on a preset reply, or tap Custom and then enter your own message.

4. To set up a reminder, tap Remind Me and then tap In One Hour or When I Leave to be reminded when you leave your current location.

Change Your Ringtone

1. The music or sound that plays when a call is coming in is called a ringtone. Your phone is set up with a default ringtone, but you can choose among a large number of Apple-provided choices. Tap Settings.

2. Tap Sounds and then tap Ringtone.

3. Scroll down the list of ringtones and tap on one to preview it (see **Figure 4-14**).

4. When you have selected the ringtone that you want in the list of ringtones, tap Sounds to return to the Sounds settings with your new ringtone in effect.

••••oo Verizon 🔋   11:56 AM   ⌁ ✻ ▬▭

❮ Sounds   **Ringtone**   Store

Vibration   Alert ❯

RINGTONES

Opening (Default)

Apex

Beacon

Bulletin

By The Seaside

Chimes

✓ Circuit

Constellation

Figure 4-14

 You can also set custom ringtones for contacts using the Contacts app to give that person's calls a unique sound. Open a contact's record, tap Edit, and then tap the Ringtone setting to display a list of ringtones. Tap one and then tap Done to save it.

Managing Contacts

*C*ontacts is the iPhone equivalent of the dog-eared address book that used to sit by your phone. The Contacts app is simple to set up and use, and it has some powerful features beyond simply storing names, addresses, and phone numbers.

For example, you can pinpoint a contact's address in iPhone's Maps app. You can use your contacts to address email and Facebook messages and Twitter tweets quickly. If you store a contact record that includes a website, you can use a link in Contacts to view that website instantly. And, of course, you can easily search for a contact by a variety of criteria, including how people are related to you, such as family or mutual friends, or by groups you create.

In this chapter, you discover the various features of Contacts, including how to save yourself time spent entering contact information by syncing a contacts list from services such as Google, Facebook, or Yahoo! to your iPhone.

Chapter
5

Get ready to . . .

Add a Contact

1. Tap Phone on the Home screen and then tap the Contacts icon at the bottom of the screen. An alphabetical list of contacts appears, like the one shown in **Figure 5-1**.

2. Tap the Add button, the button with the small plus sign (+) on it. A blank Info page opens (see **Figure 5-2**). Tap in any field, and the onscreen keyboard displays.

Add button

Figure 5-1

Figure 5-2

3. Enter any contact information you want. (Only one of the First, Last, or Company fields is required.)

4. To scroll down the contact's page and see more fields, flick up on the page with your finger.

5. If you want to add information such as a mailing or street address, you can tap the relevant Add field, which opens additional entry fields.

6. To add an information field such as Nickname or Job Title, tap Add Field toward the bottom of the page. In the Add Field dialog that appears (see **Figure 5-3**), choose a field to add. (You may have to flick the page up with your finger to view all the fields.)

7. Tap the Done button when you finish making entries. The new contact appears in your address book. Tap it to see details (see **Figure 5-4**).

Figure 5-3

Figure 5-4

If your contact has a name that's difficult for you to pronounce, consider adding the Phonetic First Name or Phonetic Last Name field, or both, to that person's record (refer to Step 6).

You can choose a distinct ringtone or text tone for a new contact. Just tap the Ringtone or Text Tone field in the New Contact form to see a list of options. When that person calls either on the phone or via FaceTime, or texts you via SMS, MMS, or iMessage, you will recognize him or her from the tone that plays.

Sync Contacts with iCloud

1. You can use your iCloud account to sync contacts from your iPad to iCloud to back them up. These also become available to your email account, if you set one up. On the Home screen, tap Settings and then tap iCloud.

2. In the iCloud settings shown in **Figure 5-5,** make sure that the On/Off switch for Contacts is set to On in order to sync contacts.

3. Tap the Back button in the top-left corner of the screen to return to Settings.

4. To choose which email account to sync with, tap Mail, Contacts, Calendars, and then tap iCloud.

5. In the following screen (see **Figure 5-6**), tap to turn Contacts on to merge contacts from that account via iCloud.

You can also use iTunes to sync contacts among all your Apple devices and even a Windows PC. See Chapter 3 for more about making iTunes settings.

You can use the iTunes Wi-Fi sync feature in iPhone Settings under General to sync with iTunes wirelessly from a computer connected to the same Wi-Fi network.

Set this to On   Set this to On

Figure 5-5   **Figure 5-6**

Assign a Photo to a Contact

1. With Contacts open, tap a contact to whose record you want to add a photo.

2. Tap the Edit button.

3. On the Info page that appears (see **Figure 5-7**), tap Add Photo.

4. In the dialog that appears, tap Choose Photo to choose an existing photo. You could also choose Take Photo to take that contact's photo on the spot.

5. In the Photos dialog that appears, choose a source for your photo (such as Recently Added, Photo Sharing, or other album).

6. In the photo album that appears, tap a photo to select it. The Move and Scale dialog, shown in **Figure 5-8**, appears.

Tap here to add photo

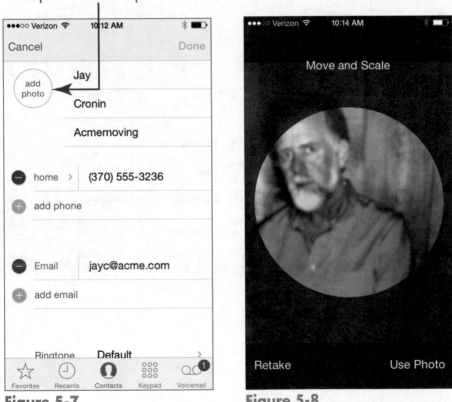

Figure 5-7   **Figure 5-8**

7. Tap the Choose button to use the photo for this contact.

8. Tap Done to save changes to the contact. The photo appears on the contact's Info page (see **Figure 5-9**).

Figure 5-9

While in the Photos dialog, in Step 6, you can modify the photo before saving it to the contact information. You can unpinch your fingers on the iPhone screen to expand the photo and move it around the space to focus on a particular section and then tap the Choose button to use the modified version.

Add Twitter or Facebook Information

1. Since iOS 5, iPhone users have been able to add Twitter information to their Contacts so that they can quickly tweet (send a short message to) others using Twitter. You

can also add Facebook or LinkedIn information so that
you can post a message to your contact's Facebook or
LinkedIn account. With Contacts open, tap a contact.

2. Tap the Edit button.

3. Scroll down and tap Add Field.

4. In the list that appears (see **Figure 5-10**), tap Add Social
Profile.

5. Tap in the Twitter Social Profile field and enter the contact's username information for an account.

 If you prefer to add Facebook information instead of
Twitter, tap Add Social Profile just under the Twitter
field in Step 5 and enter the contact's Facebook information. (You can also click the Add Social Profile
link again and choose Flickr, LinkedIn, Myspace, Sina
Welbo, or Add Custom Service in the fields that
appear.)

6. Tap Done, and the information is saved. The account is
now displayed when you select the contact, and you can
send a tweet or Facebook message by simply tapping
the username, tapping the service you want to use to
contact the person, and then tapping the appropriate
command (such as Facebook posting, as shown in
Figure 5-11).

 To update contact information for people who use
social media such as Twitter or Facebook, open
Settings and scroll down to the service. Tap it and
then tap Update Contacts. iPhone updates your contacts with any new or changed information that the
person has posted to the social media site.

Tap this option

Figure 5-10

Figure 5-11

Designate Related People

1. You can quickly designate relationships in a contact record if those people are saved to Contacts. One great use for this feature is using Siri to simply say "Call Manager" to call someone who is designated in your contact information as your manager. Tap a contact and then tap Edit.

2. Scroll down the record and tap Add Related Name.

3. The field labeled Mother (see **Figure 5-12**) now appears.

4. Tap the Add Related Name, and the Father field appears. Tap a field such as Mother or Father to change the label by tapping another relationship in the list that appears, if you wish.

5. Tap the blue Information arrow in the field, and your Contacts list appears. Tap the person's name, and it appears in the field (see **Figure 5-13**).

Figure 5-12　　　　**Figure 5-13**

 After you add relations to a contact record, when you select the person in the Contacts main screen, all the related people for that contact are listed there.

 There's a setting for Linked Contacts in the Contacts app when you're editing a contact's record. Using this setting isn't like adding a relation; rather, if you have records for the same person that have been imported into Contacts from different sources such as Google or Twitter, you can link them to show only a single contact.

Set Ringtones and Text Tones

1. If you want to hear a unique tone when you receive a phone or FaceTime call from a particular contact, you can set up this feature in Contacts. For example, if you want to be sure that you know instantly whether your spouse, sick friend, or boss is calling, you can set a unique tone for that person. To do so, tap to add a new contact or select a contact in the list of contacts and tap Edit.

2. Tap the Ringtone field in a new contact or tap Edit and then the Ringtone field in an existing contact, and a list of tones appears (see **Figure 5-14**).

●●●○○ Verizon 📶	10:30 AM	✳ ▪️🔋
Cancel	**Ringtone**	Done

　　　Buy More Tones

DEFAULT

✓　Bell Tower

RINGTONES

　　Apex

　　Beacon

　　Bulletin

　　By The Seaside

　　Chimes

　　Circuit

Figure 5-14

3. Tap a tone, and it previews. When you hear one you like, tap Done.

If you set a custom tone for someone, that tone will be used when that person calls or contacts you by FaceTime. You can also set a custom text tone to be used when the person sends you a text message — tap Text Tone instead of Ringtone in Step 2 in the preceding steps and follow the remaining steps.

 If your Apple devices are synced via iCloud, setting a unique ringtone for an iPhone contact also sets it for use with FaceTime and Messages on your iPad and Mac. See Chapter 3 for more about iCloud.

Search for a Contact

1. With Contacts open, tap in the Search field at the very top of your contacts list (see **Figure 5-15**). The onscreen keyboard opens.

2. Type the first letter of either the first or last name or company. All matching results appear, as shown in **Figure 5-16**. For example, typing *Me* might display *Megan and Melrose* and email addresses including *@metro* in the results, all of which have *Me* as the first two letters of the first or last part of the name or address.

3. Tap a contact in the results to display that person's Info page.

 You can search by phone number simply by entering the phone number in the Search field until the list narrows to the person you're looking for. This might be a good way to search for all contacts in your town or company, for example.

 You can use the alphabetical listing along the right side and tap a letter to locate a contact. Also, tap and drag to scroll down the list of contacts on the All Contacts page.

Search field

Search results

●●●○○ Verizon 🛜   10:40 AM   ❋ ■▶

Q |Search   Cancel

Q W E R T Y U I O P

A S D F G H J K L

⬆ Z X C V B N M ⌫

123 ☺ 🎤   space   Search

Figure 5-15

●●●○○ Verizon 🛜   10:39 AM   ❋ ■▶

Q Me   ⊗ Cancel

Meghan **Blan**▮▮▮   >

Meb **Bod**▮▮   >

MElle▮▮▮▮▮▮ ▮▮▮   >

MEnoc▮▮▮▮▮▮ ▮▮▮   >

Me   >

Rev **Men**▮▮   >

MEnnis   >

Q W E R T Y U I O P

A S D F G H J K L

⬆ Z X C V B N M ⌫

123 ☺ 🎤   space   Search

Figure 5-16

Go to a Contact's Website

1. If you entered website information in the Home Page field, it automatically becomes a link in the contact's record. Tap the Contacts app icon in the Extras folder to open Contacts.

2. Tap a contact's name to display the organization or person's contact information, locate the Home Page field, and then tap the link (see **Figure 5-17**).

3. The Safari browser opens with the web page displayed (see **Figure 5-18**).

Tap this link

Figure 5-17

Figure 5-18

 You can't go directly back to Contacts after you follow a link to a website. You have to press the Home button and then tap the Contacts app again to reenter the application or use the multitasking feature by pressing the Home button twice and choosing Contacts from the icons that appear along the bottom of the screen.

Address Email Using Contacts

1. If you entered an email address for a contact, the address automatically becomes a link in the contact's record. Tap the Phone icon on the Home screen and then tap Contacts.

2. Tap a contact's name to display the person's contact information, and then tap the email address link in the field labeled Email (see **Figure 5-19**).

3. The New Message dialog appears, as shown in **Figure 5-20**. Initially, the title bar of this dialog reads *New Message,* but as you type a subject, *New Message* changes to the specific title.

●●●○○ Verizon 🛜   11:34 AM   ❊ ◼▷

❮ All Contacts   Edit

Nancy Anderson

FaceTime   ▢◁ ☏

Email
apapermoon@live.com   ◯ ✉

Send Message

Share Contact

Block this Caller

☆   🕑   👤   ⦂⦂⦂   ◠◯¹
Favorites Recents Contacts Keypad Voicemail

Figure 5-19

●●●○○ Verizon 🛜   11:34 AM   ❊ ◼▷

Cancel   **New Message**   Send

To: apapermoon@live.com

Cc/Bcc, From: calyndra@icloud.com

Subject:

Sent from my iPhone

Figure 5-20

4. Tap in a field and use the onscreen keyboard to enter a subject and message.

5. Tap the Send button. The message goes on its way.

Share a Contact

1. After you've entered contact information, you can share it with others via an email message, text message, or Tweet. With Contacts open, tap a contact name to display its information.

2. On the Information page, scroll down and tap the Share Contact button. In the dialog that appears, shown in **Figure 5-21,** tap Mail (at this point you could also tap Message or Twitter). A New Message form appears.

 To share with an AirDrop-enabled device that is nearby, use the AirDrop button in the screen shown in **Figure 5-21.** Just select a nearby device, and your contact is transmitted to that person's device (such as a smartphone, Mac with OS X Yosemite, or tablet).

Figure 5-21

3. In the New Message form, use the onscreen keyboard to enter the recipient's email address. Note that if the person is saved in Contacts, you can just type his or her name here.

4. Enter information in the Subject field.

5. If you like, enter a message and then tap the Send button. The message goes to your recipient with the contact information attached as a .vcf file. (This *vCard* format is commonly used to transmit contact information.)

 When somebody receives a vCard containing contact information, he or she needs only to click the attached file to open it. At this point, depending on the email or contact management program, the recipient can perform various actions to save the content. Other iPhone, iPod touch, iPad, or iPhone users can easily import .vcf records as new contacts in their own Contacts apps.

View a Contact's Location in Maps

1. If you've entered a person's address in Contacts, you have a shortcut for viewing that person's location in the Maps application. Tap the Phone app on the Home screen and then tap Contacts.

2. Tap the contact you want to view to display that contact's information.

3. Tap Add Address and enter the address information. Tap Done and then tap the Address field. Maps opens and displays a map of the address (see **Figure 5-22**).

Figure 5-22

 This task works with more than your friends' addresses. You can save information for your favorite restaurant or movie theater or any other location and use Contacts to jump to the associated website in the Safari browser or to the address in Maps. For more about using Safari, see Chapter 10. For more about the Maps application, see Chapter 19.

Delete a Contact

1. When it's time to remove a name or two from your Contacts, it's easy to do. With Contacts open, tap the contact you want to delete.

2. On the Information page (refer to **Figure** 5-4), tap the Edit button.

3. On the Info page that displays, drag your finger upward to scroll down and then tap the Delete Contact button at the bottom (see **Figure** 5-23).

4. The confirming dialog shown in **Figure** 5-24 appears; tap the Delete Contact button to confirm the deletion.

Figure 5-23

Figure 5-24

During this process, if you change your mind before you tap Delete, tap the Cancel button in Step 4. But be careful: After you tap Delete, there's no going back! Your contact is deleted from not only your iPhone but also any other device that syncs to your iPhone via iCloud, Google, or other means.

Using Handy Utilities

*U*tilities are simple apps that can be very useful indeed to help with common tasks such as calculating your meal tip or finding your way on a hike in the woods.

In this chapter, I help you explore two apps contained in the Extras folder on the second Home screen: Compass to help you find your way, and Voice Memos so that you can record your best ideas for posterity. I also help you out with using the Calculator app on the second Home screen to keep your numbers in line. (Note that the fourth app in the Extras folder, Contacts, is covered in Chapter 5).

Use the Calculator

1. This one won't be rocket science. The Calculator app works like just about every calculator app you've ever used. Go to the second Home screen and tap Calculator to display the app (see **Figure 6-1**).

2. Tap a few numbers (see **Figure** 6-2) and then use any of these functions and additional numbers to perform calculations:

- **+, −, ×, and** ÷: These familiar buttons add, subtract, multiply, and divide the number you've entered.

- **+/−:** If the calculator is displaying a negative result, tap this to change it to a positive result, and vice versa.

- **AC/C:** This is the clear button; its name will change depending on whether you've entered one item or several. (AC clears all; C clears just the last entry.)

- **=:** This button produces the result of whatever calculation you've entered.

Figure 6-1   **Figure 6-2**

If you have a scientific nature, you'll be delighted to see that if you turn your phone to a landscape orientation, you get additional features that turn the basic calculator into a scientific calculator so that you can play with calculations involving such functions as cosines and tangents. You can also use memory functions to work with stored calculations.

Find Your Way with Compass

1. Compass is a handy tool for finding your way, assuming that you get 3G or 4G reception wherever you are. Tap the Extras folder on the second Home screen to open it and then tap Compass. The first time you do this, if you haven't enabled location access, a message appears, asking if iPhone can use your current location to provide information. Tap OK.

2. If you're using Compass for the first time, you'll be asked to tilt the screen to roll a little red ball around a circle; this helps iPhone to calibrate the Compass app. When you've completed this exercise, the Compass app appears (see **Figure 6-3**). Move around with your iPhone, and the compass indicates your current orientation in the world.

3. Tap the bold white line indicating your current location, as shown in **Figure 6-4,** and the display changes to True North and indicates with a red wedge how far off True North you are when you move the compass; tap it again to display Magnetic North.

4. Swipe to the left to view a compass view with information about how many degrees off of zero a surface is (see **Figure 6-5**). If a surface beneath your phone is flat, the screen turns green. Use this to check to see whether a surface is level.

Figure 6-3   Figure 6-4

 True North refers to the direction you follow from where you are to get to the North Pole; Magnetic North is correlated relative to the Earth's magnetic field. True North is the more accurate measurement because of the tilt of the Earth.

 You will know that you have a 4G connection if you see LTE in the Status bar. Not every location has this capability yet, so this is a good way to check whether you're connected.

Figure 6-5

Record Voice Memos

1. Voice Memos is perhaps the most robust of the three apps covered in this chapter. The app allows you to record memos, edit memos by trimming them down, share them via email or instant message with Messages, and label recordings so that you find them again. On the second Home screen, tap the Extras folder to open it and then tap Voice Memos.

2. In the Voice Memos app (see **Figure 6-6**), tap the red Record button to record a memo. (This button changes to a red Pause button when you're recording.)

3. A blue line moving from left to right shows that you're in recording mode (see **Figure 6-7**). While recording, you can tap the red Pause button to pause the recording and then tap Done to stop recording.

Record button

Pause button

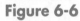

| 00:00 | 00:01 | 00:0 | 00:03 | 00:04 | 00:0 |

00:00.00

New Recording
7/1/14

Done

No recordings

Figure 6-6

| 00:04 | 00:05 | 00:06 | 00:07 | 00:08 | 00:09 |

00:06.90

New Recording
7/1/14

Done

New Recording
7/1/14   0:00:07

Figure 6-7

4. When you're done recording, a New Voice Memo dialog
appears where you can enter a name for the recording
and tap Save. A list of recorded memos appears (see
Figure 6-8). Tap one to play it back, share it via AirDrop,
Messages, or Mail; edit it, or delete it.

AirDrop is a feature that, with a fifth-generation
iPhone or later, allows you to share items such as
photos, voice memos, music, and more with another
person who has an AirDrop-enabled device and is
nearby. New with iOS 8 is the ability to share via
AirDrop with a Mac using OS X Yosemite. Learn
more about AirDrop in Chapter 10.

●●●○○ Verizon 🛜   12:29 PM   ⁂ ▭
Edit   Voice Memos   ◀))

Novel
7/1/14   0:00:03

New Recording
7/1/14   0:00:22

Figure 6-8

Trim a Voice Memo

1. Perhaps you repeated yourself at the beginning of your
memo. If you want to cut part of a recorded memo, you
can trim it. With the list of recordings displayed (refer to
Figure 6-8), tap any recording. The recording details display, as shown in **Figure 6-9**.

2. Tap Edit.

3. In the Edit screen shown in **Figure 6-10**, tap the Trim
button (it's a little square with dots coming off of the left
and right side) and then drag the lines on the right or left
of the memo bar and drag inward to trim a portion of
the recording.

Trim button

●●●○○ Verizon 🗢   12:32 PM   ❋ ▭

Voice Memos   ◀))

Novel
7/1/14   0:00:03

New Recording
7/1/14   0:00:22

▶ 0:00 |▬▬▬▬▬▬▬▬▬   -0:22

⬆️   Edit   🗑

Figure 6-9

●●●○○ Verizon 🗢   12:50 PM   ❋ ▭

Record   ◀))

00:00   00:01   00:02

00:00.00

New Recording
7/1/14

▶   ⬤   Done

Novel
7/1/14   0:00:03

New Recording
7/1/14   0:00:22

Figure 6-10

4. Tap Trim and a dialog appears. Tap Trim Original to apply the trim and save the recording, or Save As New Recording to apply the trim and save it as a new version of the recording.

 If you begin to trim a memo and change your mind, tap the Cancel button in the dialog mentioned in Step 4.

Rename a Voice Memo

1. You may occasionally have to rename a voice memo. With the list of memos displayed (refer to **Figure 6-8**), tap a memo to display its details.

2. Tap the name of the recording to display the settings shown in **Figure 6-11**.

3. Tap Backspace on your iPhone keyboard to delete the current name; enter a new name and then tap the name of the recording at the bottom of the screen to return to the list of memos, where you see the memo now named with the label you just gave it (see **Figure 6-12**).

Figure 6-11

Figure 6-12

Share a Voice Memo

1. Tap a memo in the list of memos (refer to **Figure 6-8**) to select it.

2. Tap the Share button (the box with an arrow pointing out of the top), shown in **Figure 6-13**.

Share button

Figure 6-13

3. In the menu shown in **Figure 6-14,** tap Mail to display
an email form or Message to display a Messages form to
send an instant message with the voice memo attached
(see **Figure 6-15**).

4. Fill in the recipient's information, a subject if you're
sending an email, and a message, and tap Send. The voice
memo and your message go on their way.

Tap this option

Figure 6-14

Figure 6-15

Making Your iPhone More Accessible

Chapter 7

*i*Phone users are all different, and some face visual, motor, or hearing challenges. If you're one of these folks, you'll be glad to hear that iPhone offers some handy accessibility features.

To make your screen easier to read, you can adjust the brightness or change wallpaper. You can also set up the VoiceOver feature to read onscreen elements out loud. Then there are a slew of features you can turn on or off, including Zoom, Invert Colors, Speak Selection, Large Type, and more

If hearing is your challenge, you can do the obvious and adjust the system volume. If you wear hearing aids, you can choose the correct settings for using Bluetooth or another hearing aid mode. The iPhone also has settings for Mono Audio (useful when you're wearing headphones), Speak Auto-text, using an LED flash when an alert sounds, and a Phone Noise Cancellation feature.

Features that help you deal with physical and motor challenges include an Assistive Touch feature for those who have difficulty using the iPhone touchscreen, Switch Control for

Get ready to . . .

working with adaptive accessories, and the Home Click Speed and Call Audio Routing settings that allow you to adjust how quickly you have to tap the iPhone screen to work with features and whether you can use a headset or speaker to answer calls.

Finally, the Guided Access feature provides help for those who have difficulty focusing on one task. It also provides a handy mode for showing presentations of content in settings where you don't want users to flit off to other apps, as in school or a public kiosk.

Set Brightness

1. Especially when using iPhone as an e-reader, you may find that a slightly less-bright screen reduces strain on your eyes. To adjust screen brightness, tap the Settings icon on the Home screen.

2. In Settings, tap Display & Brightness.

3. To control brightness manually, tap the Auto-Brightness On/Off switch (see **Figure 7-1**) to turn off this feature.

4. Tap and drag the Brightness slider (refer to **Figure 7-1**) to the right to make the screen brighter, or to the left to make it dimmer.

5. Press the Home button to close Settings.

 If glare from the screen is a problem for you, consider getting a *screen protector*. This thin film not only protects your screen from damage but also can reduce glare.

 In the iBooks e-reader app, you can set a sepia tone for the page, which might be easier on your eyes. See Chapter 14 for more about using iBooks.

Brightness slider

Tap here to turn off
Auto-Brightness

Figure 7-1

Change the Wallpaper

1. The picture of a night sky — the default iPhone background image — may be pretty, but it may not be the
one that works best for you. Choosing different wallpaper
may help you to see all the icons on your Home screen.
Start by tapping the Settings icon on the Home screen.

2. In Settings, tap Wallpaper.

3. In the Wallpaper settings that appear, tap Choose a New
Wallpaper and then tap a wallpaper category such as
Dynamic or Photos, as shown in **Figure 7-2**, to view
choices. Tap a sample to select it; if you choose Photos
on the Wallpaper screen, tap an album in Photos to
locate a picture to use as your wallpaper and tap it.

4. In the preview that appears, (see **Figure 7-3**), use your fingers to move the image and then tap Set.

5. In the following menu, tap either Set Lock Screen (the screen that appears when you lock the iPhone by tapping the power button), Set Home Screen, or Set Both.

6. Press the Home button to return to your Home screen with the new wallpaper set as the background.

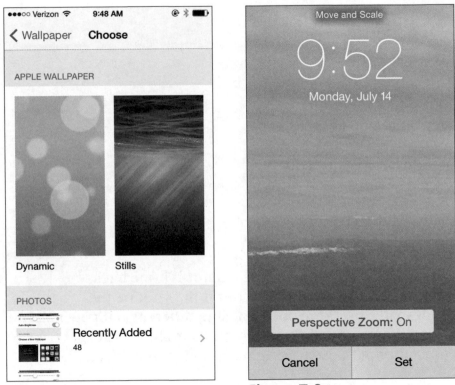

Figure 7-2   Figure 7-3

Set Up VoiceOver

1. VoiceOver reads the names of screen elements and set-tings to you, but it also changes the way you provide input to the iPhone. In Notes, for example, you can have VoiceOver read the name of the Notes buttons to you, and when you enter notes, it reads words or characters that you've entered. It can also tell you whether features such as Auto-Correction are on. To turn on this feature, tap the Settings icon on the Home screen. Tap General and then tap Accessibility.

2. In the Accessibility pane, shown in **Figure** 7-4, tap the VoiceOver button.

3. In the VoiceOver pane, shown in **Figure** 7-5, tap the VoiceOver On/Off switch to turn on this feature. With VoiceOver on, you must first single-tap to select an item such as a button, which causes VoiceOver to read the name of the button to you. Then you double-tap the button to activate its function. (VoiceOver reminds you about this if you turn on Speak Hints, which is helpful when you first use VoiceOver, but it soon becomes annoying.)

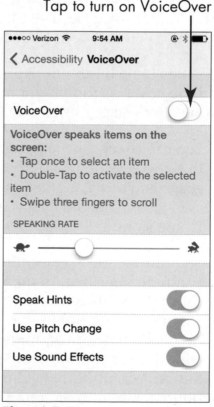

Tap this option   Tap to turn on VoiceOver

Figure 7-4   **Figure 7-5**

4. Tap the VoiceOver Practice button to select it; then double-tap the button to open VoiceOver Practice. (This is the new method of tapping that VoiceOver activates.) Practice using gestures such as pinching or flicking left, and VoiceOver tells you what action each gesture initiates.

5. Tap the Done button and then double-tap the same button to return to the VoiceOver dialog. Tap the Speak Hints On/Off switch and then double-tap the switch; VoiceOver speaks the name of each tapped item.

6. If you want VoiceOver to read words or characters to you (for example, in the Notes app), scroll down and then tap and double-tap Typing Feedback.

7. In the Typing Feedback dialog, tap and then double-tap to select the option you prefer. The Words option causes VoiceOver to read words to you, but not characters, such as the "dollar sign" ($). The Characters and Words option causes VoiceOver to read both, and so on.

8. Press the Home button to return to the Home screen. Read the next task to find out how to navigate your iPhone after you've turned on VoiceOver.

 You can change the language that VoiceOver speaks. In General settings, tap International and then Language and select another language. This action, however, also changes the language used for labels on Home icons and various settings and fields in iPhone.

 You can use the Accessibility Shortcut setting to help you more quickly turn the VoiceOver, Zoom, Switch Control, Assistive Touch, Grayscale, or Invert Colors features on and off. In the Accessibility dialog, tap Accessibility Shortcut. In the dialog that appears, choose what you want three presses of the Home button to activate. Now three presses with a single finger on the Home button provide you with the option you selected wherever you go in iPhone.

Use VoiceOver

After VoiceOver is turned on, you need to figure out how to use it. I won't kid you — using it is awkward at first, but you'll get the hang of it! Here are the main onscreen gestures you should know how to use:

⟹ **Tap an item to select it.** VoiceOver then speaks its name.

⟹ **Double-tap the selected item.** This action activates the item.

⟹ **Flick three fingers.** It takes three fingers to scroll around a page with VoiceOver turned on.

Table 7-1 provides additional gestures to help you use VoiceOver. If you want to use this feature often, I suggest that you read the VoiceOver section of the iPhone online *User Guide,* which goes into great detail about using VoiceOver. You'll find the *User Guide* at `http://manuals.info.apple.com/MANUALS/1000/MA1565/en_US/iphone_user_guide.pdf`. You can also get an iBooks version of the manual through that app in the iBookstore.

Table 7-1	VoiceOver Gestures
Gesture	*Effect*
Flick right or left.	Select the next or preceding item.
Tap with two fingers.	Stop speaking the current item.
Flick two fingers up.	Read everything from the top of the screen.
Flick two fingers down.	Read everything from the current position.
Flick three fingers up or down.	Scroll one page at a time.
Flick three fingers right or left.	Go to the next or preceding page.
Tap three fingers.	Speak the scroll status (for example, line 20 of 100).
Flick four fingers up or down.	Go to the first or last element on a page.
Flick four fingers right or left.	Go to the next or preceding section (as on a web page).

If tapping with two or three fingers seems difficult for you, try tapping with one finger from one hand and one or two from the other. When double- or triple-tapping, you have to perform these gestures as quickly as you can for them to work.

 Check out some of the settings for VoiceOver, including a choice for Braille, Language Rotor for making language choices, the ability to navigate images, and a setting to have iPhone speak notifications.

Several Vision features are simple on/off settings, so rather than repeatedly give you the steps to get to those settings, I provide this useful bullet list of additional features that you can turn on or off after you tap Settings⇨General⇨Accessibility:

➡ **Zoom:** The Zoom feature enlarges the contents displayed on the iPhone screen when you double-tap the screen with three fingers. The Zoom feature works almost everywhere in iPhone: in Photos, on web pages, on your Home screens, in your Mail, in Music, and in Videos — give it a try!

➡ **Invert Colors:** The Invert Colors setting reverses colors on your screen so that white backgrounds are black and black text is white.

 The Invert Colors feature works well in some places and not so well in others. For example, in the Photos application, pictures appear almost as photo negatives. Your Home screen image will likewise look a bit strange. And don't even think of playing a video with this feature turned on! However, if you need help reading text, White on Black can be useful in several apps.

➠ **Larger Text:** If having larger text in apps such as Contacts, Mail, and Notes would be helpful to you, you can turn on the Larger Text feature and choose the text size that works best for you.

➠ **Bold Text:** Turning on this setting restarts your iPhone (after asking you for permission to do so) and then causes text in various apps and in Settings to be bold.

➠ **Increase Contrast:** Use this setting to set up backgrounds in some areas of iPhone and apps with greater contrast, which should improve visibility.

➠ **Reduce Motion:** Tap this accessibility feature and then tap the On/Off setting to turn off the parallax effect, which causes the background of your home screens to appear to float as you move the phone around.

➠ **On/Off Labels:** If you have trouble making out colors and therefore find it hard to tell when an On/Off setting is On (green) and Off (white), use this setting to add a circle to the right of a setting when it's off and a white vertical line to a setting when it's on (see **Figure 7-6**).

On/Off Labels option

Figure 7-6

Use iPhone with Hearing Aids

1. If you have Bluetooth enabled or use another style of hearing aid, your iPhone may be able to detect it and work with its settings to improve sound on your phone calls. Tap Settings on the Home screen and then tap General.

2. Tap Accessibility and then scroll down to the Hearing section and tap Hearing Aids.

3. On the following screen, shown in **Figure 7-7**, your iPhone searches for hearing aid devices; when yours appears, tap it.

4. Tap Hearing Aid Mode to turn on a feature that could improve audio quality when you're using your hearing aid.

Figure 7-7

Adjust the Volume

1. Though individual apps such as Music and Video have their own volume settings, you can set your iPhone system volume for your ringer and alerts as well to help you better hear what's going on.

2. Tap Settings on the Home screen and then tap Sounds.

3. In the Sounds settings that appear (see **Figure 7-8**), tap and drag the Ringer and Alerts slider to the right to increase the volume of these audible attention grabbers, or to the left to lower it.

●●●○○ Sprint 🛜   4:04 PM   ✳ ▬▮

❮ Settings   **Sounds**

VIBRATE

Vibrate on Ring   ⬤▬

Vibrate on Silent   ▬◯

RINGER AND ALERTS

◀ ━━━━━━━◯━━━━ ◀))) ──── Adjust iPhone volume here

Change with Buttons   ⬤▬

The volume of the ringer and alerts can be
adjusted using the volume buttons.

SOUNDS AND VIBRATION PATTERNS

Ringtone   Piano Riff ❯

Text Tone   Vibrate Only ❯

New Voicemail   Tri-tone ❯

Figure 7-8

4. Press the Home button to return to the Home screen.

In the Sounds settings, you can turn on or off the sounds that iPhone makes when certain events occur (such as receiving new Mail or Calendar alerts). These sounds are turned on by default.

Even those of us with perfect hearing sometimes have trouble hearing a phone ring, especially in busy public places. Consider using the Vibrate settings in the Sounds settings to have your phone vibrate when a call is coming in.

Set Up Subtitles and Captioning

1. Closed captioning and subtitles help folks with hearing challenges enjoy entertainment and educational content. Tap Settings on the Home screen, tap Accessibility, and then scroll down to the Media section and tap Subtitles and Captioning.

2. On the following screen, shown in **Figure 7-9,** tap the On/Off switch to turn on Closed Captions and SDH (Subtitles for the Deaf and Hard of Hearing). If you'd like, you can also tap Style and choose a text style for the captions.

3. Press the Home button to return to the Home screen.

Figure 7-9

Manage Other Hearing Settings

Several hearing accessibility settings are simple On/Off settings, including:

➡ **Use Mono Audio:** Using the stereo effect in head-phones or a headset breaks up sounds so that you hear a portion in one ear and a portion in the other ear. The purpose is to simulate the way your ears process sounds. If there is only one channel of sound, that sound is sent to both ears. However, if you're hard of hearing or deaf in one ear, you're hearing only a portion of the sound in your hearing ear, which can be frustrating. If you have such hearing challenges and want to use iPhone with a headset connected, you should turn on Mono Audio. When it's turned on, all sound is combined and distributed to both ears.

➡ **Have iPhone Speak Auto-text:** The Speak Auto-text feature, which you access through the Speech selection under Accessibility, speaks autocorrections and autocapitalizations. (You can turn on both these features using Keyboard settings.) When you enter text in an app such as Notes or Mail, the app then makes either type of change, while Speak Auto-text lets you know what change was made.

 Why would you want iPhone to tell you whenever an autocorrection has been made? If you have vision challenges and you know that you typed *ain't* when writing dialogue for a character in your novel, but iPhone corrected it to *isn't,* you would want to know. Similarly, if you type the poet's name *e.e. cummings* and autocapitalization corrects it (incorrectly), you need to know immediately so that you can change it back again!

➡ **Turn on LED Flash for Alerts:** If you need a visual clue when an alert is spoken, turn this setting on.

 Use Phone Noise Cancellation: If you're annoyed at ambient noise when you make a call in public (or noisy private) settings, with an iPhone 5 or later, turn on the Phone Noise Cancellation feature. When you hold the phone to your ear during a call, this feature reduces background noise to some extent.

Turn On and Work with AssistiveTouch

1. The AssistiveTouch Control panel helps those who have challenges working with buttons to provide input to iPhone using the touchscreen. To turn on AssistiveTouch, tap Settings on the Home screen and then tap General and Accessibility.

2. In the Accessibility pane, scroll down and tap Assistive-Touch. In the pane that appears, tap the On/Off switch for AssistiveTouch to turn it on (see **Figure 7-10**). A gray square (called the AssistiveTouch Control panel) then appears on the right side of the screen. This square now appears in the same location in whatever apps you display on your iPhone, though you can move it around with your finger.

 3. Tap the AssistiveTouch Control panel to display options, as shown in **Figure 7-11**. New in iOS 8, the panel now includes Notification Center and Control Center options.

4. You can tap Favorites or Device on the panel to see additional choices, tap Siri to activate the personal assistant feature, tap Notification Center or Control Center to display those panels, or press Home to go directly to the Home screen. After you've chosen an option, pressing the Home button takes you back to the Home screen.

Tap to turn on AssistiveTouch

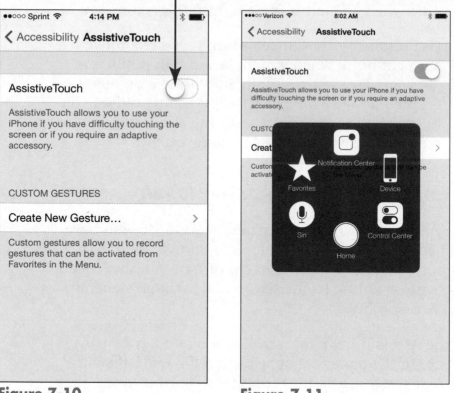

Figure 7-10   **Figure 7-11**

Table 7-2 shows the major options available in the AssistiveTouch Control panel and their purpose.

Table 7-2	AssistiveTouch Controls
Control	**Purpose**
Siri	Activates the Siri feature, which allows you to speak questions and make requests of your iPhone.
Favorites	Displays a set of gestures with only the Pinch gesture preset; you can tap any of the other blank squares to add your own favorite gestures.
Device	You can rotate the screen, lock the screen, turn the volume up or down, mute or unmute sound, or shake iPhone to undo an action using the presets in this option.
Home	Sends you to the Home screen.

Control	Purpose
Control Center	Open the Control Center common commands.
Notification Center	Open Notification Center with reminders, Calendar appointments, and so on.

Turn On Additional Physical and Motor Settings

Use these On/Off settings in the Accessibility settings to help you deal with how fast you click and how you answer phone calls:

→ **Home-press Speed:** Sometimes if you have dexterity challenges, it's hard to double-press or triple-press the Home button fast enough to make an effect. Choose the Slow or Slowest option when you tap this setting to allow you a bit more time to make that second or third tap.

→ **Call Audio Routing:** If you prefer to use your speaker phone to receive incoming calls, or you typically use a headset with your phone that allows you to tap a button to receive a call, click this option and then choose Headset or Speaker. Speakers and headsets can both provide a better hearing experience for many.

 If you have certain adaptive accessories that allow you to control devices with head gestures, you can use them to control your iPhone, highlighting features in sequence and then selecting one. Use the Switch Control feature in the Accessibility settings to turn this mode on and make settings.

Focus Learning with Guided Access

1. Guided Access is a feature that you can use to limit a user's access to iPhone to a single app, and even limit access in that app to certain features. This feature is useful in several settings, ranging from a classroom, for use by someone with attention deficit disorder, and even to a public setting such as a kiosk where you don't want users to be able to open other apps. Tap Settings and then tap General.

2. Tap Accessibility and then scroll down and tap Guided Access; then, on the screen that follows (see **Figure 7-12**), tap Guided Access to turn the feature on.

3. Tap Passcode Settings and then tap Set Guided Access Passcode to activate a passcode so that those using an app cannot return to the Home screen to access other apps. In the Set Passcode dialog that appears (see **Figure 7-13**), enter a passcode using the numeric pad. Enter the number again when prompted.

4. Press the Home button and tap an app to open it.

5. Press the Home button three times. You are presented with an Option button along the bottom of the screen; tap the button to display these options:

- **Sleep/Wake Button:** You can put your iPhone to sleep or wake it up with three presses of the Home button.

- **Volume Buttons:** You can tap Always On or Always Off. If you don't want users to be able to adjust volume using the volume toggle on the side of the iPhone, for example, use this setting.

- **Motion:** Turn this setting off if you don't want users to move the iPhone around — for example, to play a race car driving game.

- **Keyboards:** Use this setting to prohibit people using this app from entering text using the keyboard.

- **Touch:** If you don't want users to be able to use the touchscreen, turn this off.

- **Time Limit:** Tap this and use settings that are displayed to set a time limit for the use of the app.

6. At this point, you can also use your finger to circle areas of the screen that you want to disable, such as a Store button in the Music app.

7. Press the Home button three times the Home button and then enter your passcode, if you set one, to return to the Home screen.

Tap to turn on Guided Access

Figure 7-12

Figure 7-13

Talking to Your iPhone with Siri

One of the hottest features on iPhone is Siri, a personal assistant feature that responds to the commands you speak to your iPhone 4s or later. With Siri, you can ask for nearby restaurants, and a list appears. You can dictate your email messages rather than type them. You can open apps with a voice command, and with iOS 8, for the first time, Siri can open the App Store. Calling your mother is as simple as saying, "Call Mom." Want to know the capital of Rhode Island? Just ask. Siri checks several online sources to answer questions ranging from the result of a mathematical calculation to the next scheduled flight to Dubai. You can also have Siri perform tasks such as returning calls and controlling iTunes Radio. Finally, you can even play music, and with iOS 8 comes integration with Shazam, a music identifier service that can identify tagged songs (songs that contain embedded information that identifies them by categories such as artist or genre of music) for you.

If you don't have an iPhone 4s or later, you can skip this chapter and dream of the day when you can upgrade your phone.

Get ready to . . .

Activate Siri

When you first go through the process of registering your phone, making settings for your location, using iCloud, and so on, at one point you will see the screen in **Figure 8-1**. To activate Siri at this point, just tap Use Siri. As you begin to use your phone, iPhone reminds you about using Siri by displaying a message.

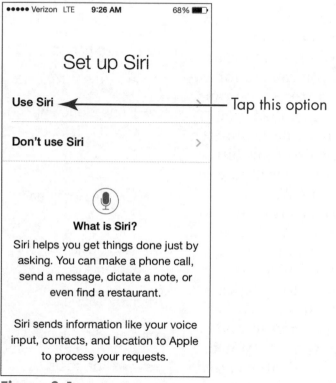

Figure 8-1

If you didn't activate Siri during the registration process, you can use Settings to turn Siri on by following these steps:

1. Tap the Settings icon on the Home screen.

2. Tap General and then tap Siri (see **Figure 8-2**).

3. In the dialog in **Figure 8-3**, tap the On/Off switch to turn Siri on.

Tap this option   Tap to turn Siri on

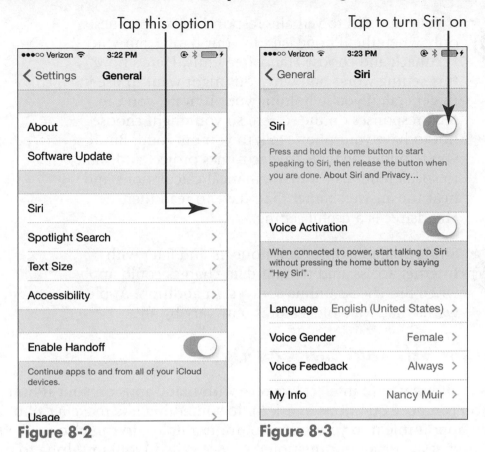

Figure 8-2   Figure 8-3

4. If you wish to change the language Siri uses, tap Language and choose a different language in the list that appears.

5. To change the gender of Siri's voice from female to male, tap Voice Gender and then tap Male.

6. If you want to be able to activate Siri Hands-Free (a new feature in iOS 8), tap the Voice Activation switch to turn on the feature. With your iPhone plugged into an outlet, car, or computer, just say "Hey, Siri" and Siri opens up, ready for a command. In addition, with streaming voice recognition, Siri displays in text what it's hearing as you speak, so you can verify that it has understood you instantly. This streaming feature makes the whole process of interacting with Siri faster.

If you want Siri to verbally respond to your requests only when the iPhone isn't in your hands, tap Voice Feedback and choose Handsfree Only. Here's how this setting works and why you might want to use it: In general, if you're holding your iPhone, you can read responses on the screen, so you might choose not to have your phone talk to you out loud. But if you're puttering with an electronics project and want to speak requests for mathematical calculations and hear the answers rather than have to read them, Handsfree is a useful setting.

 Siri is available only on iPhone 4s and later with Internet access, and cellular data charges could apply when Siri checks online sources. In addition, Apple warns that available features may vary by area.

Understand All That Siri Can Do

Siri allows you to interact by voice with many apps on your iPhone. You can pose questions or ask to do something like make a call or add an appointment to your calendar, for example. Siri can also search the Internet or use an informational service called Wolfram Alpha to provide information on just about any topic.

Siri also checks with Wikipedia, Bing, and Twitter to get you the information you ask for. In addition, you can now use Siri to tell iPhone to return a call, play your voice mail, open and search the App Store, or control iTunes Radio playback.

Siri knows what app you're using, though you don't have to have that app open to make a request involving it. However, if you are in the Messages app, you can make a statement like "Tell Susan I'll be late," and Siri knows that you want to send a message.

Siri requires no preset structure for your questions; you can phrase things in several ways. For example, you might say, "Where am I?" to see a map of your current location, or you could say, "What is my current location?" or "What address is this?" and get the same results.

If you ask a question about, say, the weather, Siri responds to you both verbally and with text information (see **Figure 8-4**) or by opening a form, as with email, or by providing a graphic display for some items such as maps. When a result appears, you can tap it to make a choice or open a related app.

Siri works with Phone, the App Store, Music, Messages, Reminders, Calendar, Maps, Mail, Weather, Stocks, Clock, Contacts, Notes, social media apps such as Twitter, Safari, and iTunes Radio (see **Figure 8-5**). In the following tasks, I provide a quick guide to some of the most useful ways you can use Siri.

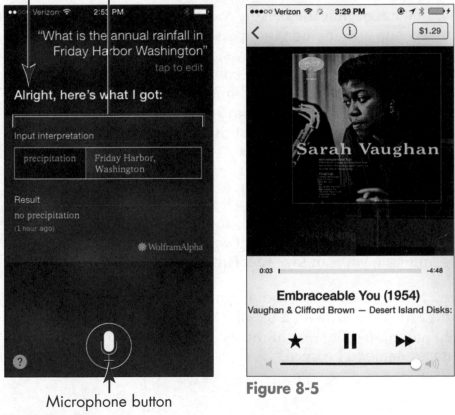

Siri's reply   Related info

"What is the annual rainfall in Friday Harbor Washington"
tap to edit

Alright, here's what I got:

Input interpretation

| precipitation | Friday Harbor, Washington |

Result

no precipitation
(1 hour ago)

✳ WolframAlpha

Microphone button

Figure 8-4

$1.29

Sarah Vaughan

0:03   -4:48

Embraceable You (1954)
Vaughan & Clifford Brown — Desert Island Disks:

★   ❚❚   ▶▶

Figure 8-5

If you want to dictate text in an app like Notes, use the Dictation key on the onscreen keyboard in iOS 8 to do so. See the task "Use Dictation," later in this chapter, for more about this feature.

Note that no matter what kind of action you wish to perform, first press and hold the Home button until Siri opens.

 With iOS 8, Siri now supports 22 languages, so you can finally show off those language lessons you took in high school.

Call Contacts

First, make sure that the person you want to call is entered in your Contacts app and include that person's phone number in his record. If you want to call somebody by stating your relationship to her, such as "Call sister," be sure to enter that relationship in the Related field in her contact record. Also make sure that the settings for Siri (refer to **Figure 8-3**) include your own contact name in the My Info field. (See Chapter 5 for more about creating contact records.) Follow these steps:

1. Press and hold the Home button until Siri appears.

2. Speak a command such as "Call Harold Smith," "Return Joe's call," or "Call Mom." If you want to make a FaceTime call, you can say "FaceTime Mom."

3. If you have two contacts who might match a spoken name, Siri responds with a list of possible matches (see **Figure 8-6**). Tap one in the list or state the correct contact's name to proceed.

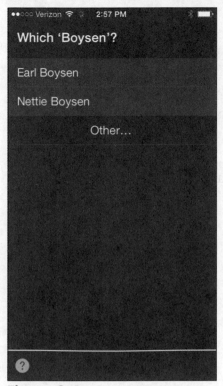

Figure 8-6

4. The call is placed. To end the call before it completes, press the Home button and then tap End.

 To cancel any spoken request, you have three options: Say "Cancel," tap the Microphone button on the Siri screen, or press the Home button. If you're using a headset or Bluetooth device, tap the end button on the device.

You can also access your voice mail using Siri. Just press and hold the Home button until Siri activates and then say something like "Check voice mail." Siri responds by telling you whether you have a new voice mail message and displays a list of any new messages. Tap one and then tap the Play button to play it back. If you want to get rid of it, tap Delete. It's that simple.

Create Reminders and Alerts

1. You can also use Siri with the Reminders app. To create a reminder or alert, press and hold the Home button and then speak a command, such as "Remind me to call Dad on Thursday at 10 a.m." or "Wake me up tomorrow at 7 a.m."

2. A preview of the reminder or alert is displayed (see **Figure** 8-7), and Siri asks you whether it should create the reminder. Tap or say Confirm to create it or Cancel.

Figure 8-7

3. If you want a reminder ahead of the event you created, activate Siri and speak a command, such as "Remind me tonight about the play on Thursday at 8 p.m." A second reminder is created, which you can confirm or cancel if you change your mind.

Add Tasks to Your Calendar

1. You can also set up events on your Calendar using Siri. Press and hold the Home button and then speak a phrase, such as "Set up meeting at 10 a.m. on October 12th."

2. A sample calendar entry appears, and Siri asks whether you want to confirm it.

3. If there's a conflict with the appointment, Siri tells you that an appointment already exists at that time (see **Figure 8-8**) and asks whether you still want to set up the new appointment. You can say "Yes" or "Cancel" at that point, or tap the Yes or Cancel button.

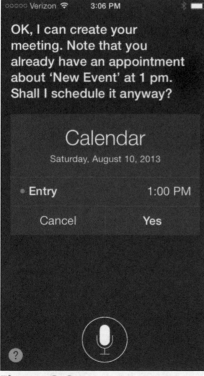

Figure 8-8

Play Music

1. You can use Siri to play music from the Music app and iTunes Radio. Press and hold the Home button until Siri appears.

2. To play music, speak a command, such as "Play music" or "Play Jazz radio station" to play a specific song, album, or radio station.

3. When music is playing, use commands, such as "Pause music," "Next track," or "Stop music" to control playback.

4. You can use the new integration of iPhone with Shazam, a music identifier app that comes in iOS 8, to identify tagged music. First, when you're near an audio source playing music, press the Home button twice to activate Siri.

5. Ask Siri a question such as "What music is playing?" or "What's this song?"

6. Siri listens for a bit and if Siri recognizes the song, it shows you the song name, artist, any other available information, and the ability to purchase the music in the iTunes Store.

Get Directions

You can use the Maps app and Siri to find your current location, get directions, find nearby businesses such as restaurants or a bank, or get a map of another location. Be sure to turn on Location Services to allow Siri to know your current location (go to Settings and tap Privacy⇨ Location Services: make sure Location Services is on and that Siri is turned on further down in these settings).

Here are some of the commands that you can try to get directions or a list of nearby businesses:

➡ **"Where am I?"**

Displays a map of your current location.

➡ **"Where is Apache Junction, Arizona?"**

Displays a map of that city.

➡ **"Find restaurants."**

Displays a list of restaurants near your current location; tap one to display a map of its location.

➡ **"Find Bank of America."**

Displays a map with the location of the indicated business (or in some cases, several nearby locations, such as a bank branch and all ATMs), as shown in **Figure 8-9.**

➡ **Get directions to the Empire State Building.**

Loads a map with a route drawn and provides a narration of directions to the site from your current location.

 After a location is displayed on a map, tap the Information button on the location's label to view its address, phone number, and website address, if available.

Figure 8-9

Ask for Facts

Wolfram Alpha is a self-professed online computational knowledge engine. That means that it's more than a search engine because it provides specific information about a search term rather than multiple search results. If you want facts without having to spend time browsing websites to find those facts, Wolfram Alpha is a very good resource.

Siri uses Wolfram Alpha and sources such as Wikipedia and Bing to look up facts in response to questions, such as "What is the capital of Kansas?" "What is the square root of 2003?" or "How large is Mars?" Just press and hold the Home button and ask your question; Siri consults its resources and returns a set of relevant facts.

You can also get information about other things, such as the weather, stocks, or the time. Just say a phrase like one of these to get what you need:

➠ **"What is the weather?"**

This shows the weather report for your current location. If you want weather in another location, just specify the location in your question.

➠ **"What is the price of Apple stock?"**

Siri tells you the current price of the stock or the price of the stock when the stock market last closed.

➠ **"What time is it?"**

Siri tells you the time and displays a clock for your location (see **Figure 8-10**).

Figure 8-10

Search the Web

Although Siri can use its resources to respond to specific requests such as "Who is the Queen of England?" more general requests for information will cause Siri to search further on the web. Siri can also search Twitter for comments related to your search.

For example, if you speak a phrase such as "Find a website about birds" or "Find information about the World Series," Siri can respond in a couple of ways. The app can simply display a list of search results by using the default search engine specified in your settings for Safari or by suggesting, "If you like, I can search the web for such and such." In the first instance, just tap a result to go to that website. In the second instance, you can confirm that you want to search the web or cancel.

Send Email, Messages, or Tweets

You can create an email or an instant message using Siri and existing contacts. For example, if you say, "Email Jack Wilkes," a form opens that is already addressed to that contact. Siri asks you what to say. Speak your message and then say "Send" to speed your message on its way.

Siri also works with messaging apps such as Messages. If you have the Messages app open and you say, "Tell Sarah I'll call soon," Siri creates a message for you to approve and send.

 Siri can also tweet, connect with Flickr and Vimeo, and post to Facebook. Go to Settings and turn on Flickr, Vimeo, Twitter, or Facebook support and provide your account information. Now you can say things to Siri such as "Post Tweet" or "Post to Facebook" and Siri asks what you want to say, lets you review it, and posts it.

Use Dictation

1. Text entry isn't Siri's strong point. Instead, you can use the Dictation key that appears with a microphone symbol on the onscreen keyboard (see **Figure 8-11**) to speak text rather than type it. This feature is called Dictation. Go to any app where you enter text, such as Notes or Mail, and tap in the document or form. The onscreen keyboard appears.

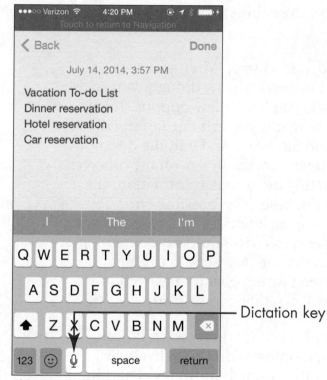

Dictation key

Figure 8-11

2. Tap the Dictation key on the keyboard and speak your text.

3. To end the dictation, tap Done.

When you finish speaking text, you can use the keyboard to make edits to the text Siri entered, although as voice recognition programs go, Dictation is pretty darn accurate. If a word sports a blue underline, which means there may be an error, you can tap to select it and make edits to it.

Get Helpful Tips

I know you're going to have a wonderful time learning the ins and outs of Siri, but before I close this chapter, here are some tips to get you going:

➡ **If Siri doesn't understand you:** When you speak a command and Siri displays what it thought you said, if it misses the mark, you have a few options. To correct a request you've made, you can tap Tap to Edit under the command Siri heard and edit the question by typing or tapping the Dictation key on the onscreen keyboard and dictating the correct information. If a word is underlined in blue, it's a possible error. Tap the word and then tap an alternative that Siri suggests. You can also simply speak to Siri and say something like "I meant Sri Lanka" or "No, send it to Sally." If even corrections aren't working, you may need to restart your phone to reset the Siri software.

➡ **Headsets and earphones:** If you're using iPhone earphones or a Bluetooth headset to activate Siri, instead of pressing the Home button, press and hold the center button (the little button on the headset that starts and stops a call).

➡ **Using Find My Friends:** There is a free app you can download from the App Store called Find My Friends that, in addition to allowing you to use it with keyboard input, allows you to ask Siri to locate your friends geographically.

➡ **Getting help:** To get help with Siri features, just press
   and hold the Home button and ask Siri, "What can
   you do?"

➡ **Joking around:** If you need a good laugh, ask Siri to
   tell you a joke. It has quite the sense of humor.

 If you're becoming a Siri groupie, you might want
to purchase *Siri For Dummies,* by Marc Saltzman
(Wiley).

Getting Social with FaceTime, Twitter, and iMessage

Chapter

9

FaceTime is an excellent video-calling app that's located on the second Home screen of iPhone out of the box. The app lets you call people who have FaceTime on their devices using either a phone number or an email address. You and your friend, colleague, or family member can see each other as you talk, which makes for a much more personal calling experience.

Twitter is a social networking service, referred to as a *microblog* because it involves only short, posted messages. Twitter is incorporated into the iOS n a way that allows you to tweet people from within Safari, Photos, Camera, Maps, and many other apps. You can also set up Twitter credentials in Settings and use them to post tweets whenever you like.

Finally, iMessage is a feature available through the preinstalled Messages app for instant messaging (IM). IM involves sending a text message to somebody's iPhone, iPod touch, Mac running OS X 10.8 or later, or iPad (using the person's phone number or email address to carry on an instant conversation). With iOS 8 comes several new features for Messages, including the capability to send audio and video via Messages.

In this chapter, I introduce you to FaceTime, Twitter, and the Messages app and review their simple controls. In no time, you'll be socializing with all and sundry.

Understand Who Can Use FaceTime

Here's a quick rundown of the device and information you need for using FaceTime's various features:

➡ You can use FaceTime to call people who have an iPhone 4 or later, an iPad 2 or a third-generation iPad or later, a fourth-generation iPod touch or later, or a Mac (running Mac OS X 10.6.6 or later).

➡ You can use a phone number to connect with anybody with either an iOS device or Mac and an iCloud account.

➡ The person you're contacting has to have allowed FaceTime to be used in Settings.

Get an Overview of FaceTime

FaceTime works with the iPhone's built-in cameras so that you can call other folks who have a device that supports FaceTime. You can use FaceTime to chat while sharing video images with another person. This preinstalled app is useful for seniors who want to keep up with distant family members and friends and see (as well as hear) the latest-and-greatest news.

You can make and receive calls with FaceTime using a phone number or an email account to those with an iCloud account and show the person on the other end what's going on around you. Just remember that you can't adjust audio volume from within the app or record a video call. Nevertheless, on the positive side, even though its features are limited, this app is straightforward to use.

You can use your Apple ID and iCloud account to access FaceTime, so it works pretty much right away. See Chapter 3 for more about getting an Apple ID.

If you're having trouble using FaceTime, make sure that the FaceTime feature is turned on. That's quick to do: Tap Settings on the Home screen, tap FaceTime, and then tap the On/Off switch to turn it on, if necessary. On this Settings screen, you can also select the phone number and/or email addresses that others can use to make FaceTime calls to you, as well as which one of those is displayed as your caller ID.

Make a FaceTime Call with Wi-Fi or 3G/4G

1. If you know that the person you're calling has FaceTime on an iPhone 4 or later, an iPad 2 or later, an iPod touch, or a Mac, adding that person to your iPhone Contacts is a good idea. Tap Phone in the dock, tap Contacts, and then tap the plus sign (Add) button; see Chapter 5 for more details about adding contacts.

2. Tap the FaceTime button on the second Home page. Tap to choose a Video or Audio call at the top of the screen. Video includes your voice and image; Audio includes only your voice.

3. If your contact doesn't appear in the Recents list, tap the Enter Name, Email, or Number field and begin to enter a contact's name; a list of matching contacts appears. You can also tap the plus sign (+) to open your complete contacts list, scroll to locate a contact who has associated a device with FaceTime, and click the appropriate method to initiate a call (see **Figure 9-1**).

You'll see a Camera button if that contact's device supports FaceTime video and a Phone button if the contact's device supports FaceTime audio.

(Note that if you haven't recorded this person in your contacts and you know the phone number to call or email, you can just enter that information in the Enter Name, Email, or Number field).

 When you call somebody using an email address, the person must be signed in to his Apple iCloud account and have verified that the address can be used for FaceTime calls. You can make this setting by tapping Settings and then FaceTime⇨Use Your Apple ID for FaceTime; FaceTime for Mac users make this setting by selecting FaceTime⇨Preferences.

4. When the person accepts the call, you see a large screen that displays the recipient's image and a small screen referred to as a Picture in Picture (PiP) containing your image superimposed (see **Figure 9-2**).

 To view recent calls, tap the FaceTime app on the second Home screen and then tap the Information button on a recent call, and iPhone displays that person's information. You can tap the contact to call the person back.

 If you have iOS 6 or later, you can use FaceTime over both a Wi-Fi network and your iPhone 3G or 4G connection. However, remember that if you use FaceTime over a phone connection, you may incur costly data usage fees. To avoid this, in Settings under FaceTime, set the iPhone Cellular Calls switch to Off.

Tap this for video

Figure 9-1

Figure 9-2

Accept and End a FaceTime Call

1. If you're on the receiving end of a FaceTime call, accepting the call is about as easy as it gets. When the call comes in, tap the Accept button to take the call or tap the Decline button to reject it (see **Figure 9-3**).

2. Chat away with your friend, swapping video images. To end the call, tap the End button (see **Figure 9-4**).

 To mute sound during a call, tap the Mute button, which looks like a microphone with a line through it (refer to **Figure 9-4**). Tap the button again to unmute your iPhone.

Figure 9-3   **Figure 9-4**

 If you'd rather not be available for calls, you can go to Settings and turn on the Do Not Disturb feature. This stops any incoming calls or notifications other than for the people you've designated as exceptions to Do Not Disturb. After you turn on Do Not Disturb, you can schedule when it's active, allow calls from certain people, or allow a second call from the same person in a three-minute interval to go through by using the Do Not Disturb settings.

Switch Views

1. When you're on a FaceTime call, you might want to use iPhone's built-in, rear-facing camera to show the person

you're talking to what's going on around you. Tap the
Switch Camera button (refer to **Figure** 9-4) to switch
from the front-facing camera that's displaying your image
to the back-facing camera that captures whatever you're
looking at (see **Figure 9-5**).

2. Tap the Switch Camera button again to switch back to
   the front camera displaying your image.

Figure 9-5

Experience Twitter on iPhone

Twitter is a social networking service for *microblogging,* which involves
posting very short messages (limited to 140 characters) online so that
your friends can see what you're up to. You can go to your Settings from
the Home screen and install the app from the Twitter settings. After you
have an account, you can post tweets for all to see, have people follow
your tweets, and follow the tweets that other people post.

The ability to tweet is integrated into several apps. You can post tweets using the Share button within Safari, Voice Memos, Photos, Camera, Maps and many third-party apps. First, using your computer or the Safari browser on your iPhone, sign up for a Twitter account at `https://twitter.com`. Go to Settings and tap Twitter. Then click Install and sign in to the iTunes Store. iPhone installs the Twitter app automatically.

Now when you're using Safari, Photos, Voice Memos, Camera, or Maps, you can choose Twitter in the screen that appears when you tap the Share button (see **Figure 9-6**). You'll see a tweet form. Just type your brief message in the form and then tap Send.

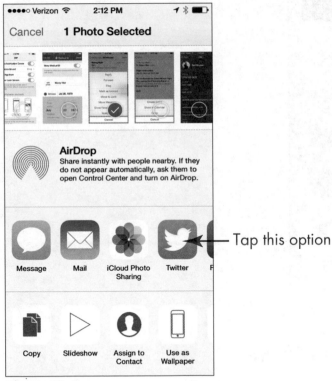

Tap this option

Figure 9-6

 See Chapters 10 and 16 for more about tweeting in the Safari and Photos apps.

Set Up an iMessage Account

1. iMessage is a feature available through the preinstalled Messages app that allows you to send and receive instant messages (IMs) to others using an Apple iOS device or suitably configured Macs. Instant messaging differs from email or tweeting in an important way. Whereas you might email somebody and wait for days or weeks before that person responds, or you might post a tweet that could sit there awhile before anybody views it, with instant messaging, communication happens almost immediately. You send an IM, and it appears on somebody's Apple device right away. Assuming that the person wants to participate in a live conversation, the chat begins immediately, allowing a back-and-forth dialogue in real time. To set up Messages, tap Settings on the Home screen.

2. Tap Messages, and the settings shown in **Figure** 9-7 appear.

Set this to On

Figure 9-7

3. If iMessage isn't set to On (refer to **Figure 9-7**), tap the On/Off switch to turn it on.

4. Check to be sure that the phone number and/or email account associated with your iPhone under the Send & Receive setting is correct. (This should be set up automatically based on your iCloud settings.) If it's not, tap the Send & Receive field, add an email or phone, and then tap Messages to return to the previous screen.

5. To allow a notice to be sent to the sender when you've read a message, tap the On/Off switch for Send Read Receipts. You can also choose to show a subject field in your messages.

6. Press the Home button to leave Settings.

 To change the email account used by Messages, tap Send & Receive, tap the Information button to the right of an email address, and then tap Remove This Email and then confirm the deletion; next, follow the preceding steps to add another account.

Use Messages to Address, Create, and Send Messages

1. Now you're ready to use Messages. From the Home screen, tap the Messages button. Tap the New Message button in the top-right corner to begin a conversation.

2. In the form that appears (see **Figure 9-8**), you can address a message in a couple of ways:

- Begin to type a name in the To field, and a list of matching contacts appears.

- Tap the Dictation key on the onscreen keyboard and speak the address.

- Tap the plus (+) button on the right side of the address field, and the All Contacts list is displayed.

3. Tap a contact on the list you chose from in Step 2. If the contact has both an email address and a phone number stored, the Info dialog appears, allowing you to tap one or the other, which addresses the message.

4. To create a message, simply tap in the message field near the bottom of the screen (see **Figure 9-9**) and type your message.

Message field

Send button

Figure 9-8

Figure 9-9

5. To send the message, tap the Send button (refer to **Figure 9-9**). When your recipient (or recipients) responds, you'll see the conversation displayed on the screen. Tap in the message field again to respond to the last comment.

 You can address a message to more than one person by simply choosing more recipients in Step 2 of the preceding list.

Read Messages

1. Tap Messages on the Home screen.

2. When the app opens, you see a list of all text messages and all attachments that have appeared in your Message app.

3. Tap a message to see the message string, including all attachments, as shown in **Figure 9-10**.

Figure 9-10

4. To view all attachments of a message, tap Details and scroll down.

Clear a Conversation

1. When you're done chatting, you might want to delete a conversation to remove the clutter before you start a new chat. With Messages open and your conversations displayed, swipe to the right on the message you want to delete.

2. Tap the Delete button next to the conversation you want to get rid of (see **Figure 9-11**).

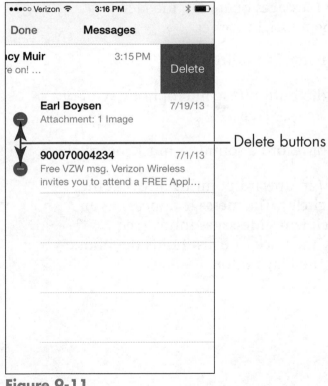

Figure 9-11

3. Tap Delete.

 You can tap the Contact button in the top-right corner of a conversation screen and choose to place a call or a FaceTime call, or to get more information about a participant at any time. You can text contacts who don't have an iCloud account but who do have cell numbers in your contacts list. Just be aware that the message may have limited characters and may not support photo, video, or audio attachments.

Send and Receive Audio

1. When you're creating a message, you can also create an audio message. With Messages open, tap the New Message button in the top-right corner.

2. Enter an addressee's name in the To field.

3. Tap and hold the Audio button (the microphone symbol to the right of the screen).

4. Speak your message or record a sound or music near you.

5. Tap the Send button (an upward-pointing arrow at the top of the recording circle). The message appears as an audio track in the recipient's Messages inbox (see **Figure 9-12**). To play the track, she just holds the phone up to her ear or taps the Play button.

Send button

Figure 9-12

Send a Photo or Video

1. When you're creating a message, you can also create a short video message. With Messages open, tap the New Message button in the top-right corner.

2. Press and hold the Camera button. In the tool palette that appears (see **Figure 9-13**), tap the Camera button to take a picture and then return to the message.

3. If you prefer to capture a video, with the palette in Figure 9-13 displayed, move the phone around to take a video and tap the red Stop button when you've recorded what you want to record. Tap the Send button (an upward-pointing arrow). Your video is attached to your message.

4. To send multiple photos or videos, repeat these steps and then tap Send to send your message and attachments.

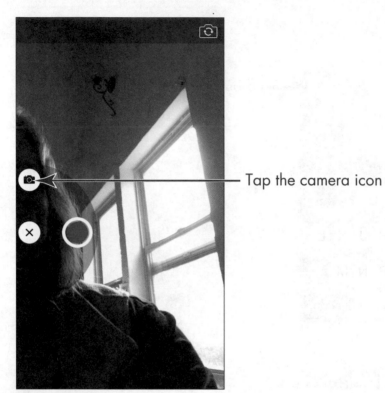

Tap the camera icon

Figure 9-13

Send a Map of Your Location

When sending a message, you can also send a map showing your current location. Tap a message and then tap Details.

Tap Send My Current Location (see **Figure 9-14**), and a map will be inserted as a message attachment.

Figure 9-14

 You can also share your location in the middle of a conversation rather than send a map attachment with your message. In the screen shown in **Figure 9-14**, tap Share My Location and then tap Share for One Hour, Share Until End of Day, or Share Indefinitely. A map showing your location appears above your conversation until you stop sharing.

Understand Group Messaging

If you want to start a conversation with a group of people, you can use group messaging. Group messaging is great for keeping several people in the conversational loop.

With iOS 8 comes a lot of group messaging functionality, including the following features:

➡ When you participate in a group message, you see all participants in the Details for the message (see **Figure 9-15**). With iOS 8, you can drop people whom you don't want to include any longer and leave the conversation yourself when you want to by simply tapping Details and then tapping Leave This Conversation.

➡ When you turn on Do Not Disturb by tapping Details in a message (see **Figure 9-15**), you won't get notifications of messages from this group, but you can still read the group's messages at a later time (this also works for individuals).

Figure 9-15

Taking you further into the workings of group messages is beyond the scope of this book, but if you're intrigued, go to www.apple.com/ios/ios8/messages/ for more information.

Activate the Do Not Disturb Feature

1. If you don't want to get notifications of new messages from an individual or group for a while, you can use the Do Not Disturb feature. With a message open, tap Details.

2. Tap the Do Not Disturb switch to turn the feature on (refer to **Figure 9-15**).

3. Later, return to Details and tap the Do Not Disturb switch again to turn the feature off.

> You can turn on the Do Not Disturb feature for everyone in the Control Center (drag up from the bottom edge of the screen to display it). You can also allow selected callers to get through in the Do Not Disturb settings by choosing everyone, no one, people you've tagged as favorites, or people in one or more groups.

Part III
Taking the Leap Online

Visit www.dummies.com/extras/iphoneforseniors for more ideas about apps you can buy in the App Store that you might find useful.

Browsing the Internet with Safari

Getting on the Internet with your iPhone is easily done using its Wi-Fi or 3G/4G capabilities. After you're online, the built-in browser (software that helps you navigate the Internet's contents), *Safari*, is your ticket to a wide world of information, entertainment, education, and more. Safari will look familiar to you if you've used it on a PC or Mac device before, though the way you move around by using the iPhone touchscreen might be new to you. In case you've never used Safari, this chapter takes you by the hand and shows you all the basics of making it work for you.

In this chapter, you discover how to go online with your iPhone. You see how to navigate among web pages and use iCloud tabs to share your browsing experience among devices. Along the way, you see how to place a bookmark for a favorite site or place a web clip on your Home screen. You can also view your browsing history, save online images to your Photo Library, post photos to sites from within Safari, or email or tweet a link to a friend. Two Safari features are Shared Links, which let you see URLs posted to your Twitter timeline, and iCloud Keychain, which is used

Get ready to . . .

for storing passwords in one handy, safe place online. You also explore Safari's Reader and Reading List features and learn how to keep yourself safer while online by using private browsing. Finally, you review the simple steps involved in printing what you find online.

Connect to the Internet

How you connect to the Internet depends on what connections are available:

➡ You can connect to the Internet via a Wi-Fi network. You can set up this type of network in your own home using your computer and some equipment from your Internet provider. You can also connect over public Wi-Fi networks, referred to as *hotspots*. You'll probably be surprised to discover how many hotspots your town or city has. Look for Internet cafés, coffee shops, hotels, libraries, and transportation centers such as airports or bus stations, for example. Many of these businesses display signs alerting you to their free Wi-Fi.

➡ You can also use the paid data network provided by AT&T, Sprint, T-Mobile, or Verizon to connect using 3G or 4G from just about anywhere you can get cellphone coverage via a cellular network.

To enable 3G/4G data, tap Settings and then Cellular. Tap to turn on the Cellular Data setting. Do note that browsing the Internet using a 3G/4G connection can eat up your data plan allotment quickly if your plan doesn't include unlimited data access.

To connect to a Wi-Fi network, you have to complete a few steps.

1. Tap Settings on the Home screen and then tap Wi-Fi. Be sure that Wi-Fi is set to On and choose a network to connect to. Network names should appear automatically when you're in range of them. When you're in range of a public hotspot, if access to several nearby networks is available, you may see a message asking you to tap a network name to select it. After you select one (or if only one network is available), you may see a message asking for your password. Ask the owner of the hotspot (for example, a hotel desk clerk or business owner) for this password, or if you're connecting to your home network, enter your network password.

2. Tap the Join button, and you're connected. Your iPhone will now recognize the network and be able to connect without entering the password.

Free public Wi-Fi networks typically don't require passwords, or the password is posted prominently for all to see. However, remember that after you connect, someone else can track your online activities because these are *unsecured* networks. Avoid accessing financial accounts or sending emails with sensitive information in them when connected to a public hotspot.

Explore Safari

1. After you're connected to a network, tap Safari on the Home screen. Safari opens, probably displaying the Apple iPhone Home page the first time you go online (see **Figure 10-1**).

2. Put two fingers together on the screen and unpinch them to expand the view. Double-tap the screen with a single finger to restore the default view size.

3. Put your finger on the screen and flick upward to scroll down on the page.

4. To return to the top of the web page, put your finger on the screen and drag downward or tap the Status bar at the very top of the screen.

Status bar

Address/Search field

Previous button

Next button

Share button

Bookmarks button

Show/Hide Tabs button

Figure 10-1

 Using your fingers on the screen to enlarge or reduce the size of a web page allows you to view what's displayed at various sizes, giving you more flexibility than the double-tap method.

 When you enlarge the display, you gain more control using two fingers to drag from left to right or from top to bottom on the screen. On a reduced display, one finger works fine for making these gestures.

Navigate Among Web Pages

1. Tap in the Address field just under the Status bar. The onscreen keyboard appears (see **Figure 10-2**).

2. Enter a web address; for example, you can go to www. wiley.com.

3. Tap the Go key on the keyboard (see **Figure** 10-2). The website appears.

- If, for some reason, a page doesn't display, tap the Reload button at the right end of the Address field.

- If Safari is loading a web page and you change your mind about viewing the page, you can tap Cancel, which appears at the right end of the Address field during this process, to stop loading the page.

4. Tap the Previous button to go to the last page you displayed.

5. Tap the Next button to go forward to the page you just backed up from.

6. To follow a link to another web page (links are typically indicated by colored text or graphics), tap the link with your finger. To view the destination web address of the link before you tap it, just touch and hold the link; a menu appears that displays the address at the top, as shown in **Figure** 10-3.

 By default, AutoFill is turned on in iPhone, causing entries you make in fields such as the Address field to automatically display possible matching entries. You can turn off AutoFill by using iPhone Settings for Safari.

With iOS 8, Apple QuickType has been added to support predictive text in the onscreen keyboard. This feature adds the capability for iPhone to spot what you probably intend to type from text you've already entered and suggests it to save you time typing.

Go key   Delete key   The link's web address

Figure 10-2   Figure 10-3

Use Tabbed Browsing

1. *Tabbed browsing* is a feature that allows you to have several websites open at one time so that you can move easily among those sites. With Safari open and a web page already displayed, tap the Show/Hide Tabs button in the bottom-right corner (refer to **Figure 10-1**). The new Tab view appears.

2. To add a new page (meaning that you're opening a new website), tap the New Page button (shaped like a plus [+] symbol) in the lower-middle of the screen (see **Figure 10-4**). A page with your Favorite sites and an address bar appears. (Note that you can get to the same new page by simply tapping in the address bar from any site.)

Private   + ⟵   Done ————— New Page button

Figure 10-4

3. Tap in the Address field and use the onscreen keyboard to enter the web address for the website you want to open. Tap the Go key. The website opens on the page.

 Repeat Steps 1–3 to open as many new web pages as you'd like.

4. You can now switch among open sites by tapping outside the keyboard to close it and tapping the Show/Hide Tabs button and scrolling among recent sites. Find the one you want and then tap it.

5. To delete a tab, tap the Show/Hide Tabs button, scroll to locate the tab, and then tap the Close button in the upper-left corner of the tab.

Using multipage browsing, you can make available not only a site but also a search results screen. If you recently searched for something, those search results will be on your Recent Searches list.

View Browsing History

 1. As you move around the web, your browser keeps a record of your browsing history. This record can be handy when you want to visit a site that you viewed previously but whose address you've now forgotten. With Safari open, tap the Bookmarks button.

2. On the menu shown in **Figure 10-5**, tap the History item.

3. In the History list that appears (see **Figure 10-6**), tap a site to navigate to it. Tap Bookmarks and then Done to leave the History and then Bookmarks feature.

 After you master the use of the Bookmarks button options, you might prefer a shortcut to view your History list. Tap and hold the Previous button at the bottom left on any screen, and your browsing history for the current session appears. You can also tap and hold the Next button to look at sites you backtracked from.

To clear the history, tap the Clear button (refer to **Figure 10-6**) and on the screen that appears, tap an option: The Last Hour, Today, Today and Yesterday, or All Time. This button is useful when you don't want your spouse or grandchildren to see where you've been browsing for anniversary, birthday, or holiday presents!

Tap this item   History list   Clear button

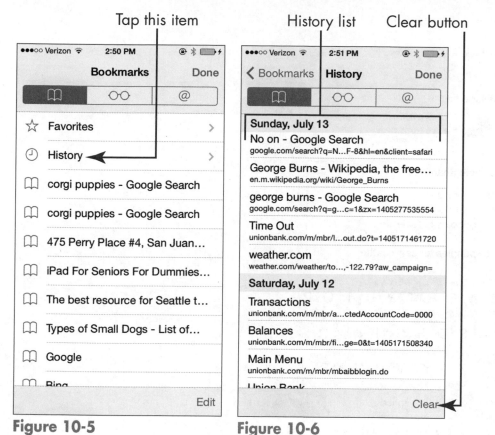

Figure 10-5   Figure 10-6

Search the Web

1. If you don't know the address of the site you want to visit (or you want to research a topic or find other information online), get acquainted with Safari's Search feature on iPhone. By default, Safari uses the Google search engine. With Safari open, tap in the Search field (refer to **Figure 10-1**). The onscreen keyboard appears.

2. Enter a search term. With the latest version of Safari, the search term can be a topic or a web address because of what's called the Unified smart search field. You can tap one of the suggested sites or complete your entry and tap the Go key (see **Figure 10-7**) on your keyboard.

Enter the search term here

History list

Go key

Figure 10-7

3. In the search results that are displayed, tap a link to visit that site.

 To change your default search engine from Google to Yahoo!, Bing, or DuckDuckGo, from the Home screen, tap Settings, tap Safari, and then tap Search Engine. Tap Yahoo!, Bing, or DuckDuckGo, and your default search engine changes.

 You can browse for specific items such as images, videos, or news by tapping the corresponding link at the top of the search results screen. Also, tap the More button in this list to see additional options to narrow your results, such as searching for books or shopping resources on the subject.

Add and Use Bookmarks

1. Bookmarks are a way to save favorite sites so that you can easily visit them again. With a site that you want to bookmark displayed, tap the Share button.

2. On the menu that appears (see **Figure 10-8**), tap Add Bookmark.

3. In the Add Bookmark dialog, shown in **Figure 10-9**, edit the name of the bookmark if you want. To do so, tap the name of the site and use the onscreen keyboard to edit its name.

Tap this option

Edit the name here

Figure 10-8

Figure 10-9

4. Tap the Save button.

5. To go to the bookmark, tap the Bookmarks button.

6. On the Bookmarks menu that appears (see **Figure 10-10**), tap the bookmarked site that you want to visit.

Figure 10-10

Tap a bookmarked site to visit it

If you want to sync your bookmarks on your iPhone browser, go to Settings on iPhone and make sure that iCloud is set to sync with Safari.

When you tap the Bookmarks button, you can tap Edit and then use the New Folder option to create folders to organize your bookmarks or folders. When you next add a bookmark, you can then choose, from the dialog that appears, any folder to which you want to add the new bookmark.

Save Links and Web Pages to Safari Reading List

 1. The Safari Reading List provides a way to save content that you want to read at a later time so that you can easily call up that content again. You essentially save the content rather than a web page address, which allows you to read the content even when you're offline. You can scroll from one item to the next easily. With a site that you want to add to your Reading List displayed, tap the Share button.

2. On the menu that appears (refer to **Figure 10-8**), tap the Add to Reading List link. The site is added to your Reading List.

 3. To view your Reading List, tap the Bookmarks button and then tap the Reading List tab (the middle tab with the eyeglasses icon near the top of the page).

4. On the Reading List that appears (see **Figure 10-11**), tap the content that you want to revisit and resume reading.

 If you want to see both the Reading List material you've read and the material you haven't read, tap the Show Unread button in the Reader View. To see all reading material, tap the Show All button.

To save an image to your Reading List, tap and hold the image until a menu appears, and then tap Add to Reading List (this is available for only some images).

To delete an item, with the Reading List displayed, swipe left or right on an item, and a Delete button appears. Tap this button to delete the item from the Reading List.

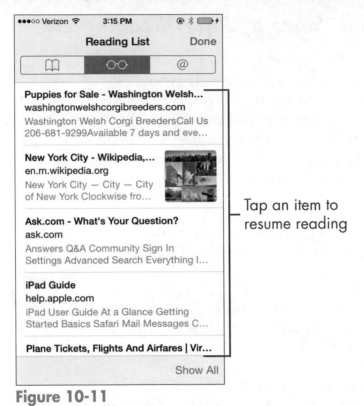

Tap an item to resume reading

Figure 10-11

Enjoy Reading More with Safari Reader

1. The Safari Reader feature gives you an e-reader type of experience right within your browser, removing other stories and links as well as those distracting advertisements. When you're on a site where you're reading content such as an article, Safari displays a Reader button on the left side of the Address field for sites that support this feature (see **Figure 10-12**). Tap the Reader button. The content appears in a reader format (see **Figure 10-13**).

2. Scroll down the page. The entire content is contained in this one long page.

Reader button

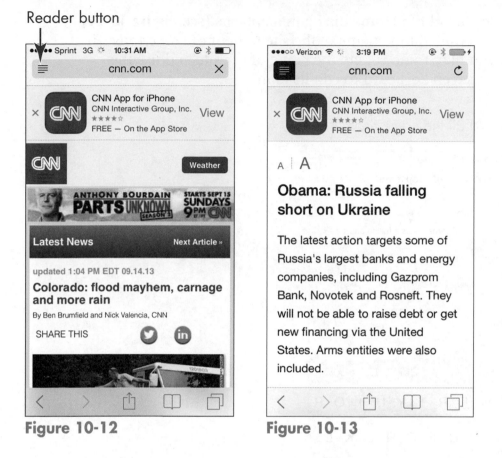

Figure 10-12

Figure 10-13

3. When you finish reading the material, just tap the Previous button to go back to its source.

 Tap the small or large letter *A* at the top of the screen to adjust the font size for the article.

Add Web Clips to the Home Screen

1. The Web Clips feature allows you to save a website as an icon on your Home screen so that you can go to the site at any time with one tap. With Safari open and displaying the site you want to add, tap the Share button.

2. On the menu that appears (refer to **Figure 10-8**), tap Add to Home Screen.

3. In the Add to Home dialog that appears (see **Figure 10-14**), you can edit the name of the site to be more descriptive, if you like. To do so, tap the name of the site and use the onscreen keyboard to edit its name.

Edit the name here

Figure 10-14

4. Tap the Add button. The site is added to your Home screen.

 Remember that you can have as many as 11 Home screens on your iPhone to accommodate all the web clips you create and apps you download (there is a limit to how many will fit on these screens; however, you can place an unlimited number of apps in folders on Home screens. If you want to delete an item from a Home screen for any reason, press and hold the icon on the Home screen until all items on the screen start to jiggle and Delete badges appear on all items except preinstalled apps. Tap the Delete badge (the X) on each item that you want to delete, and it's gone. (To get rid of the jiggle, press the Home button.)

Save an Image to Your Photo Library

1. Display a web page that contains an image you want to copy.

2. Press and hold the image. The menu shown in **Figure 10-15** appears.

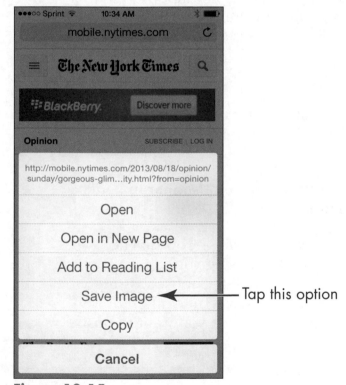

Tap this option

Figure 10-15

3. Tap the Save Image option (refer to **Figure 10-15**). The image is saved to your camera roll.

 Be careful about copying images from the Internet and using them for business or promotional activities. Most images are copyrighted, and you may violate the copyright even if you simply use an image in (say) a brochure for your association or a flyer for your community group. Note that some search engines' advanced search settings offer the option of browsing only for images that aren't copyrighted.

 Some websites are set up to prevent you from copying images on them, or they display a pop-up stating that the contents on the site are copyrighted and should not be copied.

Post Photos from Safari

1. You can post photos to sites such as eBay, Craig's List, or Facebook from within Safari. For this example, go to Facebook and sign in.

2. Tap a Photo or an Add Photo/Video or similar link, like the one shown in **Figure 10-16**.

3. In the case of Facebook, you now tap a Choose File button, and a menu displays, allowing you to take a photo or choose an existing one. Tap Choose Existing and then tap a photo source such as Camera Roll or My Photo Stream. Tap the photo or video you want to post.

4. Tap the Post button.

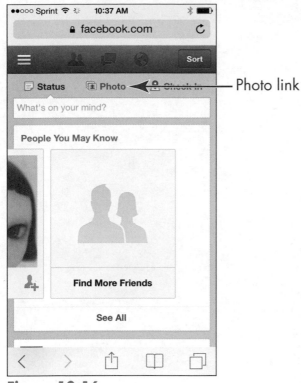

Photo link

Figure 10-16

Send a Link

1. If you find a great site that you want to share, you can do so easily by sending a link in an email (this also works for sending a site via Twitter or Facebook). With Safari open and the site you want to share displayed, tap the Share button.

2. On the menu that appears (refer to **Figure 10-8**), tap Mail.

3. On the message form that appears (see **Figure 10-17**), enter a recipient's email address, a subject, and your message.

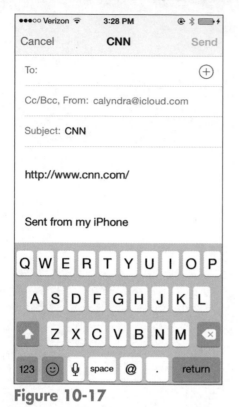

Figure 10-17

4. Tap Send, and the email is sent.

 The email is sent from the default email account that you have set up on iPhone. For more about setting up an email account, see Chapter 11.

 To tweet the link using your Twitter account, in Step 2 of this task, choose Tweet, enter your tweet message in the form that appears, and then tap Send. For more about using Twitter with iPhone, see Chapter 9. You can also choose AirDrop in the same menu with any fifth-generation iPhone or later to share with someone in your immediate vicinity who has an AirDrop-enabled device.

Make Private Browsing and Cookie Settings

Apple has provided some privacy settings for Safari that you should consider using. Private Browsing automatically stops Safari from using AutoFill to save information used to complete your entries in the Search or Address fields as you type, and erases some browsing history information. These features can keep your online activities more private.

Go to Settings from the Home screen and turn on the Block Cookies setting, which allows you to stop the downloading of *cookies* (small files that document your browsing history so that you can be recognized by a site the next time you go to or move within that site) to your iPhone.

Tap to turn on the Do Not Track feature (see **Figure 10-18**). Tap the arrow on Block Cookies and choose to always block cookies, never block cookies, or block cookies only from third parties and advertisers.

Figure 10-18

You can also tap the Clear History and Website Data option (refer to **Figure** 10-18) to manually clear your browsing history, saved cookies, and other data.

Print a Web Page

1. If you have a wireless printer that supports Apple's AirPrint technology, you can print web content using a wireless connection. With Safari open and the site you want to print displayed, tap the Share button.

2. On the menu that appears (refer to **Figure** 10-8), scroll to the right in the bottom row of buttons and then tap Print.

3. In the Printer Options dialog that appears (see **Figure** 10-19), tap Select Printer. In the list of printers that appears, tap the name of your wireless printer.

●●●○○ Sprint 📶   10:45 AM   ✳ ▬▬▶

Cancel   **Printer Options**

Printer   Select Printer ❯ ← Tap this option

1 Copy   ⊟ ⊞ ⊞ ⊞

Print

Figure 10-19

4. Tap either the plus or minus button in the Copy field to adjust the number of copies to print. If your printer supports two-sided printing, you'll also see a Double-Sided On/Off switch.

5. Tap Print to print the displayed page.

 The Mac applications Printopia and HandyPrint make any shared or network printer on your home network visible to your iPhone. Printopia has more features, but will cost you, whereas HandyPrint is free.

 If you don't have an AirPrint-compatible wireless printer or don't wish to use an app to help you print wirelessly, just email a link to the web page to yourself, open the link on your computer, and print from there.

Understand iCloud Tabs

1. The iCloud Tabs feature allows you to access all browsing history among your different devices from any device. If you begin to research a project on your iPad before you leave home, you can then pick up where you left off as you sit in a waiting room with your iPhone.

2. Tap Settings and then tap iCloud to make sure that all devices are using the same iCloud account.

3. Open Safari on another device and tap the Show/Hide Tabs button. Scroll down to see a list of iCloud tabs for every device using your iCloud account. All items in your iPhone's browsing history are displayed.

Working with Email in Mail

Chapter 11

S taying in touch with others by using email is a great way to use your iPhone. You can access an existing account using the handy Mail app supplied with your iPhone or sign in to your email account using the Safari browser. Using Mail involves adding an existing email account by way of Settings. Then you can use Mail to write, format, retrieve, and forward messages from that account.

Mail offers the capability to mark the messages you've read, delete messages, and organize your messages in a small set of folders, as well as use a handy search feature. You can create a VIP list so that you're notified when that special person sends you an email.

Several new features for Mail arrived with iOS 8, including a feature that makes jumping between a draft email and your inbox possible; the ability to quickly swipe to mark an email as read or flag it for future action; and the ability to create an event from information about a reservation, flight number, or phone number within an email.

In this chapter, you read all about Mail and its various features.

Add an Email Account

1. You can add one or more email accounts, including the email account associated with your iCloud account, using iPhone Settings. If you have an iCloud, Microsoft Exchange (often used for business accounts), Gmail, Yahoo!, AOL, or Outlook.com (this includes Microsoft accounts from Live, Hotmail, and so on) account, iPhone pretty much automates the setup. To set up iPhone to retrieve messages from your email account at one of these popular providers, first tap the Settings icon on the Home screen.

2. In Settings, tap Mail, Contacts, Calendars. The settings shown in **Figure 11-1** appear.

3. Tap Add Account. The options shown in **Figure 11-2** appear.

Tap this option   Select your email provider

Figure 11-1

Figure 11-2

4. Tap iCloud, Gmail, Yahoo!, AOL, Exchange, or Outlook. com. Enter your account information in the form that appears (see **Figure 11-3**) and tap Next.

| No Service | 10:51 AM | ☀ ▭◆ |
| Cancel | **Gmail** | Next |

Name	John Appleseed
Email	example@gmail.com
Password	Required
Description	My Gmail Account

— Enter account info here

Figure 11-3

5. After iPhone takes a moment to verify your account information, on the next screen you can tap any On/Off switch to have Mail, Contacts, Calendars, Reminders, or Notes from that account synced with iPhone.

6. When you're done, tap Save. The account is saved, and you can now open it using Mail.

Set Up a POP3 Email Account

1. You can also set up most popular email accounts, such as those available through Earthlink or a cable provider's service, by obtaining the host name from the provider. To set up an existing account with a provider other than iCloud, Gmail, Yahoo!, AOL, Exchange, or Outlook.com, you enter the account settings yourself. First, tap the Settings icon on the Home screen.

2. In Settings, tap Mail, Contacts, Calendars, and then tap the Add Account button (refer to **Figure 11-1**).

3. On the screen that appears (refer to **Figure 11-2**), tap Other.

4. On the screen shown in **Figure 11-4**, tap Add Mail Account.

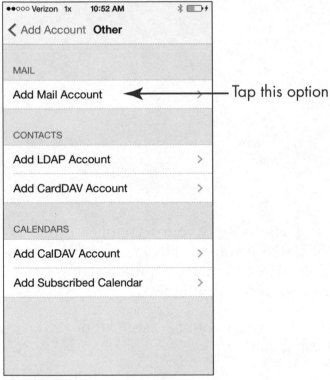

Figure 11-4

5. In the form that appears (refer to **Figure 11-3**), enter your name and an account address, password, and description, and then tap Next. iPhone takes a moment to verify your account and then returns you to the Mail, Contacts, Calendars page, with your new account displayed.

 iPhone will probably add the outgoing mail server (SMTP) information for you, but if it doesn't, you may have to enter it yourself. If you have a less mainstream email service, you may have to enter the mail server protocol (POP3 or IMAP — ask your provider for this information) and your password.

6. To make sure that the Account field is set to On for receiving email, tap the account name. In the dialog that appears, tap the On/Off switch for the Mail field and then tap the Mail button to return to Mail settings. You can now access the account through iPhone's Mail app.

 If you turn on Calendars in the Mail account settings, any information that you've put into your calendar in that email account is brought over into the Calendar app on your iPhone and reflected in the Notification Center (discussed in more detail in Chapter 22).

Open Mail and Read Messages

1. Tap the Mail app icon, located in the Dock on the Home screen (see **Figure 11-5**). A red circle on the icon, called a badge, indicates the number of unread emails in your Inbox.

2. In the Mail app (see **Figure 11-6**), tap the Inbox whose contents you want to display.

Tap the Mail app

Figure 11-5

Figure 11-6

3. Tap a message to read it. It opens (see **Figure 11-7**).

4. If you need to scroll to see the entire message, just place your finger on the screen and flick upward to scroll down. You can swipe right while reading a message to open the Inbox's list of messages, and then swipe from right to left to return to your list of mailboxes.

 You can tap the Next or Previous buttons (top-right corner of the message) to move to the next or previous message in the Inbox or tap All Inboxes in the top-left corner to return to your Inbox.

Next and Previous buttons

Reply/Forward button

Figure 11-7

 Email messages that you haven't read are marked with a blue circle in your Inbox. After you read a message, the blue circle disappears. You can mark a read message as unread to help remind you to read it again later. With a message open and details about it displayed, swipe to the right and then tap Mark as Unread.

 If you have an iPhone 6 Plus and you hold it horizontally, you will view both the Inbox and currently selected message. This is because the larger 5.5" screen can accommodate more content, and apps such as Mail and Weather take advantage of this.

 To escape your email now and then (or to avoid having messages retrieved while you're at a public Wi-Fi hotspot), you can stop retrieval of data including email by tapping Settings, Cellular, and then the On/Off switch on the Cellular Data option. Now you'll get data on your device only if you're logged in to a Wi-Fi network.

Reply To or Forward Email

1. With an email message open (see the previous task), tap the Reply/Forward button, which looks like a left-facing arrow (refer to **Figure 11-7**). Then tap Reply, Reply All (available if there are multiple recipients), or Forward in the menu that appears (see **Figure 11-8**).

2. In the form that appears (see **Figure 11-9**), tap in the To field and enter another addressee if you like (you have to do this if you're forwarding); next, tap in the message body and enter a message (see **Figure 11-10**).

Tap here to enter a recipient

Figure 11-8

Figure 11-9

Send button

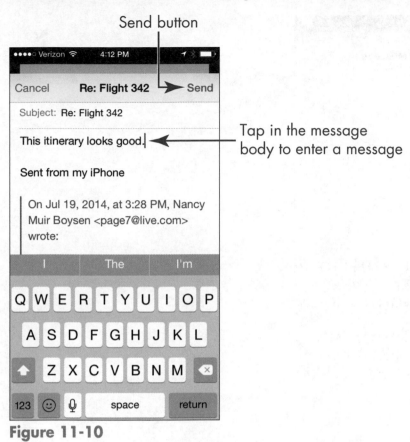

Tap in the message
body to enter a message

Figure 11-10

3. Tap the Send button. The message goes on its way.

 If you want to move an address from the To field to the Cc or Bcc field, tap and hold the address and drag it to the other field.

 If you tap Forward to send the message to somebody else and the original message had an attachment, you're offered the option of including or not including the attachment.

Create and Send a New Message

1. With Mail open, tap the New Message button in the bottom-right corner (this looks like a page with a pen on it). A blank message form appears (see **Figure 11-11**).

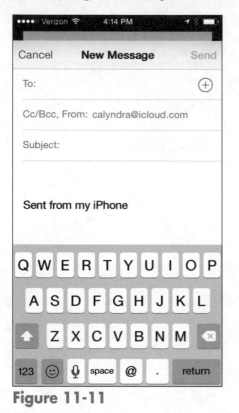

Figure 11-11

2. Enter a recipient's address in the To field. If you have
saved addresses in Contacts, tap the plus sign (+) in the
Address field to choose an addressee from the Contacts
list that appears.

3. If you want to send a copy of the message to other
people, tap the Cc/Bcc field. When the Cc and Bcc fields
open, enter addresses in either or both. Use the Bcc field
to specify recipients of blind carbon copies, which means
that no other recipients are aware that that person
received this reply.

4. Enter the subject of the message in the Subject field.

5. Tap in the message body and type your message.

6. If you want to check a fact or copy and paste some part of another message into your draft message, swipe down near the top of the email to display your Inbox and other folders. Locate the message, and when you're ready to return to your draft, tap the Subject of the email, which is displayed near the bottom of the screen.

7. When you've finished creating your message, tap Send.

Format Email

1. You can apply some basic formatting to email text. You can use bold, underline, and italic formats, and indent text using the Quote Level feature.

2. Press and hold the text in a message you're creating and choose Select or Select All to select a single word or all the words in the email. Note that when you make a selection, handles appear that you can drag to add adjacent words to your selection. If the menu disappears after you select the text, just tap one of the selection handles and it will reappear.

3. To see more tools, tap the arrow on the toolbar that appears; to apply bold, italic, or underline formatting, tap the B*I*U button (see **Figure 11-12**).

4. In the toolbar that appears (see **Figure 11-13**), tap Bold, Italics, or Underline to apply formatting.

5. To change the indent level, tap and hold at the beginning of a line and then tap the arrow at the far end of the toolbar (refer to **Figure 11-12**). In the toolbar that appears, tap Quote Level.

Tap this option   Make your selection here

Figure 11-12

Figure 11-13

6. Tap Increase to indent the text or Decrease to move
indented text farther toward the left margin.

 To use the Quote Level feature, make sure that it's on.
From the Home screen tap Settings, tap Mail, Contacts,
Calendars, and then tap the Increase Quote Level
On/Off switch to turn it on.

Search Email

1. What do you do if you want to find all messages from a
certain person or containing a certain word in the Subject
field? You can use Mail's handy Search feature to find
these emails (though you can't search message contents).
With Mail open, tap an account to display its Inbox.

2. In the Inbox, tap and drag down near the top of the Inbox to display the Search field. Tap in the Search field, and the onscreen keyboard appears.

3. Enter a search term or name, as shown in **Figure 11-14**. Matching emails are listed in the results (refer to **Figure 11-14**).

Figure 11-14

4. Tap the All Mailboxes tab to view messages that contain the search term in one of those fields in any mailbox, or tap the Current Mailbox tab to see only matches within the current mailbox (refer to **Figure 11-14**).

 You can also use the Spotlight Search feature covered in Chapter 2 to search for terms in the To, From, or Subject lines of mail messages.

To start a new search or go back to the full Inbox, tap the Delete icon (the circled X) on the far-right end of the Search field to delete the term or just tap the Cancel button.

Mark Email as Unread or Flag for Follow-Up

1. With a new feature in iOS 8, you can use a simple swipe to access tools that either mark an email as unread after you've read it (placing a blue dot before the message) or flag an email (which places an orange circle before it). These methods help you to remember to reread an email that you've already read or to follow up on a message at a later time. With Mail open and an Inbox displayed, swipe to the left to display three options: More, Flag, and Trash.

2. Tap More. On the menu shown in **Figure 11-15**, you're given several options, including Mark as Unread and Flag. Tapping either command applies it and returns you to your Inbox. Tap Mark as Unread. Note that you can also get to this command by swiping to the right on a message displayed in your Inbox.

3. Swipe to the left on another email and then tap Flag. An orange circle appears before the email.

You can either mark an email as unread or flag it; you can't do both. Either action provides a visual clue that you need to revisit this message before deleting it.

In the menu shown in Figure 11-15, you can also select Notify Me. This option causes Mail to notify you whenever somebody replies to this email thread.

Figure 11-15

Create an Event from Email Contents

1. A neat feature in Mail is the ability to create a Calendar event from within an email. To check this out, create an email to yourself mentioning a reservation on a specific airline on a specific date and time; you can also mention another type of reservation, such as for dinner, or mention a phone number.

2. Send the message to yourself and then open Mail.

3. In your Inbox, open the email. Note that the pertinent information is displayed in blue, underlined text.

4. Tap the underlined text, and in the menu shown in **Figure 11-16**, tap Create Event. A New Event form from Calendar appears. Enter additional information about the event and then tap Done.

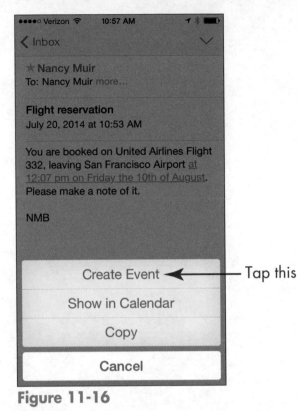

Figure 11-16

Delete Email

1. When you no longer want an email cluttering your Inbox, you can delete it. With the Inbox displayed, tap the Edit button. Circular check boxes are displayed to the left of each message (see **Figure 11-17**).

2. Tap the circle next to the message that you want to delete. (You can tap multiple items if you have several emails to delete.) A message marked for deletion shows a check mark in the circular check button (refer to **Figure 11-17**).

3. Tap the Trash button at the bottom of the Inbox dialog. The message is moved to the Trash folder. Note that some email services use different terms for Trash; for example, Google calls this feature Archive, and its button and menu options vary accordingly.

Figure 11-17

 You can also delete an open email by tapping the Trash Can icon on the toolbar that runs across the bottom of the screen, or swiping left on a message displayed in an Inbox and tapping the Trash button that appears.

Organize Email

1. You can move messages into any of several predefined folders in Mail (these will vary depending on your email provider and the folders you've created on your provider's server). After displaying the folder containing the message you want to move (for example, Trash or Inbox), tap the Edit button. Circular check boxes are displayed to the left of each message (refer to **Figure 11-17**).

2. Tap the circle next to the message you want to move.

3. Tap the Move button.

4. In the Mailboxes list that appears (see **Figure 11-18**), tap the folder where you want to store the message. The message is moved.

```
•••••○ Verizon 🗢      4:33 PM        ⬆ ✳ 🔋
         Move this message to a new mailbox.
 ⟨ Accounts    Outlook           Cancel

   ┌──┐
   │  │    Nancy Muir Boysen
   └──┘    Flight 342

   ⌂  Inbox

      🗁  2013 CC purchases supplies

      🗁  betas

      🗁  Business Receipts

   ◁  Sent

      🗁  Cordova

   ⊠  Junk

   🗑  Trash                          27

      🗁  POP
```

Figure 11-18

Create a VIP List

1. A VIP list is a way to create a list of senders. When any of these senders sends you an email, you'll be notified of it through the Notifications feature of iPhone. In the list of all Mailboxes, tap the Info button to the right of VIP (see **Figure 11-19**).

2. Tap Add VIP (see **Figure 11-20**), and your Contacts list appears. Tap a contact to add that person to the VIP list.

Tap this button   Tap this option

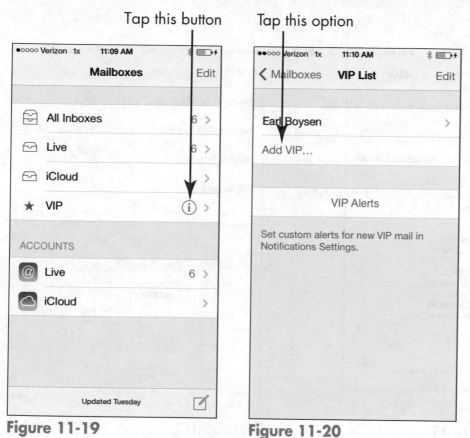

Figure 11-19   Figure 11-20

3. Press the Home button and then tap Settings.

4. Tap Notifications and then tap Mail. In the settings that appear, shown in **Figure 11-21**, tap VIP.

5. Tap the Show in Notification Center On/Off switch to turn on notifications for VIP mail.

6. Tap an alert style and choose what Notification Sound should play or what badge icon should appear. You can also choose to have the notification displayed on your Lock screen (see **Figure 11-22**).

Tap this

Figure 11-21

Figure 11-22

7. Press the Home button to close Settings. New mail from your VIPs should now appear in Notification Center when you swipe down from the top of the screen, and, depending on the settings you chose, may cause a sound to play or a badge icon to appear on your Lock screen, and a blue star icon to appear to the left of these messages in the Inbox in Mail.

Shopping the iTunes Store

Chapter 12

*T*he iTunes Store app that comes preinstalled in iPhone lets you easily shop for music, movies, TV shows, and audiobooks. If you've downloaded the free iTunes U app, you can even install online classes. And, as Chapter 14 explains, you can get electronic books via the iBooks app.

In this chapter, you discover how to find content in the iTunes Store. You can download the content directly to your iPhone or to another device and then sync it to your iPhone. With the new Family Sharing feature, which I cover in this chapter, as many as six people in a family can share purchases, and they can all use the same credit card. Finally, I cover a few options for buying content from other online stores.

Note that I cover opening an iTunes account and downloading iTunes software to your computer in Chapter 3. If you need to, read Chapter 3 to see how to handle these two tasks before digging into this chapter.

Get ready to . . .

Explore the iTunes Store

1. Visiting the iTunes Store from your iPhone is easy with the built-in iTunes Store app. Tap the iTunes Store icon on the Home screen.

2. If you're not already signed in to iTunes, the dialog shown in **Figure 12-1** appears, asking for your iTunes password. Enter your password and tap OK.

Enter your password here

Figure 12-1

3. Tap the Music button (if it isn't already selected) in the row of buttons at the bottom of the screen. You see several rows of categories of selections such as Albums and EPs, What's Hot, and New Releases.

4. Flick your finger up to scroll through the featured selections or tap the See All button to see more selections in any category, as shown in **Figure 12-2.**

5. Tap the Charts tab at the top of the screen. This displays lists of bestselling songs, albums, and music videos in the iTunes Store.

6. Tap any listed item to see more detail about it, as shown in **Figure 12-3,** and hear a brief preview when you tap the number to the left of a song.

Figure 12-2   **Figure 12-3**

The navigation techniques in these steps work essentially the same in any of the content categories (the buttons at the bottom of the screen), which include Music, Movies, and TV Shows, Audiobooks, and Tones (the last two are accessed through the More button at the bottom of the iTunes screen). Just tap one to explore it.

If you want to use the Genius playlist feature, which recommends additional purchases based on the contents of your library in the iTunes app on your iPhone, tap the More button at the bottom of the screen and then tap Genius. If you've made enough purchases in iTunes, song and album recommendations appear based on those purchases as well as the content in your iTunes Match library (a fee-based service), if you have one.

The Podcast app is a preinstalled app in iPhone that you can use to find and download podcasts from your phone. To use iTunes U courses, you have to install an app. Go to the App Store on your iPhone, search for iTunes U, and install this free app to get access to this additional content.

Find a Selection

You can look for a selection in the iTunes Store in several ways. You can use the Search feature, search by genre or category, or view artists' pages. Here's how these work:

⇒ Tap the Search button at the bottom of the screen and the Search field shown in **Figure 12-4** appears. Enter a search term using the onscreen keyboard. Tap the Search button on the keyboard or, if a suggestion in the list of search results appeals to you, just tap that suggestion.

⇒ Tap an item such as Music at the bottom of the screen; then tap the Genres button at the top of the screen. A list of genres like the one shown in **Figure 12-5** appears.

⇒ On a description page that appears when you tap a selection, you can find more offerings by the people involved with that particular work. For example, for a music selection, tap to display details about it and then tap the Reviews tab at the middle of the page to see all reviews of the album (see **Figure 12-6**). For a movie (tap Movies at the bottom of the iTunes Store Home page), tap to open details and then tap Reviews, or tap the Related tab to see more movies starring any of the lead actors.

Enter a search term here

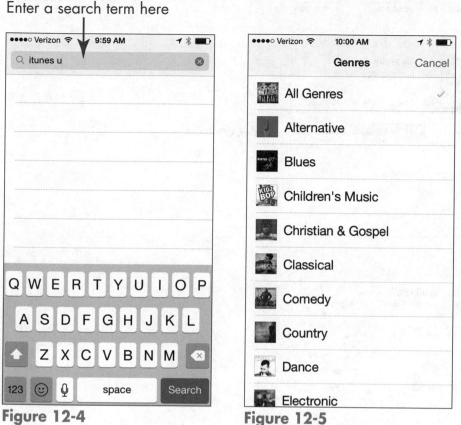

Figure 12-4

Figure 12-5

If you find a selection that you like, tap the Share button at the top of its description page to share your discovery with a friend via AirDrop, Mail, Message, Twitter, or Facebook. A message form appears with a link that your friend can tap to view information about the selection. Note that you must have set up an associated account (such as Twitter) before you can use this feature. Tap Settings from the Home screen to set up an account.

Reviews tab

Figure 12-6

Preview Music, a Video, or an Audiobook

1. Because you've already set up an iTunes account (or if you haven't done so yet, refer to Chapter 3), when you choose to buy an item, it's automatically charged to the credit or debit card you have on file, to your PayPal account, or against any allowance you have outstanding from an iTunes gift card. You might want to preview an item before you buy it. If you like it, buying and down-loading are then easy and quick. Open iTunes and use any method outlined in earlier tasks to locate a selection that you might want to buy.

2. Tap the item to see detailed information about it, as shown in **Figure 12-7**.

3. For audiobooks, tap the Preview button to play a preview. For a TV show, tap an episode to get further information (refer to **Figure 12-7**). If you're looking at a music selection, tap the track number or name of a selection to play a preview. For a movie or audiobook selection, tap the Trailers Play button (movies) shown in **Figure 12-8**, or the Preview button (audiobooks).

Tap an episode to get
additional info

Play button

Figure 12-7

Figure 12-8

Buy a Selection

1. When you find an item that you want to buy, tap the button that shows either the price (if it's a selection available for purchase; see **Figure** 12-9) or the button with the word *Free* on it (if it's a selection available for free).

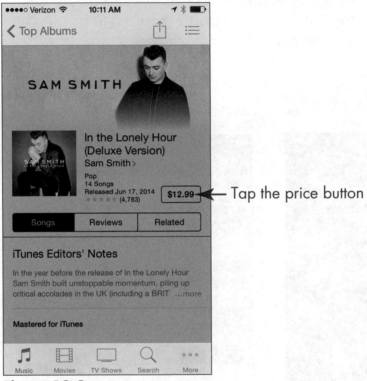

Figure 12-9

The button label changes to Buy X, where X is the type of content, such as a song or album, that you're buying. If the item is free, the label changes to Install.

2. Tap the Buy X button. The iTunes Password dialog appears (refer to **Figure** 12-1).

3. Enter your password and tap OK. The item begins down-loading, and the cost, if any, is automatically charged against your account. When the download finishes, you can view the content using the Music or Video app, depending on the type of content.

 If you want to buy music, you can open the description page for an album and tap the album price, or buy individual songs rather than the entire album. Tap the price for a song and then proceed to purchase it.

 Note the Redeem button on some iTunes screens. Tap this button to redeem any iTunes gift certificates that you might get from your generous friends, or from yourself.

If you don't want to allow purchases from within apps (for example, Music or Videos) but rather want to allow purchases only through the iTunes Store, you can go to the Settings app, tap General, tap Restrictions, and then tap Enable Restrictions and enter a passcode. After you've set a passcode, you can tap individual apps to turn on restrictions for them, as well as for actions such as sharing via AirDrop, deleting apps, or using Siri.

You can allow content to be downloaded over your 3G/4G cellular network if you're not near a Wi-Fi hotspot. Be aware, however, that you could incur hefty data charges with your provider if you run over your allotted data. However, if you aren't near a Wi-Fi hotspot, downloading over your cellular network might be your only option. Tap Settings, tap iTunes & App Store, scroll down, and set the Use Cellular Data setting switch to On.

Rent Movies

1. In the case of movies, you can either rent or buy content. If you rent, which is less expensive but a one-time deal, you have 30 days from the time you rent the item to begin to watch it. After you have begun to watch it, you have 24 hours from that time left to watch it on the same device, as many times as you like. With iTunes open, tap the Movies button.

2. Locate the movie you want to rent and tap it, as shown in **Figure 12-10.**

3. In the detailed description of the movie that appears, tap the Rent button (if it's available for rental); see **Figure 12-11.**

Rent button

Figure 12-10   **Figure 12-11**

4. The gray Rent button changes to a green Rent Movie button; tap it to confirm the rental. The movie begins to download to your iPhone immediately, and your account is charged the rental fee.

5. After the download is complete, you can use the Videos app to watch it. (See Chapter 17 to read about how this app works.)

 Some movies are offered in high-definition versions. These HD movies look pretty good on that crisp, colorful iPhone screen.

 You can also download content to your computer and sync it to your iPhone. Refer to Chapter 3 for more about this process.

Shop Anywhere Else

One feature that's missing from the iPhone is support for Adobe Flash, a format of video playback that many online video-on-demand services and interactive games use. However, most online stores that sell content such as movies and music have added iPhone-friendly videos to their collections, so you do have alternatives to iTunes for your choice of movies and TV shows. You can also shop for music from sources other than iTunes, such as Amazon.com.

You can open accounts at one of these stores by using your computer or your iPhone's Safari browser and then following the store's instructions for purchasing and downloading content.

The following content providers offer iPhone-compatible video content, and more are opening all the time:

➡ **ABC:** `http://abc.go.com`

➡ **CBS News:** `www.cbsnews.com`

➡ **TV.com:** `www.tv.com`

➡ **Netflix:** `www.netflix.com`

➡ **Ustream:** `www.ustream.tv`

➡ **iMP4hub:** `www.imp4hub.com`

 For non–iPhone-friendly formats, you can download the content on your computer and stream it to your iPhone using Air Video (for $2.99) on the iPhone and Air Video Server (for free) using your Mac or Windows computer. For more information, go to `www.inmethod.com/air-video/index.html`.

Will Apple Pay change the way you shop?

With iPhone 6 and 6 Plus, Apple also announced a new electronic payment service, Apple Pay. Called a mobile wallet, this service uses the Touch ID feature in your iPhone's Home button to identify you and any credit cards you've stored at the iTunes Store to make payments via a feature called Passbook. Your credit card information isn't stored on your phone, and Apple doesn't know a thing about your purchases. In addition, Apple considers Apple Pay to be safer because the store cashier doesn't even have to know your name.

There are 220,000 merchant locations that are set up to use Apple Pay, which launches late fall 2014 and is supported by Amex, Visa, MasterCard, and six of the largest banks in the United States.

Enable Auto-Downloads of Purchases from Other Devices

1. With iCloud, you can make a purchase or download free content on any of your Apple devices, and iCloud automatically shares those purchases with all your Apple devices. To enable this auto-download feature on iPhone, start by tapping Settings on the Home screen.

 To use iCloud, first set up an iCloud account. See Chapter 3 for detailed coverage of iCloud, including setting up your account.

2. Tap iTunes & App Store.

3. In the options that appear, scroll down and then set the switch to On for any category of purchases you want to auto-download to your iPhone from other Apple devices: Music, Apps, or Books (see **Figure 12-12**).

Figure 12-12

At this point, Apple doesn't offer an option of auto-downloading video content using these settings, probably because video is such a memory and bandwidth hog. You are probably better off downloading video using the iTunes app and then using iTunes to get the content onto your iPhone.

Set Up Family Sharing

Family Sharing is a new feature that allows as many as six people in your family to share whatever anybody in the group has purchased from the iTunes, iBooks, and App Stores even though you don't share Apple IDs. Your family must all use the same credit card to purchase items (tied to whichever Apple ID is managing the family), but you can approve purchases by children 13 years old and younger. You can also share calendars, photos, and a family calendar (see Chapter 21 for information about Family Sharing and Calendar and Chapter 16 for information on sharing photos in a family album). Start by turning on Family Sharing.

1. Tap Settings.

2. Tap iCloud and then tap Set Up Family Sharing.

3. Tap Get Started. On the next screen, you can add a photo for your family. Tap Continue.

4. On the Share Purchases screen, tap Share Purchases from a different account to use another Apple account.

5. Tap Continue and check the payment method that you want to use. Tap Continue.

6. On the next screen, tap Add Family Member. Enter the person's name (assuming that this person is listed in your contacts) or email address. An invitation is sent to the person's email. When the invitation is accepted, the person is added to your family (see **Figure 12-13**).

Figure 12-13

 Note that the payment method for this family is displayed under Shared Payment Method in this screen. All those involved in a family have to use a single payment method for family purchases.

 There's also a link called Create an Apple ID for a Child. When you click this link and enter information to create the ID, the child's account is automatically added to your Family and retains the child status until he or she turns 13. If a child accesses iTunes to buy something, he or she gets a prompt to ask permission. You get an Ask to Buy notification on your phone as well as via email. You can then accept or decline the purchase, giving you control over family spending in the iTunes Store.

Expanding Your iPhone Horizons with Apps

Some *apps* (short for *applications*) come pre-installed on your iPhone, such as Contacts and Videos. But you can choose from a world of other apps out there for your iPhone, some for free (such as iBooks) and some for a price (typically, ranging from 99 cents to about $10, though some can top out at $90 or more).

Apps range from games to financial tools such as loan calculators to apps that help you when you're planning or taking a trip.

In this chapter, I suggest some apps that you might want to check out and explain how to use the App Store feature of iPhone to find, purchase, and download apps.

Explore Senior-Recommended Apps

As I write this book, new iPhone apps are in development, so even more apps that could fit your needs will be available. Still, to get you exploring what's possible, I provide a quick list of apps that might whet your appetite.

Access the App Store by tapping the App Store icon on the Home screen. You can start by exploring the Featured or Top Choices categories (see the buttons along the bottom of the screen). Or you can tap Explore and find apps divided into categories. Tap an app to see more information about it.

Here are some interesting apps to explore:

➡ **Sudoku2 (free):** If you like this mental logic puzzle in print, try it out on your iPhone (see **Figure 13-1**). It has three lessons and several levels ranging from easiest to nightmare, making it a great way to make time fly by in a doctor's or dentist's waiting room.

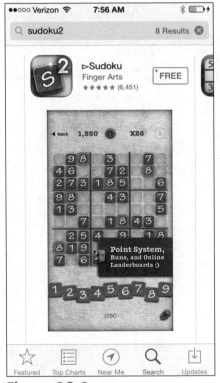

Figure 13-1

➡ **StockWatch Portfolio Tracking ($2.99):** Even though there's a Stocks app on the iPhone Home screen, this app will help you keep track of your investments in a portfolio format. You can use the app to create a watch list and record your stock performance.

⟹ **SpaceEffect (free):** If you need a photo-sharing service with some cool features, try SpaceEffect. You can not only upload and share photos but also apply awesome effects to them.

⟹ **Paint Studio ($3.99):** Get creative! You can use this powerful app to draw, add color, and even create special effects.

⟹ **Virtuoso Piano Free 3 (free):** If you love to make music, you'll love this app, which gives you a virtual piano keyboard to play and compose on the fly.

⟹ **iPhoto ($4.99 and free for new iPhones purchased after 9/1/13):** This is an Apple app that provides all kinds of tools for editing those great photos that you can grab with your iPhone.

⟹ **Travelzoo (free):** Get great deals on hotels, airfare, rental cars, entertainment, and more. This app also offers tips from travel experts.

⟹ **Nike Training Club (free):** Use this handy utility to help design personalized workouts, see step-by-step instructions to help you learn new exercises, and watch video demonstrations. The reward system in this app may just keep you going toward your workout goals.

 Note that with iOS 8, iCloud Drive allows you to work on documents in the cloud. Use Keynote, Numbers, Pages, and more apps to get your work done from any device. See Chapter 3 for more about iCloud.

Search the App Store

1. Tap the App Store icon on the Home screen. The site shown in **Figure 13-2** appears.

2. At this point, you have several options for finding apps:

- Scroll downward to view various categories of Featured apps such as Best New Apps and Best New Games.

- Tap the Top Charts tab at the bottom of the screen to see bestselling apps. Tap the Explore option to display apps in categories such as Books, Education, and Finance. Tap a category to display apps that fit within it.

- Tap the Categories button in the top-left corner of the screen on the Featured and Top Charts views as an alternative way to browse by type of app such as Education or Entertainment, as shown in **Figure 13-3.**

- Tap the Search button at the bottom of the screen and then tap in the Search field, enter a search term, and tap the result you want to view.

- Tap the See All button in any category shown in the Featured view to view all the items in that category.

- In the Top Charts view, use the Paid, Free, and Top Grossing tabs to narrow your search.

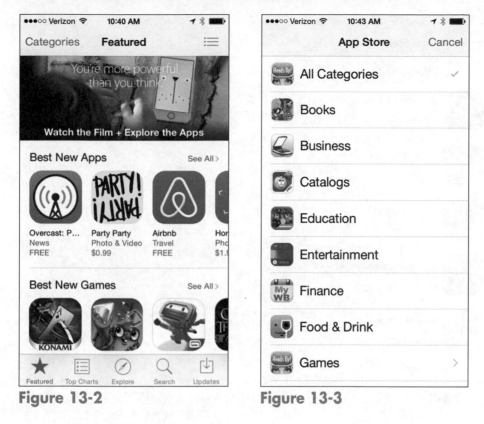

Figure 13-2   **Figure 13-3**

Get Applications from the App Store

1. Buying or getting free apps requires that you have an iTunes account, which I cover in Chapter 3. After you have an account, you can use the saved payment information there to buy apps or download free apps with a few simple steps. With the App Store open, tap the Top Charts button, and then tap the Free tab, as shown in **Figure 13-4**.

2. Tap the Free button for an app that appeals to you. (To get a *paid* app, you tap the same button, which is then labeled with a price.)

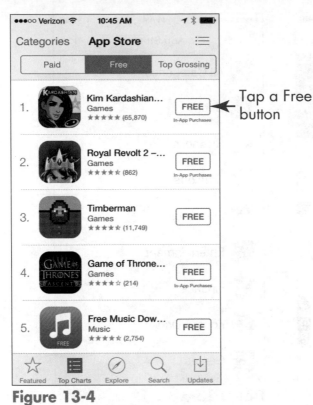

Tap a Free button

Figure 13-4

3. The Free button changes to read *Install App* (or, in the case of a paid app, the button changes to read *Buy*. Tap the button and the button changes to read *Installing*. You may be asked to enter your iTunes password; do so and then tap the OK button to proceed.

4. The app downloads, and if you purchase an app that isn't free, your credit card or gift card balance is charged at this point for the purchase price.

 Out of the box, only preinstalled apps are located on the first iPhone Home screen, with a few such as Voice Memos and Podcasts located on the second Home screen. Apps that you download are placed on available Home screens, and you have to scroll to view and use them; this procedure is covered later in this chapter. See the next task for help in finding your newly downloaded apps using multiple Home screens.

 If you've opened an iCloud account, you can set it up so that anything you purchase on your iPhone is automatically pushed to other Apple iOS devices and your iTunes library, and vice versa. See Chapter 3 for more about iCloud.

Organize Your Applications on Home Screens

1. iPhone can display up to 15 Home screens. By default, the first Home screen contains preinstalled apps, and the second contains a few more preinstalled apps, including Contacts and Calculator in the Extras folder. Other screens are created to contain any apps you download or sync to your iPhone. At the bottom of any iPhone Home screen (just above the Dock), dots indicate the number of Home screens you've filled with apps; a solid dot specifies which Home screen you're on now, as shown in **Figure 13-5**. Press the Home button to open the last displayed Home screen.

2. Flick your finger from right to left to move to the next Home screen. To move back, flick from left to right.

3. To reorganize apps on a Home screen, press and hold any app on that page. The app icons begin to jiggle (see **Figure 13-6**), and any apps you installed will sport a Delete button (a black circle with a white X on it).

4. Press, hold, and drag an app icon to another location on the screen to move it.

5. Press the Home button to stop all those icons from jiggling!

Screen you're on

A Delete button

Dots indicating the number
of Home screens

Figure 13-5

Figure 13-6

 To move an app from one page to another, while the apps are jiggling, you can press, hold, and drag an app to the left or right to move it to the next Home screen. You can also manage what app resides on what Home screen and change the order of the Home screens from iTunes when you've connected iPhone to iTunes via a cable or wireless sync.

 You can use the multitasking feature for switching between apps easily. Press the Home button twice and you get a preview of open apps. With iOS 8, you also get a row of recently used contacts with photos if the contact contains one above the apps. When you tap a contact, you then get options to call, message, or FaceTime call that person. Scroll among the apps and tap the one you want to go to. You can also swipe an app upward from this preview list to close it.

Organize Apps in Folders

iPhone lets you organize apps in folders so that you can find them more easily. The process is simple:

1. Tap and hold an app until all apps do their jiggle dance.

2. Drag one app on top of another app. The two apps appear in a box with a placeholder name in a strip above them (see **Figure 13-7**).

Placeholder name

Figure 13-7

3. To change the name, tap in the field at the end of the placeholder name, and the keyboard appears.

4. Tap the Delete key to delete the placeholder name and type one of your own.

5. Tap Done, and then tap anywhere outside the box to close it.

6. Press the Home button to stop the icons from dancing around, and you'll see your folder appear on the Home screen where you began this process.

Delete Apps You No Longer Need

1. When you no longer need an app you have installed, it's time to get rid of it. (You can't delete apps that are preinstalled on the iPhone, however.) If you use iCloud to push content across all Apple iOS devices, note that deleting an app on your iPhone won't affect that app on other devices. Display the Home screen that contains the app you want to delete.

2. Press and hold the app until all apps begin to jiggle.

3. Tap the Delete button for the app you want to delete (refer to **Figure 13-6**).

4. A confirmation like the one shown in **Figure 13-8** appears. Tap Delete to proceed with the deletion.

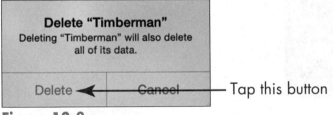

Delete "Timberman"
Deleting "Timberman" will also delete all of its data.

Delete ◄───── Cancel ───── Tap this button

Figure 13-8

 Don't worry about wiping out several apps at one time by deleting a folder. When you delete a folder, the apps that were contained within the folder are placed back on a Home screen if space is available, and you can still find the apps using the Spotlight Search feature.

Update Apps

1. App developers update their apps all the time, so you might want to check for those updates. The App Store icon on the Home screen displays the number of available updates in a red circle. Tap the App Store icon on the Home Screen.

2. Tap the Updates button to access the Updates screen and then tap any item you want to update. Note that if you have Family Sharing turned on, there will be a folder titled Family Purchases that you can tap to display apps that are shared across your family's devices. To update all, tap the Update All button.

3. On the app screen that appears, tap Update. You may be asked to confirm that you want to update, or to enter your Apple ID; after you do, tap OK to proceed. You may also be asked to confirm that you are over a certain age or agree to terms and conditions; if so, scroll down the terms dialog and, at the bottom, tap Agree. The download progress is displayed.

You can download multiple apps at one time. If you choose more than one app to update instead of downloading apps sequentially, several items will download simultaneously.

If you have an iCloud account that you have activated on several devices and update an app on your iPhone, any other Apple iOS devices are also updated automatically and vice versa.

iOS 8 performs what Apple calls "intelligently scheduled updates," meaning that updates to apps and the iOS happen at times when your iPhone isn't using much power, for example when you're connecting to the Internet via Wi-Fi. And speaking of updating, iOS 8 also studies your habits and can update apps that require updated content, such as Facebook or Stocks, around the time you usually check them so that you have instant access to current information.

Part IV
Having Fun and Consuming Media

Visit www.dummies.com/extras/iphoneforseniors for tips on getting the most out of iTunes Radio.

Using Your iPhone as an E-Reader

Chapter 14

A traditional *e-reader* is a device that's used primarily to read the electronic version of books, magazines, and newspapers. If you're happy reading on your smaller iPhone screen, your phone can be a great e-reader, although it isn't a traditional e-reader device like the Kindle because it gets its functionality from an e-reader app.

Apple's free, downloadable app that turns your iPhone into an e-reader is *iBooks*, which also enables you to buy and download books from Apple's iBookstore. You can also use one of several other free e-reader apps — for example Kindle, Stanza, or Nook. Then you can download books to your iPhone from a variety of online sources, such as Amazon and Google, so that you can read to your heart's content.

Another preinstalled reading app covered later in this chapter is Newsstand. Newsstand provides access to a different reading experience: Its focus is on subscribing to and reading magazines, newspapers, and other periodicals.

In this chapter, you discover the options available for reading material and how to buy books and subscribe to publications. You also learn how to navigate a book or periodical and adjust the brightness and type, as well as how to search books and organize your iBooks and Newsstand libraries.

Discover E-Reading

An *e-reader* is any electronic device that enables you to download and read books, magazines, PDF files, or newspapers. Many e-readers use E Ink technology to create a paperlike reading experience. These devices are typically portable and dedicated only to reading the electronic version of published materials.

The iPhone is a bit different from an e-reader. It isn't only for reading books, and you have to download an app to enable it as an e-reader (though the apps are usually free). Also, the iPhone doesn't offer the paperlike reading experience — you read from a phone screen (though you can adjust the brightness and background color of the screen).

When you buy a book online (or get one of many free publications), it downloads to your iPhone in a few seconds using a Wi-Fi or 3G/4G connection. The iPhone offers several navigation tools to move around an electronic book, which you explore in this chapter.

Find Books with iBooks

1. In Chapter 13, I walk you through the process of downloading the iBooks application in the "Get Applications from the App Store" task, so you should do that first, if you haven't already. To shop using iBooks, tap the iBooks application icon to open it. (It's probably on your second or third Home screen, so you may have to swipe your finger to the left on the screen to locate it.)

2. In the iBooks library that opens (see **Figure 14-1**), you see a bookshelf; yours probably has only one free book already downloaded to it. (If you don't see the bookshelf, tap the My Books button to go there.) Tap the Featured button, and you're taken to the iBookstore with featured titles displayed.

Figure 14-1

3. In the iBookstore, shown in **Figure 14-2,** featured titles are shown by default. You can do any of the following to find a book:

- Tap the Search button at the bottom of the screen and then tap in the Search field that appears and type a search word or phrase, using the onscreen keyboard.

- Tap the More button along the top of the screen and scroll down to Browse Categories to see links to popular categories of books, as shown in **Figure 14-3.** Tap a category to view those selections.

- Press your finger on the screen and flick up to scroll to more suggested titles on a page.

- Tap the Top Charts button at the bottom of the screen to view both Paid and Free books listed on top bestseller lists.

- Tap Purchased to see only titles that you've already purchased on any Apple device connected via iCloud.

 Scroll to the bottom of any screen to access Quick Links, which include shortcuts to Best of the Month, Free Books, and Textbooks.

- Tap a suggested selection or featured book to read more information about it.

Search button

Figure 14-2   **Figure 14-3**

Many books let you download free samples before you buy. You get to read several pages of the book to see whether it appeals to you, and it doesn't cost you a dime! Look for the Get Sample button when you view book details.

Explore Other E-Book Sources

Beyond using iBooks, the iPhone is capable of using other e-reader apps to read book content from other bookstores. You first have to download another e-reader application such as Kindle from Amazon or the Barnes & Noble Nook reader from the App Store (see Chapter 13 for how to download apps). You can also download a nonvendor-specific app such as Bluefire Reader, which handles ePub and PDF formats, as well as the format that most public libraries use (protected PDF). Then use the app's features to search for, purchase, and download content.

The Kindle e-reader application is shown in **Figure 14-4**. After downloading the free app from the App Store, you just open the app and enter the email address associated with your Amazon account and password. Any content you've already bought from the Amazon.com Kindle Store from your computer or Kindle Fire tablet is archived online and can be placed on your Kindle Home page on the iPhone for you to read anytime you like. Tap the Device tab to see titles stored on iPhone rather than in Amazon's Cloud library. To enhance your reading experience, use features such as changing the background to a sepia tone or changing font. To delete a book from this reader, press the title with your finger, and the Remove from Device button appears.

 E-books are everywhere! You can get content from a variety of other sources: Project Gutenberg, Google, some publishers like Baen, and so on. Download the content using your computer, if you like, and then just add the items to Books in iTunes and sync them to your iPhone. You can also open items from a web link or email, and they're copied to iBooks for you. Just be aware that e-books come in different formats, and your iPhone won't work with formats other than ePub or PDF (for example, it can't use formats such as the Kindle's Mobi and AZW). You can also make settings to iCloud so that books are pushed across your Apple devices or place them in an online storage service such as Dropbox and access them from there.

Figure 14-4

Buy Books

1. If you've set up an account with iTunes, you can buy books at the iBookstore using the iBooks app. (See Chapter 3 for more about iTunes.) Open iBooks and tap Featured. When you find a book in the iBookstore, either in Featured titles or by searching, you can buy it by tapping it and then tapping the Price button. The button changes to the Buy Book button, as shown in **Figure 14-5.** (If the book is free, these buttons are labeled Free and Get Book, respectively.)

2. Tap the Buy Book or Get Book button. If you haven't already signed in, the iTunes Password dialog, shown in **Figure 14-6,** appears.

 If you have signed in, your purchase is accepted immediately. No returns are allowed as they are with Amazon Kindle devices, so tap carefully!

Buy Book button

Figure 14-6

Figure 14-5

3. Enter your password and tap OK.

4. The book appears on your bookshelf, and the cost is charged to whichever credit card you specified when you opened your iTunes account.

 Books that you've downloaded to your computer can also be synced with your iPhone by using the Lightning to USB Cable and your iTunes account, or by using the wireless iTunes Wi-Fi Sync setting on the General Settings menu. Using either method, you can find lots of free books from various sources online and share them online with a service such as Dropbox, or drag them into your iTunes Book library; then simply sync them to your iPhone. See Chapter 3 for more about syncing.

Navigate a Book

1. Tap iBooks and, if your Library (the bookshelf) isn't already displayed, tap the My Books button.

2. Tap a book to open it. The book opens to its title page or the last spot you read on any compatible device, as shown in **Figure 14-7**.

3. Take any of these actions to navigate the book:

- **To go to the book's Table of Contents:** Tap the Table of Contents button at the top of the page (refer to **Figure 14-7**) and then tap the name of a chapter to go to it (see **Figure 14-8**).

- **To turn to the next page:** Place your finger anywhere along the right edge of the page and flick to the left or tap.

Table of Contents button

Tap any chapter to go to it

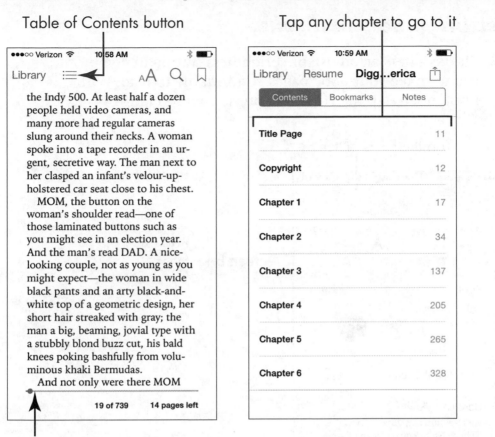

Slider to move to another page

Figure 14-7

Figure 14-8

- **To turn to the preceding page:** Place your finger anywhere on the left edge of a page and flick to the right or tap.

- **To move to another page in the book:** Tap and drag the slider at the bottom of the page (refer to **Figure 14-7**) to the right or left.

 To return to the Library to view another book at any time, tap the Library button. If the button isn't visible, tap anywhere on the page, and the button and other tools appear.

Adjust Brightness in iBooks

1. iBooks offers an adjustable brightness setting that you can use to make your book pages comfortable to read. With a book open, tap the Fonts button, shown in **Figure 14-9.**

Tap the Fonts button . . .

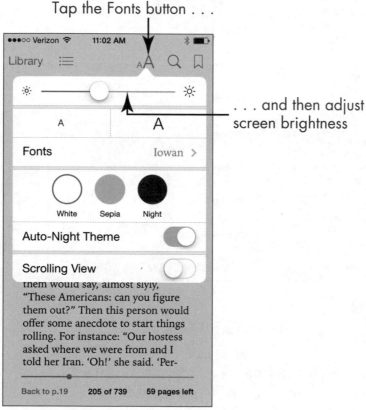

. . . and then adjust screen brightness

Figure 14-9

2. On the Brightness setting that appears (refer to **Figure 14-9**), tap and drag the slider to the right to make the screen brighter, or to the left to dim it.

3. Tap anywhere on the page to close the Fonts dialog.

Experiment with the brightness level that works for you, or try out the Sepia setting, which you find by tapping Sepia in the Fonts dialog. Bright-white screens are commonly thought to be hard on the eyes, so setting the brightness halfway relative to its default setting or less is probably a good idea (and saves on battery life).

Change the Font Size and Type

1. If the type on your screen is a bit small for you to make out, you can change to a larger font size or choose a different font for readability. With a book open, tap the Fonts button (it sports a smaller capital *A* and a larger capital *A*, as shown in **Figure 14-10**).

2. In the Fonts dialog that appears (refer to **Figure 14-10**), tap the button with a smaller *A*, on the left, to use smaller text, or the button with the larger *A*, on the right, to use larger text.

3. Tap the Fonts button. The list of fonts shown in **Figure 14-11** appears.

4. Tap a font name to select it. The font changes on the book page.

5. If you want a sepia tint on the pages, which can be easier on the eye, tap the Back button to redisplay the Fonts dialog, and then tap the Normal, Sepia, or Night setting to activate it.

6. Tap outside the Fonts dialog to return to your book.

 Some fonts appear a bit larger on your screen than others because of their design. If you want the largest font, use Iowan.

Tap the Fonts button

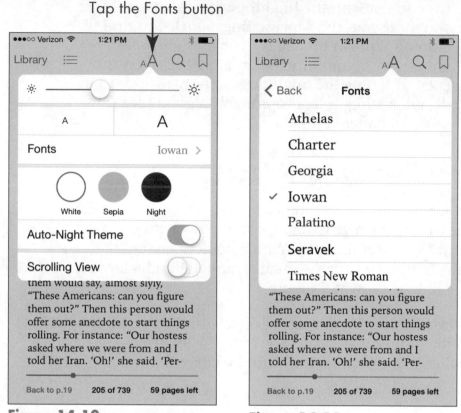

Figure 14-10

Figure 14-11

Search in Your Book

1. You may want to find certain sentences or references in your book. To do so, with a book displayed, tap the Search button shown in **Figure 14-12**. The onscreen keyboard appears.

2. Enter a search term and then tap the Search key on the keyboard. iBooks searches for any matching entries.

3. Use your finger to scroll down the entries (see **Figure 14-13**).

Search button   Scroll through the entries

Figure 14-12   **Figure 14-13**

4. Flick your finger to scroll down the search results and then use either the Search Web or Search Wikipedia button at the bottom of the Search dialog if you want to search for information about the search term online.

 You can also search for other instances of a particular word while in the book pages by pressing your finger on the word and tapping the right-facing arrow and then Search on the toolbar that appears.

Use Bookmarks and Highlights

1. Bookmarks and highlights in your e-books operate like favorite sites that you save in your web browser: They enable you to revisit a favorite passage or refresh your memory about a character or plot point. To bookmark a page, have that page displayed and just tap the Bookmark button in the top-right corner (see **Figure** 14-14).

2. To highlight a word or phrase, press a word until the toolbar shown in **Figure** 14-15 appears.

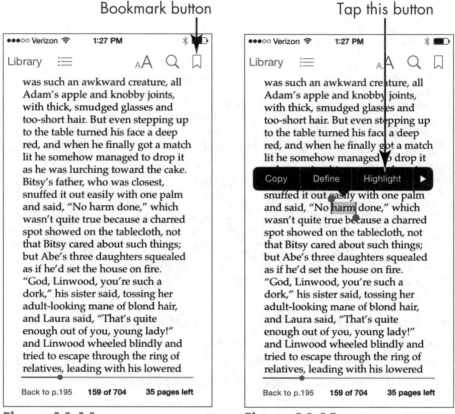

Bookmark button

Tap this button

Figure 14-14

Figure 14-15

3. Tap the Highlight button. A colored highlight is placed on the word.

4. To change the color of the highlight, add a note, or remove the highlight, tap the highlighted word. The toolbar shown in **Figure** 14-16 appears.

5. Tap one of these four buttons (from left to right):

- *Colors:* Displays a menu of colors that you can tap to change the highlight color as well as an underline option.

- *Remove Highlight:* Removes the highlight.

- *Note:* Lets you add a note to the item.

- *Share:* Allows you to share the highlighted text with others via AirDrop, Message, Mail, Twitter, or Facebook, or to copy the text.

6. You can also tap the button at the right side of the toolbar to access Copy, Define, and Search tools. Tap outside the highlighted text to close the toolbar.

7. To go to a list of bookmarks and notes (including highlighted text), tap the Table of Contents button that appears (refer to **Figure 14-7**).

8. In the Table of Contents, tap the Bookmarks tab. As shown in **Figure 14-17,** all bookmarks are displayed. If you wish to see highlighted text and associated notes, you display the Notes tab.

9. Tap a bookmark in the bookmark list to go to that location in the book.

 iPhone automatically bookmarks where you left off reading in a book so that you don't have to mark your place manually. If you use any other device registered to your iTunes or iCloud account, you also pick up where you left off reading.

Bookmarks tab

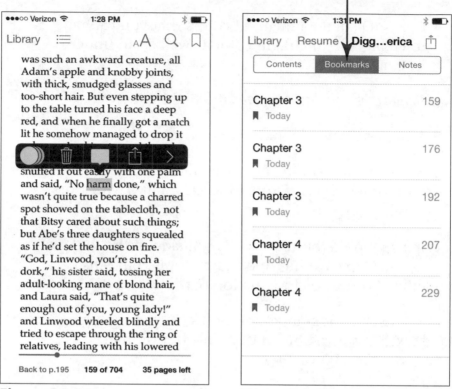

Figure 14-16   **Figure 14-17**

Check Words in the Dictionary

1. As you read a book, you may come across unfamiliar words. Don't skip over them — take the opportunity to learn a new word! With a book open, press your finger on a word and hold it until the toolbar shown in **Figure 14-18** appears.

2. Tap the Define button. A definition dialog appears, as shown in **Figure 14-19**.

3. Tap the definition and scroll down to view more.

4. When you finish reviewing the definition, tap Done, and the definition disappears.

Tap this option

Figure 14-18

Figure 14-19

 You can also tap the Search Web or Search Wikipedia buttons to look for information about a word from those sources, and tap the Manage button to choose which dictionary your definitions come from.

Organize Books in Collections

1. iBooks lets you create and name collections of books to help you organize them by your own logic, such as Tear Jerkers, Work-Related, and Great Recipes. You can place a book in only one collection, however. To create a collection from the Library bookshelf, tap Select.

2. On the screen that appears, tap a book and then tap Move. In the Collections screen shown in **Figure 14-20,**

tap New Collection. On the blank line that appears, type a name.

3. Tap Done, which closes the dialog and returns you to the Collection. To add a book to a collection from the Library, tap Select.

4. Tap a book and then tap the Move button that appears in the top of the screen (see **Figure 14-21**). In the dialog that appears, tap the collection to which you'd like to move the book, and the book now appears on the bookshelf in that collection. To change which collection you're viewing, tap the button with the current collection's name to display other collections and then tap the one you want.

Tap this   Tap this button

Figure 14-20   Figure 14-21

5. To delete a book from a collection with the collection displayed, tap Select, tap the book, and then tap Delete.

 To delete a collection with the Collections dialog displayed, select the collection that you want to delete and then tap Edit. Tap the minus sign (–) to the left of the collection and then tap Delete to get rid of it. A message appears, asking you to tap Remove (to remove the contents of the collection from your iPhone) or Don't Remove. Note that if you choose Don't Remove, all titles within a deleted collection are returned to their original collections in your library, the default one being Books.

Download Magazine Apps to Newsstand

1. Newsstand is an interface that allows you to access a collection of apps that let you subscribe to and read magazines, newspapers, and periodicals other than books. Newsstand comes preinstalled on iPhone. When you download a free publication, you're actually downloading an app to Newsstand. You can then tap that app to buy individual issues, as covered in the next section. Tap the Newsstand icon on the Home screen to open Newsstand (see **Figure 14-22**).

2. Tap the Store button (refer to **Figure 14-22**). The store opens, displaying Featured periodicals. There are also Top Charts and Explore buttons along the bottom of the screen that take you to other kinds apps (see **Figure 14-23**).

3. Tap any of the items displayed, scroll down the screen to view other choices, or tap the Search button on the bottom of the screen and enter a search term to locate a publication you're interested in.

Tap this button

Figure 14-22   **Figure 14-23**

 If you tap other icons at the bottom of the screen, such as Top Charts or Explore, you're taken to other types of content than periodicals. Also, if you tap the Featured icon again after tapping one of these icons, you're taken to other kinds of apps than periodicals. If you're focused on finding only periodicals, your best bet is to stay on the Store screen that displays when you tap the Store button in Newsstand.

4. When you find an item, tap it to view a detailed description (see **Figure 14-24**).

5. Tap the Free button and then tap Install. The app downloads to Newsstand.

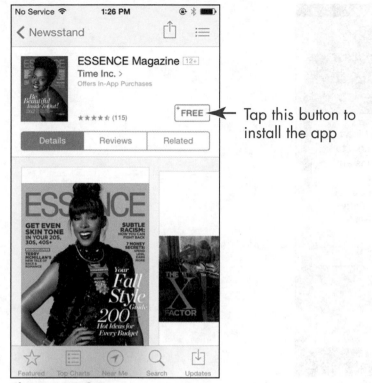

Tap this button to install the app

Figure 14-24

Preview and Buy Issues of Periodicals through Newsstand

1. Tap a periodical app that you've added to Newsstand. The message shown in **Figure 14-25** appears, asking if you'd like to be informed of new issues. Tap OK if you want to be informed.

2. Tap the Preview Issue button to take a look at a description of its content, or tap the Buy button (or, in the case of a free publication, the Download button).

3. In the purchase confirmation dialog that appears, tap Buy. The issue is charged to your iTunes account.

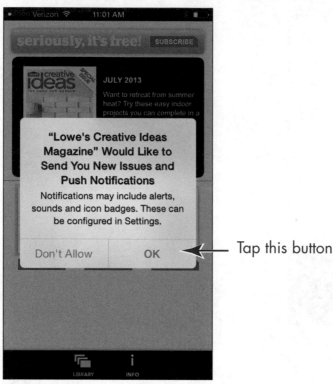

Figure 14-25

Tap this button

 Note that different stores offer different options for subscribing, buying issues, and organizing issues. Think of Newsstand as a central collection point for apps that allow you to preview and buy content in each publication's store.

Read Periodicals in Your Newsstand Apps

1. If you buy a periodical or you've downloaded a free subscription preview, such as the magazine shown in **Figure 14-26,** you can tap the publication in Newsstand to view it.

2. In the publication that appears, use your finger to swipe left, right, up, and down to view more of the pages (see **Figure 14-27**).

Figure 14-26

Figure 14-27

 Note that different publications offer different options for subscribing, buying issues, navigating, and organizing issues.

Playing with Music on iPhone

Chapter 15

*i*Phone includes an iPod-like app called Music that allows you to take advantage of its amazing little sound system to play your favorite music or podcasts and audiobooks.

In this chapter, you get acquainted with the Music app and its features that allow you to sort and find music and control playback. You also get an overview of AirPlay for accessing and playing your music over a home network or, with iOS 8, over any connected device (this also works with videos and photos). Finally, I introduce you to iTunes Radio for your listening pleasure.

View the Library Contents

1. Tap the Music app, located in the Dock on the Home screen. The Music library appears (the Artists view is shown **Figure 15-1**).

2. Tap the Playlists, Artists, or Songs buttons at the bottom of the library to view your music according to any of these criteria (refer to **Figure 15-1**).

3. Tap the More button (see **Figure 15-2**) to view music by album, genre, or composer, or to view any audiobooks you've acquired.

Tap a criterion to use   Tap this button

Figure 15-1   **Figure 15-2**

 iTunes has several free items that you can download and use to play around with the features in Music. You can also sync content, such as iTunes Smart Playlists stored on your computer or other Apple devices to your iPhone, and play it using the Music app. (See Chapter 3 for more about syncing and Chapter 12 for more about getting content from iTunes.)

Apple offers a service called iTunes Match (visit www.apple.com/itunes/ for more information). You pay $24.99 per year for the capability to match the music you've bought from other providers (and stored on your computer) to what's in the iTunes library. If there's a match (and there usually is), that content is added to your iTunes library on iCloud. Then, using iCloud, you can sync the content among all your Apple devices.

Create Playlists

1. You can create your own playlists to put tracks from various sources into collections of your choosing. Tap the Playlists button at the bottom of the Music screen.

2. Tap New Playlist. In the dialog that appears, enter a name for the playlist and tap Save. On the next screen, if necessary, tap a collection of songs, such as Purchased, to display songs.

3. In the list of selections that appears (see **Figure 15-3**), tap the plus sign next to each item you want to include.

4. Tap the Done button and then tap the Playlists button to return to the Playlists screen.

5. Your playlist appears in the list, and you can now play it by tapping the list name and then tapping a track to play it.

To search for a song in your music libraries, use the Spotlight Search feature. From your first Home screen, you can swipe down from the screen outside the Dock and enter the name of the song. A list of search results appears.

Tap the plus sign to include a song in the playlist

Figure 15-3

Search for Music

1. You can search for an item in your Music library by using the Search feature. With Music open, swipe down near the top of the screen and then tap the Search field that's displayed (see **Figure 15-4**). The onscreen keyboard appears.

2. Enter a search term in the Search field. Results are displayed, narrowing as you type, as shown in **Figure 15-5**.

3. Tap an item to play it.

 You can enter an artist's name, a lyricist's or a composer's name, or a word from the item's title in the Search field to find what you're looking for.

Tap here to search for audio   Results display here

Figure 15-4   **Figure 15-5**

Play Music

1. Locate the music that you want by using the methods described in previous tasks in this chapter.

2. Tap the item you want to play. Note that if you're displaying the Songs tab, you don't have to tap an album to open a song; you need only tap a song to play it. If you're using any other tab, you have to tap items such as albums (or multiple songs from one artist) to find the song you want to hear.

3. Tap the item you want to play from the list that appears; it begins to play (see **Figure 15-6**).

4. Use the Previous and Next buttons at the bottom of the screen shown in **Figure 15-7** to navigate the audio file that's playing. The Previous button takes you back to the beginning of the item that's playing; the Next button takes you to the next item. Use the Volume slider on the bottom of the screen (or the Volume buttons on the side of your iPhone) to increase or decrease the volume.

Progress bar

Figure 15-6

Previous Pause Volume Next
slider

Figure 15-7

5. Tap the Pause button to pause playback. Tap the button again to resume playing. Note that you can also use music controls for music that's playing from the Lock screen.

6. Tap and drag the slider that indicates the current playback location on the Progress bar to the left or right to "scrub" to another location in the song. If the slider isn't visible, tap the image of the album cover, and the Progress bar appears.

7. If you don't like what's playing, here's how to make another selection: Tap the Back to Library arrow in the top-left corner to return to the Library view or tap the Album List button in the top-right corner to show other selections in the album that's playing.

 You can use Siri to play music hands free. Just press and hold the Home button, and when Siri appears, say something like "Play 'Take the A Train'" or "Play *The White Album.*"

 Home Sharing is a feature of iTunes that you can use to share music among up to five devices that have Home Sharing turned on. After Home Sharing is set up via iTunes, any of your devices can stream music and videos to other devices, and you can even click and drag content between devices using iTunes. To play music from another device via Home Sharing, tap the More button in Music and then tap the Shared option. For more about Home Sharing, visit this site: www.apple.com/support/homesharing.

 New with iOS 8 comes Family Sharing. Using this feature, up to six members of your family can share purchased content even if they don't share the same iTunes account. You can set up Family Sharing under iCloud in Settings. See Chapter 12 for more about Family Sharing.

Shuffle Music

1. If you want to play a random selection of the music in an album on your iPhone, you can use the Shuffle feature. Tap Music on the Home screen, tap the Albums tab, and then tap an album.

2. With an album open, tap the Shuffle button, which looks like two lines crossing to form an *X* (see **Figure** 15-8). Your content plays in random order.

Shuffle button

Figure 15-8

If you're playing music and have set the Volume slider as high as it goes and you're still having trouble hearing, consider getting ear buds. These cut out extraneous noises and may improve the sound quality of what you're listening to, as well as add stereo to iPhone's mono speaker. Preferably, use 3.5 mm stereo ear buds; insert them in the headphone jack at the bottom of your iPhone.

Use AirPlay

The AirPlay streaming technology is built into the iPhone, iPod touch, Macs and PCs running iTunes, and iPad. *Streaming* technology allows you to send media files from one device to be played on another. You can send (for example) a movie that you've purchased on your iPhone or a slideshow of your photos to be played on your Apple TV and then control the TV playback from your iPhone. You can also send music to be played over compatible speakers. Check out the Apple Remote app, which you can use to control your Apple TV.

You can use the AirPlay button in the Control Center, which you display by swiping up from the bottom edge of your iPhone screen, to take advantage of AirPlay in a few ways:

➡ Purchase Apple TV and stream video, photos, and music to the TV.

➡ Purchase AirPort Express and attach it to your speakers to play music.

➡ If you buy AirPort Express, you can stream audio directly to your speakers. Because this combination of equipment varies, my advice — if you're interested in using AirPlay — is to visit your nearest Apple Store and find out which hardware combination will work best for you.

➡ Get AirPlay-compatible speakers. With these, you don't need AirPort Express at all because you can AirPlay to the speakers directly.

To use AirPlay with another AirPlay-enabled device on your network or in close proximity, swipe up from the bottom of your screen and tap the AirPlay button in the Control Center; then select the AirPlay device to stream the content to, or choose your iPhone to move the playback back to it.

 If you get a bit antsy watching a long movie, one of the beauties of AirPlay is that you can still use your iPhone to check email, browse photos or the Internet, or check your calendar while the media file is playing on the other device.

Play Music with iTunes Radio

1. You can access iTunes Radio with any Apple device that has iOS 7 or later. Begin by tapping the Music icon on the Home screen.

2. On the screen that appears, tap the Radio button at the bottom of the screen.

3. Tap a Featured Station; a featured song begins to play (see **Figure 15-9**).

4. Use the tools at the bottom of the screen (refer to **Figure 15-9**) to control playback.

5. Tap the star-shaped Favorites button at the bottom of the screen to display the options shown in **Figure 15-10**. Here you can choose to Play More Like This, Never Play This Song, or Add to iTunes Wish List. By using these settings, you help iTunes understand your musical suggestions and can even build custom radio stations.

Figure 15-9   **Figure 15-10**

Add Stations to iTunes Radio

You aren't just limited to playing featured stations. You can add a station to My Stations in a couple of ways. You can play a featured station, pause it, and then tap the Information icon (the circled *i* in the top-middle of the screen), and choose New Station from Artist or New Station from Song. You can also create a New Station of your own.

1. Tap the Music icon in the Dock.

2. Tap Radio.

3. From the iTunes Radio Home page, tap the New Station button (see **Figure 15-11**).

4. Tap a category of music such as Jazz or Latin Hits (see **Figure 15-12**). If subcategories are then offered, tap the one you prefer and then tap the Add New button that appears to the right of the category. The category is added to your stations.

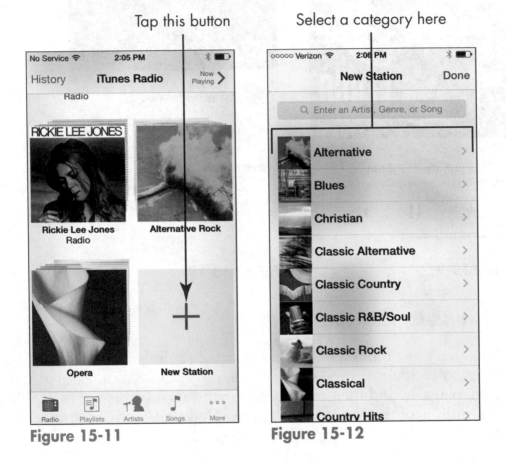

Tap this button   Select a category here

Figure 15-11   Figure 15-12

View Your iTunes Radio History

iTunes Radio offers a great way to see where you've been and where you're going, musically speaking, with its History and Wish List features.

1. Tap the Music icon in the Dock.

2. In the screen that appears (see **Figure 15-13**), tap History in the top-left corner.

3. Tap the Played tab to see the music you've listened to.

4. Tap the Wish List tab (see **Figure 15-14**) to see items that you've added to your Wish List (see the earlier task, "Play Music with iTunes Radio," to discover how to add a selection to your Wish List).

Tap this option

Wish List tab

Figure 15-13

Figure 15-14

 When a song is playing, tap the Information button and then tap Share Station to share a song via AirDrop, Message, Mail, Twitter, or Facebook.

Playing with Photos

Chapter 16

W ith its gorgeous screen, the iPhone is a natural for taking and viewing photos. It supports most common photo formats, such as JPEG, TIFF, and PNG. You can shoot your photos by using the built-in cameras in iPhone with built-in square or panorama modes. If you have an iPhone 4.5 or later, you can edit your images using smart adjustment filters. You can also sync photos from your computer, save images that you find online to your iPhone, or receive them by email, MMS, or iMessage.

The Photo Sharing feature lets you share groups of photos with people, including your family, using iCloud on an iOS device or on a Mac or Windows computer with iCloud access. Your iCloud Photo Library makes all this storage and sharing easier.

When you have photos to play with, the Photos app lets you organize photos and view photos in albums, one by one, or in a slideshow. You can also view photos by the years in which they were taken, with images divided into collections by the location or time you took them. You can also AirDrop (iPhone 5 and later), email, message, or tweet a photo to a friend, print it, share it via AirPlay, or post it

Get ready to . . .

to Facebook. Finally, you can create time-lapse videos with the Camera app, allowing you to record a sequence in time such as a flower opening as the sun warms it. You can read about all these features in this chapter.

Take Pictures with the iPhone Cameras

1. The cameras in the iPhone are just begging to be used, so no matter which phone model you have, get started! Tap the Camera app icon on the Home screen to open the app.

2. If the camera type at the bottom of the screen (see **Figure 16-1**) is set to Video, slide to the left to choose Photo (the still camera).

 iPhone's front- and rear-facing cameras allow you to capture photos and video (see Chapter 17 for more about the video features) and share them with family and friends. iPhone 6 and 6 Plus offer an 8-megapixel iSight camera with features such as Phase Detection Autofocus, image stabilization to avoid those fuzzy moving targets, and True Tone Flash, a sensor that tells iPhone when a flash is needed.

3. You can set the Pano (for panorama) and Square options using the slider control above the Capture button. These controls let you create square images like those you see on the popular Instagram site. With Pano selected, tap to begin to take a picture and pan across a view, and then tap Done to capture a panoramic display.

4. Tap the Flash button in the top-left corner of the screen when using the rear camera and tap On if your lighting is dim enough to require a flash, Off if you don't want iPhone to use a flash, or Auto if you want to let iPhone decide for you.

5. If you want a time delay before the camera snaps the picture, tap the Time Delay button at the top right of the screen and then tap 3s or 10s for a 3- or 10-second delay.

6. Move the camera around until you find a pleasing image. You can do a couple of things at this point to help you take your photo:

- Tap the area of the grid where you want the camera to autofocus.

- Pinch the screen to display a digital zoom control; drag the circle in the zoom bar to the right or left to zoom in or out on the image.

7. Tap the Capture button at the bottom center of the screen (the big, white button). You've just taken a picture, and it's stored in the Photos app gallery automatically.

 You can also use a Volume button (located on the left side of your iPhone) to capture a picture or start or stop video camera recording.

8. Tap the Switch Camera button in the top-right corner to switch between the front camera and rear camera. You can then take selfies (pictures of yourself), so go ahead and tap the Capture button to take another picture.

9. To view the last photo taken, swipe to the left or tap the thumbnail of the latest image in the bottom-left corner of the screen; the Photos app opens and displays the photo.

10. Tap the Share button (it's the box with an arrow coming out of it, located in the bottom-left corner of the screen) to display a menu that allows you to AirDrop, email, or instant message the photo, assign it to a contact, use it as iPhone wallpaper, tweet it, post it to Facebook, share via iCloud Photo Sharing, or print it (see **Figure 16-2**).

Slide to Photo

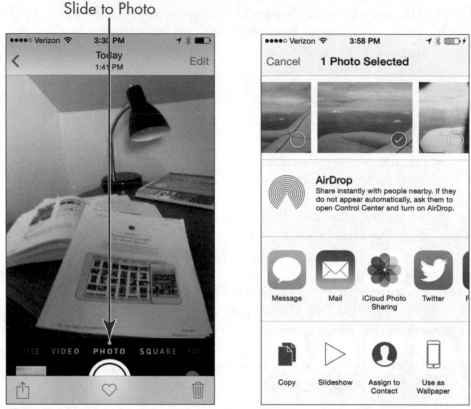

Figure 16-1   Figure 16-2

11. To delete the image, have it displayed and tap the Trash Can button in the bottom-right corner of the screen.

12. Tap Delete Photo in the confirming menu that appears.

 To go to the camera with the Lock screen displayed, swipe the Camera icon up to go directly to the Camera app.

 You can use the Photo Sharing feature to automatically sync your photos across various devices. Turn on Photo Sharing by tapping Settings on the Home screen and then tapping Photos & Camera.

Save Photos from the Web

1. The web offers a wealth of images that you can download to your Photo Library. Open Safari and navigate to the web page containing the image you want.

2. Press and hold the image. A menu appears, as shown in **Figure 16-3**.

3. Tap Save Image. The image is saved to your Recently Added album in the Photos app, as shown in **Figure 16-4**.

 For more about how to use Safari to navigate to or search for web content, see Chapter 10.

Figure 16-3

Figure 16-4

A number of sites protect their photos from being copied by applying an invisible overlay. This blank overlay image ensures that you don't actually get the image you're tapping. Even if a site doesn't take these precautions, be sure that you don't save images from the web and use them in ways that violate the rights of the person or entity that owns them.

 If you want to capture your iPhone screen, the process is simple. Press the Sleep/Wake button and Home button simultaneously. The screen capture is saved in PNG format to your Recently Added album. To save a picture sent as an email attachment in Mail, tap the attachment icon and the picture opens. Press the screen till a menu appears and then tap Save.

View an Album

1. The Photos app organizes your pictures into albums, using such criteria as the folder or album on your computer from which you synced the photos or photos captured using the iPhone camera (saved in the Recently Added folder). You may also have albums for images that you synced from other devices through iTunes or shared via Photos. To view your albums, start by tapping the Photos app icon on the Home screen.

2. Tap the Albums tab to display your albums, as shown in **Figure 16-5**.

3. Tap an album. The photos in it are displayed.

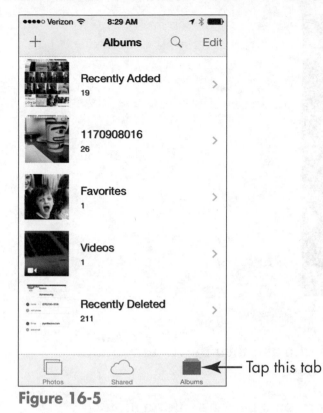

Tap this tab

Figure 16-5

View Individual Photos

1. Tap the Photos app icon on the Home screen.

2. Tap Albums (refer to **Figure 16-5**).

3. Tap an album to open it; then, to view a photo, tap it. The picture expands, as shown in **Figure 16-6**.

4. Flick your finger to the left or right to scroll through the album to look at the individual photos in it.

Figure 16-6

5. You can tap the Back button and then the Albums button to return to the Album view.

 You can place a photo on a person's information record in Contacts. For more about how to do this, see Chapter 5.

 You can associate photos with faces and events; when you do, additional tabs appear at the bottom of the screen when you display an album containing that type of photo.

Edit Photos

1. iPhone Photos isn't Photoshop, but it does provide you with some tools for editing photos, with some that arrived in iOS 8. Tap the Photos app on the Home screen to open it.

2. Using methods previously described in this chapter, locate a photo you want to edit.

3. Tap the Edit button; the Edit Photo screen shown in **Figure 16-7** appears.

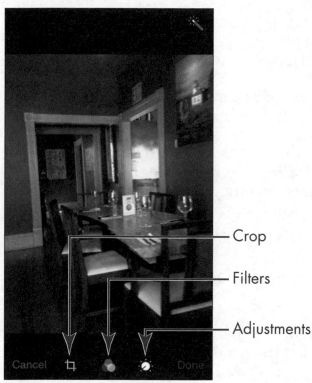

Crop

Filters

Adjustments

Figure 16-7

4. At this point, you can take three possible actions with these tools:

- *Crop:* To crop the photo to a portion of its original area, tap the Crop button. You can then tap any corner of the image and drag inward or outward to remove areas of the photo. Tap Crop and then Save to apply your changes.

- *Filters:* Apply any of nine filters such as Fade, Mono, or Noir to change the feel of your image. These effects adjust the brightness of your image or apply a black-and-white tone to your color photos. Tap the Filters button in the middle of the tools at the bottom of the screen and scroll to view available filters. Tap one and then tap Apply to apply the effect to your image.

- *Adjustments:* Tap Light, Color, or B&W to access a slew of tools that you can use to tweak contrast, color intensity, shadows, and more.

5. If you're pleased with your edits, tap the Done button, and a copy of the edited photo is saved.

 Each of the editing features has a Cancel button. If you don't like the changes you made, tap this button to stop making changes before you save the image.

Organize Photos

1. If you want to create your own album, display the Recently Added album.

2. Tap the Select button in the top-right corner and then tap individual photos to select them. Small check marks appear on the selected photos (see **Figure 16-8**).

3. Tap the Add To button and then tap New Album. (*Note:* If you've already created albums, you can choose to add the photo to an existing album at this point.)

4. Enter a name for a new album and then tap Save. If you create a new album, it appears in the Photos main screen with the other albums that are displayed.

 You can also choose the Share or Delete buttons when you've selected photos in Step 2 of this task. This allows you to share or delete multiple photos at a time.

Check marks indicate
selected photos

Figure 16-8

View Photos by Years and Location

1. You can view your photos in logical categories such as by date or a location where they were taken. These so-called smart groupings let you, for example, view all photos taken this year or all the photos from your summer vacation. Tap Photos on the Home screen to open the Photos app.

2. Tap Photos at the bottom of the screen. The display of photos by date appears (see **Figure 16-9**).

3. Tap Collections in the top-left corner; you see collections of photos by location and date (see **Figure 16-10**).

Figure 16-9   **Figure 16-10**

4. Tap a collection and you can view the individual "moments" in that collection broken down day by day.

 To go back to larger groupings, such as from a moment in a collection to the larger collection to the entire last year, just keep tapping the Back button at the top left of the screen (which will be named after the next collection up in the grouping hierarchy, such as Collections or Years).

Share Photos with Mail, Twitter, or Facebook

1. You can easily share photos stored on your iPhone by sending them as email attachments, via iMessage or MMS (text message), by posting them to Facebook, sharing them via iCloud Photo Sharing or Flickr, or as tweets on Twitter. (You have to go to Facebook or Twitter using a browser and set up an account on those services before you can use this feature.) Next, tap the Photos app icon on the Home screen.

2. Tap the Photos or Album tab and locate the photo you want to share.

3. Tap the photo to select it and then tap the Share button. (It looks like a box with an arrow jumping out of it.) The menu shown in **Figure 16-11** appears.

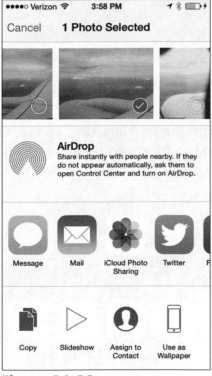

Figure 16-11

4. Tap the Mail, Message, Twitter, iCloud Photo Sharing, Facebook, or Flickr option.

5. In the message form that appears, make any modifications that apply in the To, Cc/Bcc, or Subject fields and then type a message for email, or enter your Facebook posting or Twitter tweet.

6. Tap the Send or Post button, and the message and photo are sent or posted.

 You can also copy and paste a photo into documents such as those created in the Pages word-processor application. To do this, press and hold a photo in Photos until the Copy command appears. Tap Copy and then, in the destination application, press and hold the screen and tap Paste.

Share a Photo Using AirDrop

AirDrop, available to users of iPhone 5 and later, provides a way to share content such as photos with others who are nearby and who have an AirDrop-enabled device (more recent Macs that can run OS X Yosemite). Follow the steps in the previous task to locate a photo you want to share; after you've located that photo, follow these steps:

1. Tap the Share button.

2. If an AirDrop-enabled device is in your immediate vicinity (such as within 30 feet or so), you see the device listed at the top of the screen (see **Figure 16-12**). Tap the device name and your photo is sent to the other device.

 Note that the other device has to have AirDrop enabled. To enable AirDrop, open the Control Center (swipe up from the bottom of any screen) and tap AirDrop. Choose Contacts Only or Everyone to specify who you can use AirDrop with.

AirDrop-enabled devices
within range

Figure 16-12

Share Photos Using iCloud Photo Sharing

1. iCloud Photo Sharing allows you to automatically share photos from the Moments screen. Tap Share to the right of a moment and then choose to share the whole moment or selected photos (see **Figure 16-13**).

2. In the Share screen that opens, tap iCloud Photo Sharing.

3. Tap Post, and the photos or moment are posted to your iCloud Photo Library.

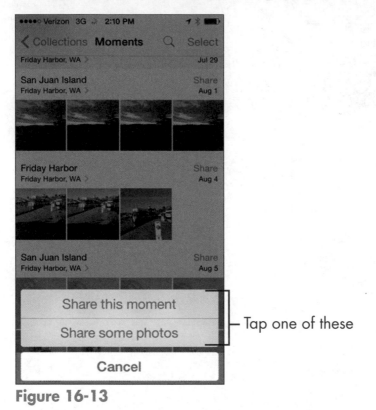

Tap one of these

Figure 16-13

Work in iCloud Photo Library

1. iCloud Photo Library automatically backs up all your photos and videos to the cloud. Tap Settings, Photos & Camera and then tap the On button for iCloud Photo Library to post all your photos to this library in the cloud.

2. Tap Home and then tap the Photos app to open it.

3. Tap Albums in the bottom-right corner to view all photos and videos stored in the iCloud Library.

 With all these photos available to you, you'll need to be able to search your library for the one you want. Tap the Search button at the top of the Photos screen. A list of so-called "smart" suggestions appears. Enter the date or time of the photo, a location, or an album name such as "Vacation" to locate the photo.

Print Photos

1. If you have a printer that's compatible with Apple's AirPrint technology, you can print photos. With Photos open, locate the photo you want to print and tap it to maximize it.

2. Tap the Share button, and on the menu that appears (refer to **Figure 16-11**), scroll in the bottom row of buttons to the far right and then tap Print.

3. In the Printer Options dialog that appears (see **Figure 16-14**), tap Select Printer. iPhone presents you with a list of any compatible wireless printers on your local network.

●●●○○ Sprint 🛜   9:37 AM   ⌁ ⁂ ▬▬

~~Touch to return to Navigation~~

Cancel	**Printer Options**

Printer   Select Printer ＞ ←— Tap this option

1 Copy   [— | +]

Print

Figure 16-14

4. Tap the plus or minus symbols in the Copy field to set the number of copies to print.

5. Tap the Print button, and your photo is sent to the printer.

Run a Slideshow

1. You can run a slideshow of your images in Photos and even play music and choose transition effects for the show. Tap the Photos app on the Home screen.

2. Display an individual photo in an album that contains more than one photo.

3. Tap the Share button and then tap Slideshow to see the Slideshow Options dialog, shown in **Figure 16-15.**

4. If you want to play music along with the slideshow, tap the On/Off switch on the Play Music field.

5. To choose music to play along with the slideshow, tap Music and, in the list that appears (see **Figure 16-16**), tap any selection from your Music library.

6. In the Slideshow Options dialog, tap Transitions and then tap the transition effect that you want to use for your slideshow.

Figure 16-15

Figure 16-16

7. Tap the Start Slideshow button. The slideshow begins. Tap the screen to stop the slideshow at any time.

 To run a slideshow that includes only the photos contained in a particular album, tap the Albums tab, tap an album to open it, and then tap the Slideshow button to make settings and run a slideshow.

Delete Photos

1. You might find that it's time to get rid of some of those old photos of the family reunion or the last community center project. If the photos weren't transferred from your computer, but instead were taken, downloaded, or captured as screenshots on the iPhone, you can delete them. Tap the Photos app icon on the Home screen.

2. Tap the Albums or Photos tab and then, if you've opened the Albums tab, tap an album to open it.

3. Locate a photo that you want to delete and then tap the Trash Can icon. In the confirming dialog that appears, tap the Delete Photo button to finish the deletion.

 If you delete a photo in Photo Sharing, it is deleted on all devices that you shared it with.

Create Time-Lapse Videos from Photos

1. New with iOS 8 is the Time Lapse feature of Camera. Capturing photos with this feature allows you to create a time-lapse photo show. iPhone captures photos at select intervals, making the capture of a dynamic scene such as a sunset possible. Tap Camera on the Home screen.

2. Swipe the listing at the bottom of the screen until Time Lapse is centered over the Capture button (see **Figure 16-17**).

3. Tap the Capture button. Leave the camera recording as long as you like and then tap the End button. Your new time-lapse images appear in the bottom-left corner. Tap the image and then tap Play.

Figure 16-17

Getting the Most Out of Video Features

Using the Videos app, you can watch downloaded movies or TV shows, as well as media that you've synced from iCloud or your Mac or PC.

In addition, iPhone 6 sports both a front and rear video camera that you can use to capture your own videos, and by downloading the iMovie app for iPhone (a more limited version of the longtime mainstay on Mac computers), you add the capability to edit those videos. The 4.7" Retina HD display on iPhone 6 and the 5.5" Retina HD display on iPhone 6 Plus offer even more pixels for better resolution than ever. An 8MP iSight camera can record high-definition video. These two phones are, quite simply, two of the best phones ever for viewing and capturing images, both still and moving.

A few other improvements to video in iPhone 6 and 6 Plus include image stabilization to avoid the shakes when recording, more frames shot per second for smoother video, and Cinematic Video Stabilization, which means that your iPhone continually autofocuses as you're recording.

In this chapter, I explain all about shooting and watching video content from a variety of sources. For practice, you might want to refer to Chapter 12 first to find out how to purchase or download one of many available TV shows or movies from the iTunes Store.

Capture Your Own Videos with the Built-In Cameras

The camera lens that comes on iPhone 6 and 6 Plus has perks for photographers, including a large aperture and highly accurate sensor, which make for better images all around. In addition, auto image stabilization makes up for any shakiness in the hands holding the phone, and autofocus has sped up thanks to the fast A8 processor chip. For videographers, you'll appreciate a fast frames-per-second capability as well as a slow-motion feature.

1. To capture a video, tap the Camera app on the Home screen. In iPhone, two video cameras are available for capturing video, one from the front and one from the back of the device. (See more about this topic in the next task.)

2. The Camera app opens (see **Figure 17-1**). Tap and slide the camera-type options above the red Record button to the right until Video rests above the button; this is how you switch from the still camera to the video camera.

3. If you want to switch between the front and back cameras, tap the Switch Camera button in the top-right corner of the screen (refer to **Figure 17-1**).

4. Tap the red Record button to begin recording the video. (The red dot in the middle of this button turns into a red square when the camera is recording.) When you're finished, tap the Record button again. Your new video is now listed in the bottom-left corner of the screen. Tap the video to play it, share it, or delete it. In the future, you can find and play the video in your Camera Roll when you open the Photos app.

Switch Camera button

Flash button

Last media capture

Record button

Figure 17-1

Before you start recording, remember where the camera lens is — while holding the iPhone and panning, you can easily put your fingers directly over the lens! Also, you can't pause your recording; when you stop, your video is saved, and when you start recording, you're creating a new video file.

Play Movies or TV Shows with Videos

1. When you first open the Videos app, you may see relatively blank screens with a note that you don't own any videos and a link to the iTunes Store. After you've purchased TV shows and movies or rented movies from the iTunes Store (see Chapter 12 to learn how) or other sources, you'll see tabs of the different kinds of content you own. Tap the Videos app icon on the Home screen to open the application.

If your iPhone is on the same Wi-Fi network as your computer and both are running iTunes, with the iPhone and iTunes set to use the same Home Sharing account, you see the Shared List. With this setup, you can stream videos from iTunes on your computer to your iPhone.

2. On a screen like the one shown in **Figure 17-2,** tap the appropriate category at the bottom of the screen (TV, Podcasts, or Movies, depending on the content you've downloaded) and then tap the video you want to watch. Information about the movie or TV show episodes appears, as shown in **Figure 17-3.** TV Shows include an Episodes, Details, and Related tab; Movies contain a Details, Chapters, and Related tab.

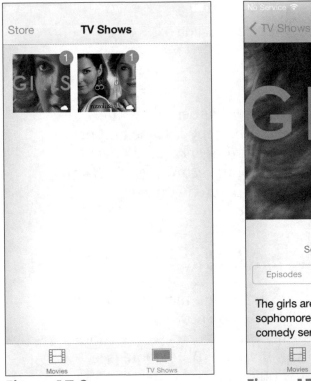

Figure 17-2   Figure 17-3

3. For TV Shows, tap the Episodes tab to display episodes that you can tap to play; for Movies, the Play button appears no matter which tab is selected. Tap the Play button (see Figure 17-4) and the movie or TV show begins playing. (If you see a small, cloud-shaped icon instead of a Play button, tap it and the content is downloaded from iCloud.) Note that the progress of the playback is displayed on the Progress bar showing how many minutes you've viewed and how many remain. If you don't see the bar, tap the screen once to display it briefly, along with a set of playback tools at the bottom of the screen.

Figure 17-4

4. With the playback tools displayed, take any of these actions:

   • Tap the Pause button to pause playback.

- Tap either Go to Previous Chapter or Go to Next Chapter to move to a different location in the video playback. Note that if a video has chapter support, another button appears here for displaying all chapters so that you can move more easily from one to another.

- Tap the circular button on the Volume slider and drag the button left or right to decrease or increase the volume, respectively.

5. To stop the video and return to the information screen, tap the Done button to the left of the Progress bar.

 Note that if you've watched a video and stopped it partway, it opens by default to the last location that you were viewing. To start a video from the beginning, tap and drag the circular button (called the *playhead*) on the Progress bar all the way to the left.

 If your controls disappear during playback, just tap the screen and they'll reappear.

 If you download the free iTunes U app, you can access educational video content that you can play back using the Videos app.

Turn On Closed-Captioning

1. iTunes and iPhone offer support for closed-captioning and subtitles. If a movie has either closed-captioning or subtitles, you can turn on the feature in iPhone. Look for the CC logo on media that you download to use this feature; be aware that video you record won't have this capability. Begin by tapping the Settings icon on the Home screen.

2. Tap General⇨Accessibility. On the screen that appears, scroll down and tap Subtitles & Captioning.

3. On the menu that displays (see **Figure** 17-5), tap the Closed Captions + SDH switch to turn on the feature. Now when you play a movie with closed-captioning, you can tap the Audio and Subtitles button to the left of the playback controls to manage these features.

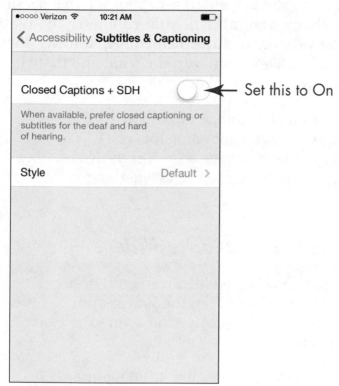

Figure 17-5

Delete a Video from the iPhone

You can buy videos directly from your iPhone, or you can sync via iCloud or iTunes to place content you've bought or created on another device on your iPhone.

When you want to get rid of video content on your iPhone because it's a memory hog, you can delete it by going to the Home screen and tapping Settings⇨General⇨Usage. Tap Manage Storage and then tap

Videos to see a list of videos stored on your iPhone. Flick to the left over the video that you want to delete and then tap the Delete button that appears.

You can also delete it by using iTunes and then sync again, removing it from your iPhone. If you buy a video using iTunes and sync to download it to your iPhone and then delete it from your iPhone, it's still saved in your iTunes library. You can sync your computer and iPhone again to download the video once more. Remember, however, that rented movies, once deleted, are gone with the wind and that video doesn't sync to iCloud as photos and music do.

 iPhone has a much smaller storage capacity than your typical computer, so downloading lots of TV shows or movies can fill its storage area quickly. If you don't want to view an item again, delete it to free space.

Let Others Know about Your Favorite Videos

1. You can share your opinion about a video using AirDrop, Mail, Message, Twitter, or Facebook. Tap the Videos app to open it and then tap the Store button. Find a video you want to share and tap it.

2. In the information screen shown in **Figure 17-6**, tap the Share button (a box with an arrow at the top of it at the top of the screen). Tap AirDrop, Mail, Message, Twitter, or Facebook to use one of these methods of sharing your enthusiasm for the item (see **Figure 17-7**).

3. In the corresponding form, enter a recipient in the To field and add to the message, if you like. If you chose to post to your Facebook page, enter your message in the Facebook form.

Share button

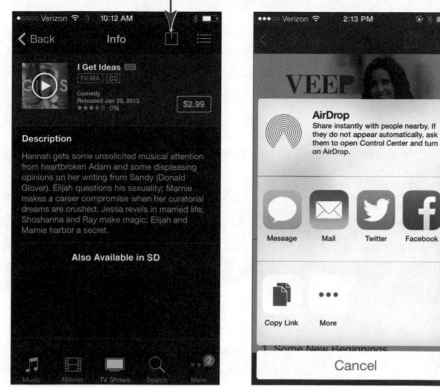

Figure 17-6

Figure 17-7

4. Tap the appropriate Send button to send your recommendation by your preferred method.

Playing Games

The iPhone is super for playing games, with its bright screen, portable size, and ability to rotate the screen as you play and track your motions. You can download game apps from the App Store and play them on your device. You can also use the preinstalled Game Center app to help you find and buy games, add friends to play against, share, and track scores.

In this chapter, you get an overview of game playing on your iPhone, including opening a Game Center account, adding a friend, purchasing and downloading games, and playing basic games solo or against friends.

 Of course, you can also download games from the App Store and play them on your iPhone without having to use Game Center. What Game Center provides is a place where you can create a gaming profile, add a list of gaming friends, keep track of and share your scores and perks, and shop for games (and only games) in the App Store, which includes listings of top-rated games and game categories to choose from.

Get ready to . . .

Open an Account in Game Center

1. Using the Game Center app, you can search for and buy games, add friends with whom you can play those games, and keep records of your scores for posterity. From the Home screen, tap the Game Center icon. If you've never used Game Center, you're asked whether to allow *push notifications.* If you want to receive these notices, which alert you that your friends want to play a game with you, tap OK. You should, however, be aware that push notifications can drain your iPhone's battery.

2. On the Game Center opening screen, you're asked to sign in (see **Figure 18-1**). If you want to use Game Center with another Apple ID, tap Create New Apple ID and follow the onscreen instructions, which ask you to enter your birthdate, agree to terms, choose a security question and so forth; or enter your current account information and tap the Go button.

3. The screen that appears after you've signed in shows games you've downloaded, requests from other players, friends, and so on (see **Figure 18-2**). You can tap any of the floating balloons to get to these categories, or tap a button along the bottom of the screen.

 When you first register for Game Center, if you use an e-mail address other than the one associated with your Apple ID, you may have to create a new Apple ID and verify it by responding to an email message that's sent to your email address. See Chapter 3 for more about creating an Apple ID when opening an iTunes account.

Figure 18-1

Figure 18-2

Create a Profile

1. When you have an account with which you can sign in to Game Center, you're ready to specify some account settings. On the Home screen, tap Settings.

2. Tap Game Center, and in the dialog that appears (see **Figure 18-3**), if you don't want other players to be able to invite you to play games when Game Center is open, tap the Allow Invites switch to turn off the feature.

3. Tap the account name under Game Center Profile and sign in to the account, if requested to do so.

4. If you want your friends to be able to send you requests for playing games via email, check to see whether the Primary email address listed on this screen is the one you want them to use (see **Figure 18-4**). If not, tap Add Another Email and enter another email address.

Allow Invites option

Primary email address

Figure 18-3

Figure 18-4

5. In the Nickname field, enter the handle that you want to be known by when playing games.

6. Tap Allow Invites or Nearby Players; the latter allows players to find you and invite you to games.

7. If you want others to see your profile, including your real name, tap the Public Profile switch to turn on Public Profile (refer to **Figure 18-4**).

8. Tap Done when you're finished with the settings and then tap Game Center on the Home screen; You return to the Game Center Home screen, already signed in to your account with information displayed about friends, games, and gaming achievements (all at zero, initially).

 After you create an account and a profile, whenever you go to the Game Center, you log in by entering your email address and password and then tapping Sign In.

Add Friends

1. If you want to play Game Center games with others who have an Apple ID and an iPad, iPod touch, Mac running Mountain Lion, Mavericks, or Yosemite, or an iPhone, add them as friends so that you can invite them to play. From the Game Center Home screen, tap the Friends button at the bottom of the screen.

2. On the Friends page, tap the Add Friends button in the top-right corner (the button is shaped like a plus sign). Note that you also have the option of tapping the Requests button and tapping Add Friends from there.

3. Enter an email address in the To field (see **Figure 18-5**) and edit the invitation, if you like.

4. Tap the Send button. After your friend accepts your invitation, his or her name is listed on the Friends screen.

 Game Center contains a Friend Recommendations feature. Tap the Friends tab and then tap the A-Z button in the top-left corner. A Recommendations section appears above the list of your current friends. These are people who play the same or similar games, so if you like, try adding one or two as friends. You can tap the Points tab to view the points these folks have accumulated so that you can stay in your league.

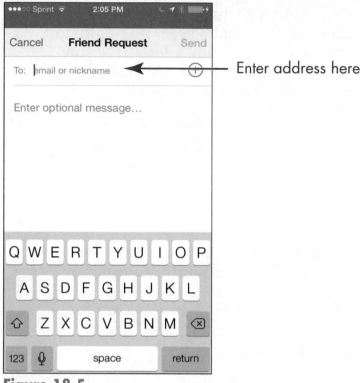

Enter address here

Figure 18-5

 You will probably also receive requests from friends who know you're on Game Center. When you get one of these email invitations, be sure that you know the person sending it before you accept; otherwise, you could be enabling a stranger to communicate with you.

 Although a few games have versions for both Mac and iOS users, the majority are either Mac-version only or iOS-version only — something to be aware of when you buy games.

Purchase and Download Games

1. Time to get some games to play! Open Game Center and sign in to your account.

2. Tap the Games button at the bottom of the screen, and under the Recommended category, tap Show More.

3. Scroll through the list of games that appears and tap one that appeals to you to display details about achievements and players (see **Figure 18-6**). Note that you can tap the Store button from here to go to the iTunes Store to view more games.

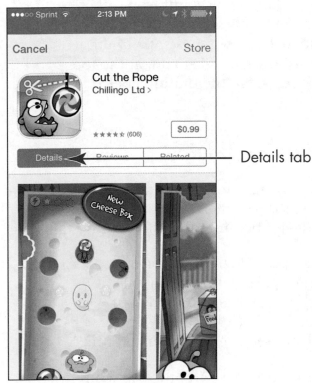 ———— Details tab

Figure 18-6

4. To buy a game, tap the button labeled with either the word *free* or the price (such as $1.99). Then tap the button again, which is now labeled Buy if it has a price or Install if it's free.

5. A dialog appears, asking for your Apple ID and password. Enter these and tap OK.

6. Another dialog appears, asking you to sign in. Follow the instructions on the next couple of screens to enter your password and verify your payment information if this is the first time you've signed in to your account from this device.

7. When the confirmation dialog appears, tap Buy or Install. The game downloads.

 If you've added friends to your account, you can go to the Friends screen and view games that your friends have downloaded. To purchase one of these games, just tap it in your friend's list and, at the top of the screen that appears, tap the button labeled with the game's price.

Master iPhone Game-Playing Basics

It's almost time to start playing games, but first let me give you an idea of iPhone's gaming strengths. For many reasons, iPhone is a good, smaller-screen gaming device because of the following strengths:

➡ **Fantastic-looking screen:** First, the iPhone screen offers bright colors for great gaming. In-Plane Switching (IPS) technology lets you hold your iPhone at almost any angle (it has a 178-degree viewing angle) and still see good color and contrast.

➡ **Faster processor:** The super-fast A8 processor chip in your iPhone 6 or 6 Plus is ideal for gaming.

➡ **Long battery life:** A device's long battery life (24 hours of talk with iPhone 6 and 14 with iPhone 6 Plus) means that you can tap energy from it for many hours of gaming fun.

➡ **Specialized game-playing features:** Some newer games have features that take full advantage of the iPhone's capabilities. For example, *Nova* (from Gameloft) features Multiple Target Acquisition, which lets you to target multiple bad guys in a single move to blow them out of the water with one shot. In *Real Racing Game* (Firemint), for example, you can look in your rearview mirror as you're racing to see what's coming up behind you, a feature made possible by the iPhone's large screen.

➡ **The M8 coprocessor:** iPhone contains a motion-detecting coprocessor that can interpret data from a sensor about your motion when walking or driving. Look for game and fitness app designers to begin to take advantage of that capability in the near future.

➡ **Great sound:** The built-in iPhone speaker is a powerful little item, but if you want an experience that's even more up close and personal, you can plug in a headphone, some speaker systems, or a microphone using the built-in jack.

In addition to the M8 motion coprocessor, most later iPhone models using iOS 8 have a built-in motion sensor — the *three-axis accelerometer* — as well as a gyroscope. These features provide lots of fun for people developing apps for the iPhone because they make the automatically rotating screen part of the gaming experience for you to enjoy. For example, a built-in compass reorients itself automatically as you switch your iPhone from landscape to portrait orientation. In some racing games, you can grab the iPhone as though it were a steering wheel and rotate the device to simulate the driving experience.

Play Against Yourself

Many games allow you to play a game all on your own. Each has different rules and goals, so you'll have to study a game's instructions and Help to learn how to play it, but here's some general information about these types of games:

➡ Often a game can be played in two modes: with others or in a *solitaire version*, in which you play yourself or the computer.

➡ Many games you may be familiar with in the offline world, such as *Carcassonne* or *Scrabble*, have online versions. For these, you already know the rules of play, so you simply need to figure out the execution. For example, in the online *Carcassonne* game, you tap to place a tile on the board, tap the placed tile to rotate it, and tap the check mark to complete your turn and reveal another tile.

➡ All the games you play on your own record your scores in Game Center so that you can track your progress.

Challenge Friends in Game Center

1. After you have added a friend and both of you have downloaded the same games, you can challenge your friends to beat your scores. Tap the Game Center app icon on the Home screen and sign in, if necessary.

2. Tap Friends. The Friend page (see **Figure 18-7**) appears.

3. Tap the name of the friend you want to challenge.

4. Tap the Game bubble and then tap the name of a game you have in common.

5. Tap the Achievements tab for your friend and then tap
one of her achievements. On the screen that appears (see
Figure 18-8) tap Send Challenge.

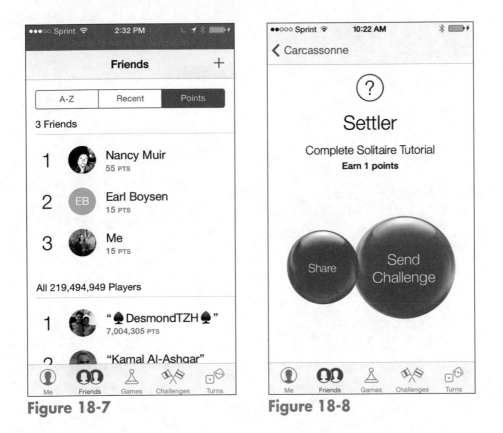

Figure 18-7   **Figure 18-8**

6. At this point, some games offer you an invitation to fill
out with a message and send to the friend. If you do that,
wait for your friend to respond, which he can do by tapping Accept or Decline on his device.

Finding Your Way with Maps

The Maps app has lots of useful functions. You can find directions with suggested alternative routes from one location to another. You can bookmark locations to return to them again. And the Maps app lets you get information about locations, such as phone numbers and web links to businesses. You can even add a location to your Contacts list or share a location link with your buddy using Mail, Messages, Twitter, or Facebook.

You're about to have some fun exploring Maps in this chapter.

Go to Your Current Location

1. iPhone can figure out where you are at any time and display your current location. From the Home screen, tap the Maps icon. Tap the Current Location button (the small arrow in the bottom-left corner; see **Figure 19-1**).

Figure 19-1

2. A map is displayed with your current location indicated (refer to **Figure 19-1**). Depending on your connection, Wi-Fi or 3G/4G (sometimes noted as LTE in Maps), a pulsating circle may appear around the pin, indicating the area surrounding your location based on cell tower triangulation. Your exact location can be anywhere within the area of the circle, and the location service is likely to be less accurate using a Wi-Fi connection than your phone's 3G or 4G connection.

3. Double-tap the screen to zoom in on your location. (Additional methods of zooming in and out are covered in the "Zoom In and Out" task, later in this chapter.)

 As mentioned previously, if you access maps via a Wi-Fi connection, your current location is a rough estimate based on a triangulation method. By using your 3G or 4G data connection, you access the global positioning system (GPS), which can more accurately pinpoint where you are. Still, if you type a starting location and an ending location to get directions, you can get pretty accurate results even with a Wi-Fi–connected iPhone.

Change Views

1. The Maps app offers three views: Standard, Satellite, and Hybrid. iPhone displays the Standard view (see the top-left image in **Figure 19-2**) by default the first time you open Maps. To change views, with Maps open, tap the Information button in the bottom-right of the screen (refer to **Figure 19-1**) to reveal the Maps menu, shown in **Figure 19-3.**

2. Tap the Satellite tab. The Satellite view (refer to the top-right image in **Figure 19-2**) appears.

3. Tap the Information button to reveal the menu again and then tap the Hybrid tab. In Hybrid view, Satellite view is displayed with street names superimposed (refer to the bottom-left image in **Figure 19-2**).

4. Finally, you can display a 3D effect on any view (refer to the bottom-right image in **Figure 19-2**) by tapping the Show 3D map option in the Maps menu.

On the Maps menu, you can also access a Traffic overlay feature. If you live in a large metropolitan area (this feature doesn't really work in small towns or rural settings), turn on this feature by tapping the Show Traffic option in the Maps menu. To help you navigate your rush-hour commute or trip to the mall, the traffic overlay shows red dashes on roads, indicating accidents or road closures; yellow dashes indicate traffic slowdowns.

Figure 19-2

Figure 19-3

 You can drop a pin to mark a location on a map that you can then return to. See the task "Drop a Pin," later in this chapter, for more about this topic.

 To print any displayed map to an AirPrint-compatible wireless printer, just tap the Share button on the Maps main screen and tap Print on the Sharing screen that appears.

Zoom In and Out

1. You'll appreciate the Zoom feature because it gives you the capability to zoom in and out to see more or less detailed maps and to move around a displayed map.

With a map displayed, double-tap with a single finger to zoom in (see **Figure 19-4**; the image on the left shows the map before zooming in, and the image on the right shows the map after zooming).

Figure 19-4

2. Double-tap with two fingers to zoom out, revealing less detail.

3. Place two fingers positioned together on the screen and move them apart to zoom in.

4. Place two fingers apart on the screen and then pinch them together to zoom out.

5. Press your finger to the screen and drag the map in any direction to move to an adjacent area.

 It can take a few moments for the map to redraw itself when you enlarge, reduce, or move around it, so be patient. Areas that are being redrawn look like blank grids but are filled in eventually. Also, if you're in Satellite or Hybrid view, zooming in may take some time; wait it out because the blurred image resolves itself.

Go to Another Location or a Favorite

1. With Maps open, tap in the Search field (see **Figure 19-5**); the keyboard opens. If you have displayed directions for a route, you won't see the Search field in the top of the screen; you may have to tap the Clear button on a directions screen to get back to the Search field.

2. Type a location, using a street address with city and state, a stored contact name, or a destination such as *Empire State Building* or *Detroit airport*. Maps may make suggestions as you type if it finds any logical matches. Tap the result you prefer. The location appears with a red pin inserted in it and an information bar with the location name with a Directions button to the left, an arrow to the right (see **Figure 19-6**). Tap the arrow, and more information is displayed. In some cases, the Street View icon is also displayed. Note that if several locations match your search term, several pins may be displayed in a suggestions list.

 Try asking for a type of business or location by zip code. For example, if you crave something with pepperoni in Spokane, WA, you might enter **99208 pizza**.

Search field

Directions button

Information bar

Figure 19-5

Figure 19-6

3. Tap Map in the top left corner, and you move back to the map where you can tap the screen and drag in any direction to move to a nearby location.

4. Tap the Share button (the symbol to the right of the Search field; refer to **Figure 19-6**), and then tap Add to Favorites. Tap Save in the screen that appears (modifying the location name first, if you like), and the location is saved to Favorites. Now when you tap in the Maps Search field, Favorites is the first result. Tap on Favorites to view and go to a favorite site.

5. To delete a location from Favorites, with Favorites displayed tap Edit, and tap the red circle to the left of any item and then tap Delete.

 If you enter a destination such as *Bronx Zoo*, you might want to also enter its city and state. Entering *Bronx Zoo* landed me in the Woodland Park Zoo in Tacoma because Maps looks for the closest match to your geographical location in a given category.

Drop a Pin

1. Pins are markers: A green pin marks a start location, a red pin marks a search result, and a blue pin (referred to as the *blue marker*) marks your iPhone's current location. If you drop a pin yourself, it appears in a lovely purple. Display a map that contains a spot where you want to drop a pin to help you find directions to or from that site.

2. If you need to, you can zoom in to a more detailed map to see a better view of the location you want to pin.

3. Press and hold your finger on the screen at the location where you want to place the pin. The pin appears, together with an information bar (refer to **Figure 19-6**).

4. Tap the arrow (refer to **Figure 19-6**) on the information bar to display details about the pin location (see **Figure 19-7**).

 If a location has associated reviews on sites such as the restaurant review site Yelp (www.yelp.com), you can display details about the location and scroll down to read the reviews.

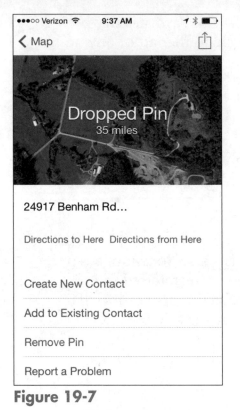

Figure 19-7

Find Directions

1. You can get directions in a couple of different ways. With at least one pin on your map in addition to your current location or a dropped pin, tap the Directions button in the top-left corner (an arrow bending to the right) and then tap Route. A line appears, showing the route between your current location and the closest pin (see **Figure 19-8**). Tap Clear to return to the Maps main screen.

2. You can also enter two locations to get directions from one to the other. Tap the Directions button in Maps and then tap in the Start field (see **Figure 19-9**). The keyboard appears.

Line indicating your route   Start field

Figure 19-8   **Figure 19-9**

3. Enter a different starting location.

4. Tap in the End field and enter a destination location. If you like, you can tap the Pedestrian or Public Transit buttons to get walking or bus/train routes rather than driving directions. Tap the Route button on the keyboard. The route between the two locations is displayed.

5. When a route is displayed, a bar appears along the bottom of the Maps screen (refer to **Figure 19-8**) with information about the distance and time it takes to travel between the two locations. Here's what you can do at this point:

- Tap the Directions button (it's the icon at the bottom of the screen that looks like a numbered list) to display written directions.

- Tap Start to begin turn-by-turn direction narration (see **Figure 19-10**).

Figure 19-10

6. If there are alternative routes, Maps notes the number of such routes in the Directions informational display and shows the routes on the map. Tap a route number to make it the active route.

View Information About a Location

1. You display the Information dialog for locations to get directions in previous tasks. In this task, you focus on the useful information displayed there. Go to a location and tap the pin.

2. On the information bar that appears above the pinned location, tap the arrow (refer to **Figure 19-6**).

3. In the Information dialog (refer to **Figure 19-7**), tap the web address listed in the Home Page field, which you can use to go the location's web page, if one is associated with it.

4. You can also press and hold either the Phone or Address field and use the Copy button (see **Figure 19-11**) to copy the phone number, for example, so that you can place it in a Notes document for future reference.

Copy button

Figure 19-11

5. Tap the Map button in the top-left corner to return to the map view.

 Rather than copy and paste information, you can easily save all information about a location in your Contacts address book. See the next task, "Add a Location to a New Contact," to find out how it's done.

Add a Location to a New Contact

1. Tap a pin to display the information bar.

2. Tap the arrow.

3. In the Information dialog that appears, tap Create New Contact or Add to Existing Contacts.

4. In the resulting dialog, scroll to the bottom and tap Create New Contact. The New Contact dialog appears (see **Figure 19-12**). (Note that if you choose Add to an Existing Contact here, you can choose a contact from your Contacts list to add the location information to).

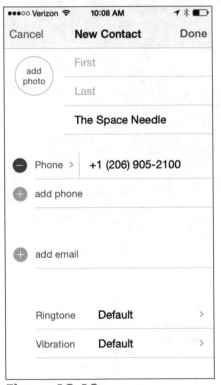

Figure 19-12

5. Whatever information was available about the location has already been entered. Enter any additional information you need, such as a name, phone number, or email address.

6. Tap Done. The information is stored in your Contacts address book.

Share Location Information

1. Tap a pin to display the information bar.

2. Tap the arrow to display more information.

3. In the Information dialog that appears, tap Share in the upper-right corner. In the dialog that appears (see **Figure 19-13**), you can choose to share via AirDrop, text message, Mail, Twitter, or Facebook. Tap Mail to see how this option works.

4. On the form that appears, use the onscreen keyboard to enter a recipient's information. (If you're using Facebook or Twitter, you enter recipient information as appropriate to the service you choose to use.)

5. Tap Send. A link to the location information in Google Maps is sent to your designated recipients.

 If you choose Twitter or Facebook in Step 3, you must have already installed and set up the Twitter or Facebook app and have a Twitter or Facebook account set up using iPhone Settings before sharing Maps content using those services. You also must have an account with these services to use them to share content.

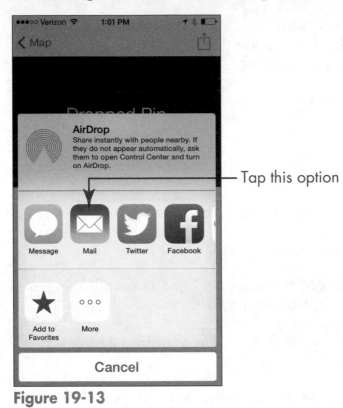

Figure 19-13

Get Turn-By-Turn Navigation Help

1. When you enter directions for a route and display that route (refer to **Figure 19-10**), you can then begin listening to turn-by-turn navigation instructions that can be helpful as you're driving. Tap the Start button at the bottom of the screen.

2. The narration begins and large text instructions are displayed. Continue driving according to the route until the next instruction is spoken.

3. For an overview of your route (as shown in **Figure 19-14**), at any time you can tap the screen and then tap the Overview button that appears in the upper-right corner.

Figure 19-14

To adjust the volume of the spoken navigation aid, tap Settings on the iPhone Home screen, tap Maps, and then adjust the Navigation Voice Volume settings to No Voice, Low, Normal Volume, or Loud Volume.

To change route information from miles to kilometers, go to Settings, tap Maps, and tap In Kilometers to change the setting.

Part V
Managing Your Life and Your iPhone

Visit http://www.dummies.com/extras/iphonefor seniors to find out how to set up the Stocks app to reflect your personal investment portfolio in Notification Center.

Getting in Step with Health

H ealth is a brand-new app that arrives with iOS 8. Essentially, Health is an aggregator for health and fitness data. You can input information about your height, weight, medications, nutrition, sleep quality, and more. You can then view that data in the Dashboard view.

In this chapter, I provide an overview of the Health app and how to get information into and out of it. I also give you a glimpse at some of the possible apps and health equipment that are slated to interact with Health to make it even more useful in months and years to come.

Get an Overview of the Health App

This has to be said right up front: Health is not ready for prime time. Although there are some apps and even equipment such as blood-pressure monitors that can connect with Health today, many more are under development.

Chapter

20

Get ready to . . .

That means that, at this point, you can mainly input data about your health and fitness manually and then view that information by displaying charts on the Dashboard or by viewing tables.

Health is divided into categories such as fitness, lab results, medication, nutrition, and sleep. When you tap the Health Data tab at the bottom of the Health Dashboard screen (see **Figure 20-1**), you see the categories listed in **Figure 20-2**. Each of these categories can have subtopics contained within it that you reach by tapping a main topic, such as Fitness.

Health Data tab

Figure 20-1
Figure 20-2

The Health app also has a medical record feature called Medical ID, which is covered in the next task.

Use Medical ID

One of the simplest and easiest to use features is Medical ID, where you can store your vital statistics. This could be useful if you're in an accident and emergency medical personnel need to access information about your blood type or allergies to medications, for example.

1. In the Health app, tap the Medical ID tab in the lower-right corner. You see an introduction to Medical ID.

2. Tap Create Medical ID.

3. In the screen that appears (see **Figure 20-3**), for items with a + sign surrounded by a green circle, tap the Add button to add a field.

4. For example, you might scroll down and tap Birthdate. When the screen in **Figure 20-4** appears, use the scrolling columns that appear at the bottom of the screen to set a birth date; for example, use your finger to scroll up and down on the month field till you find your birth month; then do the same thing to the day and year columns until your birth date is set.

5. Tap a field such as Medical Conditions to enter information using the onscreen keyboard that appears.

6. Tap Done to save your entries.

7. Tap Edit to add more fields or edit existing fields.

 On the Medical ID screen of Health is a note saying that if you choose to set the Show When Locked switch to On, emergency medical information will be available on the Lock screen.

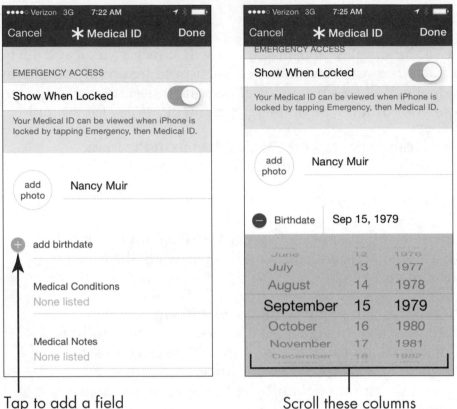

Tap to add a field
Figure 20-3

Scroll these columns
Figure 20-4

Discover How to Input Data

1. Because most entry of data in the Health app at this time is manual, knowing how to enter data is important. Tap the Health Data tab.

2. Tap a category such as Fitness.

3. Tap one of the subtopics shown in **Figure** 20-5, such as Weight.

4. On the screen shown in **Figure** 20-6, tap Add Data Point.

5. Enter data using the onscreen keypad.

6. Tap Add.

7. Tap Show All Data (see **Figure 20-6**) to see a table of
entries, including your most recent entry.

Tap a subtopic

Tap this to see data
you've entered

Figure 20-5   **Figure 20-6**

Tap this to enter data

 If you go into the Fitness Category in Health, you see
an item named Steps. According to reports, a Steps
counter is to be built into Health that can replace any
third-party pedometer app.

Import and Export Data

Because developers are just beginning to create or modify apps to work
with Health, it's hard to show you examples of importing or exporting

data. Additionally, different apps may send or receive data from Health using different interfaces and commands. But, theoretically, here's how it should work.

When you use an app that supports Health, those apps will request permission to update data. For example, a pedometer or activity tracker app might be able to upload data to Health, saving you the drudgery of manual entry. You can tap the Sources tab in Health to view supporting apps that you've downloaded and installed to your iPhone.

 See the next section for more about the types of apps that are coming down the pike that will work with Health.

In addition, you'll eventually be able to export data using apps such as Patient from the Mayo Clinic (see **Figure 20-7**) so that you can keep your physician informed about your progress or challenges.

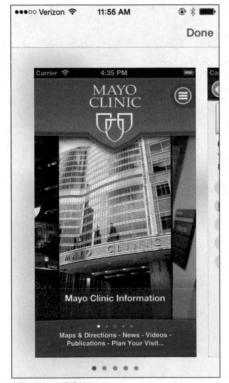

Figure 20-7

Explore Apps Health Can Work With

Health has nowhere to go but up in terms of available apps that are designed to interact with it to supply imported data such as calories consumed and steps walked. Here are some of the apps that are rumored to be in development that will work with the Health app:

➡ **Patient app by Mayo:** This app (refer to **Figure 20-7**), allows you to manage doctor appointments, get test results, and read the latest medical news. Apple is working with the Mayo Clinic to add support for the Health app.

➡ **MyChart app by Epic:** This app is very similar to Patient by Mayo, allowing you to handle appointments, get test results, and so on. This is another app that is available in the App Store today but that may take a while to become a full-fledged support tool for Health.

➡ **Nike+ apps by Nike:** Several Nike apps take advantage of iPhone and iPad's built-in accelerometer that allows the devices to handle and track movements. Track a variety of activities via Nike+ apps and integrate the data into Health.

➡ **Fitbit by Fitbit, Inc.:** FitBit wristbands measure activity, sleep, and calories. They have an app that works on the iPad and iPhone, which they are likely to connect to Health.

 Health is rumored to be getting its own pedometer, Steps, which will be built into the app, saving you the trouble of using a third-party pedometer app. Though Health is currently set up as a shell for entering fitness and health data in one central place, it may just gain its own tracking functionality.

Understand What Equipment Connects with Health

In the future, Health will connect with a variety of equipment to import data about your health and fitness. For example, LEConnect currently has treadmills that can send data on your gym accomplishments.

Withings produces a wireless blood pressure monitor and weight scales that already support iPhone apps. Omron also produces a blood-pressure monitor that can supply data wirelessly.

Glucose monitors are another likely piece of equipment for porting data to Health, though some health care proponents are concerned about this more hard-core health data and the chance for error when used with an app not produced by a medical manufacturer. In addition, some of these health monitors are subject to federal approval, and self-reporting to a medical provider is under debate because it can become part of the official patient records, so it will be interesting to see how far into this area Apple can go with its Health app.

Set Up the Dashboard

1. Open a category and then a topic, such as Carbohydrates under Nutrition.

2. Tap the Show on Dashboard switch to turn it on (see **Figure 20-8**).

3. Tap the Dashboard tab at the bottom of the screen to see the item included with other data graphs.

4. To change the increment of time displayed on Dashboard graphs, tap Day, Week, Month or Year (see **Figure 20-9**).

Tap this switch   Tap one of these

Figure 20-8   **Figure 20-9**

 To remove an item from the Dashboard, just tap the Health Data tab, tap the appropriate topic and then tap the subtopic, such as Height. Tap the Show on Dashboard switch to turn it off.

Keeping On Schedule with Calendar and Clock

*W*hether you're retired or still working, you have a busy life full of activities (even busier if you're retired, for some unfathomable reason). You may need a way to keep on top of all those activities and appointments. The Calendar app on your iPhone is a simple, elegant, electronic daybook that helps you do just that.

In addition to being able to enter events and view them in a list or by the day, week, or month, you can set up Calendar to send alerts to remind you of your obligations and search for events by keywords. You can even set up repeating events, such as birthdays, monthly get-togethers with the girls or guys, or weekly babysitting appointments with your grandchild. To help you coordinate calendars on multiple devices, you can also sync events with other calendar accounts. And by taking advantage of the new Family Sharing feature in iOS 8, you can create a Family calendar that everybody in your family can add events to.

Chapter 21

Another preinstalled app that can help you stay on schedule is Clock. Though simple to use, Clock helps you view the time in multiple locations, set alarms, check yourself with a stopwatch feature, and use a timer.

In this chapter, you master the simple procedures for getting around your calendar, creating a Family calendar, entering and editing events, setting up alerts, syncing, and searching. You also learn the simple ins and outs of using Clock.

View Your Calendar

1. Calendar offers several ways to view your schedule. Start by tapping the Calendar app icon on the Home screen to open it. Depending on what you last had open and the orientation in which you're holding your iPhone, you may see today's calendar, List view, the month, week, or an open event, or the Search screen with search results displayed.

2. Tap the Today button at the bottom of the screen to display Today's view (if it's not already displayed) and then tap the List View button to see all scheduled events for that day. The List view, shown in **Figure 21-1**, displays your daily appointments for every day in a list, with times listed on the left. Tap an event in the list to get more event details, or tap the Add button (the + symbol) to add an event.

 If you'd like to display events only from a particular calendar, such as the Birthday or US Holidays calendars, tap the Calendars button at the bottom of the List view and select a calendar to base the list on.

3. Tap Month; in the Monthly view, the List View button changes to a Combined View button. Tap this to show the month calendar at the top and a scrollable list of events at the bottom, as shown in **Figure 21-2**. Tap the button again to return to the Monthly view.

4. Tap a date in the Monthly calendar and you'll see that week at the top and the selected day's events below. Note that the Weekly view doesn't have the capability to display combined lists.

Tap to add an event   Combined View button

Figure 21-1

Figure 21-2

5. In the Monthly view, if the month displayed at the top of the screen is August, tap the arrow to its left to get a yearly display (see **Figure 21-3**) and then tap another month to display it. In the Yearly view, you see the calendar for the entire year with a red circle around today.

●●●○○ Verizon 🔵   10:15 AM   🔺 ✳ 🔋⚡

🔍   +

2014

JAN	FEB	MAR
1 2 3 4	1	1
5 6 7 8 9 10 11	2 3 4 5 6 7 8	2 3 4 5 6 7 8
12 13 14 15 16 17 18	9 10 11 12 13 14 15	9 10 11 12 13 14 15
19 20 21 22 23 24 25	16 17 18 19 20 21 22	16 17 18 19 20 21 22
26 27 28 29 30 31	23 24 25 26 27 28	23 24 25 26 27 28 29
		30 31

APR	MAY	JUN
1 2 3 4 5	1 2 3	1 2 3 4 5 6 7
6 7 8 9 10 11 12	4 5 6 7 8 9 10	8 9 10 11 12 13 14
13 14 15 16 17 18 19	11 12 13 14 15 16 17	15 16 17 18 19 20 21
20 21 22 23 24 25 26	18 19 20 21 22 23 24	22 23 24 25 26 27 28
27 28 29 30	25 26 27 28 29 30 31	29 30

JUL	AUG	SEP
1 2 3 4 5	1 2	1 2 3 4 5 6
6 7 8 9 10 11 12	3 4 5 6 7 8 9	7 8 9 10 11 12 13
13 14 15 16 17 **18** 19	10 11 12 13 14 15 16	14 15 16 17 18 19 20
20 21 22 23 24 25 26	17 18 19 20 21 22 23	21 22 23 24 25 26 27
27 28 29 30 31	24 25 26 27 28 29 30	28 29 30
	31	

OCT	NOV	DEC
1 2 3 4	1	1 2 3 4 5 6
5 6 7 8 9 10 11	2 3 4 5 6 7 8	7 8 9 10 11 12 13
12 13 14 15 16 17 18	9 10 11 12 13 14 15	14 15 16 17 18 19 20
19 20 21 22 23 24 25	16 17 18 19 20 21 22	21 22 23 24 25 26 27
26 27 28 29 30 31	23 24 25 26 27 28 29	28 29 30 31
	30	

Today   Calendars   Inbox

Figure 21-3

6. To move from one month to the next in Monthly view, you can also scroll up or down the screen with your finger.

7. To jump back to today, tap the Today button in the bottom-left corner of Calendar; the month containing the current day is displayed.

 To view any invitation that you accepted, which placed an event on your calendar, tap Inbox, and a list of invitations is displayed. Note that with iOS 8, you are able to use text within emails such as a date, flight number, or phone number to add an event to Calendar. Tap Done to return to the calendar.

 Note that if you're lucky enough to own an iPhone 6 Plus, because of its wider screen, when you hold it horizontally and you're in the Calendar app, you'll see more information on the screen than you'll see on any other iPhone. For example, in Monthly view, you'll see the entire month on the left and detailed information on events for the selected day.

Add Calendar Events

1. With any view displayed, tap the plus-symbol-shaped Add button (refer to **Figure 21-3**) to add an event. The Add Event dialog appears.

2. Enter a title for the event and, if you want, a location.

3. Tap the All-day switch to turn it on for an all-day event. Tap the Starts or Ends field; the scrolling setting for day, hour, and minute appears (see **Figure 21-4**).

●●●○○ Verizon 📶	10:21 AM	🚟 ✳ ▭✦	
Cancel	**New Event**	Add	
Title			
Location			
All-day		⬭	
Starts	July 18, 2014	10:00 AM	
Tue Jul 15	7	57	
Wed Jul 16	8	58	
Thu Jul 17	9	59	
Today	**10**	**00**	**AM**
Sat Jul 19	11	01	PM
Sun Jul 20	12	02	
Mon Jul 21	1	03	
Time Zone		Cupertino ⟩	
Ends		11:00 AM	

Figure 21-4

4. Place your finger on the date, hour, minute, or AM/PM column and move your finger to scroll up or down.

5. If you want to add notes, use your finger to scroll down in the Add Event dialog and tap in the Notes field. Type your note and then tap the Add button to save the event.

 You can edit any event at any time by simply tapping it in any view of your calendar and, when the details are displayed, tap Edit. The Edit dialog appears, offering the same settings as the Add Event dialog. Tap the Done button to save your changes or Cancel to return to your calendar without saving any changes.

Create Repeating Events

1. If you want an event to repeat, such as a weekly or monthly appointment, you can set a repeating event. With any view displayed, tap the Add button to add an event. The New Event dialog (refer to **Figure 21-4**) appears.

2. Enter a title and location for the event and set the start and end dates and times, as shown in the preceding task, "Add Calendar Events."

3. Scroll down the page if necessary and then tap the Repeat field; the Repeat dialog, shown in **Figure 21-5,** is displayed.

4. Tap a preset time interval: Every Day, Week, 2 Weeks, Month, or Year and you return to the New Event dialog. Tap Custom and make the appropriate settings if you want to set any other interval, such as every two months on the 6th of the month.

5. Tap Done. You return to the Calendar.

●●●○○ Verizon 📶   10:41 AM   ⌁ ✳ 🔋⚡

❮ New Event   **Repeat**

✓ Never

Every Day

Every Week

Every 2 Weeks

Every Month

Every Year

Custom   ❯

Figure 21-5

Other calendar programs may give you more control over repeating events; for example, you might be able to make a setting to repeat an event the fourth Tuesday of every month. If you want a more robust calendar feature, you might consider setting up your appointments in an application such as Outlook or the Mac version of Calendar and syncing them to iPhone. But if you want to create a simple repeating event in iPhone's Calendar app, simply add the first event on a Tuesday and make it repeat every week. Easy, huh?

Add Alerts

1. If you want your iPhone to alert you when an event is coming up, you can use the Alert feature. First tap the Settings icon on the Home screen and choose Sounds.

2. Scroll down to Calendar Alerts and tap it; then tap any Alert Tone, which causes iPhone to play the tone for you. When you've chosen the alert tone you want, tap Sounds to return to Sounds settings.

Press the Home button and then tap Calendar and create an event in your calendar or open an existing one for editing, as covered in earlier tasks in this chapter.

3. In the New Event (refer to **Figure 21-4**) or Edit dialog, tap the Alert field. The Event Alert dialog appears, as shown in **Figure 21-6**.

4. Tap any preset interval, from 5 Minutes to 2 Days Before or At Time of Event and tap New Event to return to the New Event dialog. (Remember that you can scroll down in the Event Alert dialog to see more options.)

5. Note that the Alert setting is shown in the New Event or Edit dialog (see **Figure 21-7**).

6. Tap Done in the Edit dialog or Add in the New Event dialog to save all settings.

 If you work for an organization that uses a Microsoft Exchange account, you can set up your iPhone to receive and respond to invitations from colleagues in your company. When somebody sends an invitation that you accept, it appears on your calendar. Check with your company network administrator (who will jump at the chance to get her hands on your iPhone)

or the *iPhone User Guide* to set up this feature if it sounds useful to you. Note that iCloud offers similar functionality to individuals.

Alert setting for an event

●●●○○ Verizon 📶 11:10 AM ⚡📶 🔋	●●●○○ Verizon 📶 11:12 AM ⚡📶 🔋
❮ New Event **Event Alert**	Cancel **New Event** Add

Figure 21-6 (left screen):

None

At time of event

5 minutes before

15 minutes before

30 minutes before

1 hour before

2 hours before

1 day before

2 days before

1 week before

Figure 21-7 (right screen):

Starts	July 28, 2014 10:00 AM
Ends	11:00 AM
Repeat	Daily >
End Repeat	Never >
Travel Time	None >
Calendar	● Work >
Invitees	None >
Alert	30 minutes before >
Second Alert	None >
Show As	Busy >

Figure 21-6   **Figure 21-7**

Create a Calendar Account

1. If you use a calendar available from an online service such as Yahoo! or Google, you can subscribe to that calendar to read events saved there on your iPhone. Note that you can only read, not edit, these events. Tap the Settings icon on the Home screen to get started.

2. Tap the Mail, Contacts, Calendars option. The Mail, Contacts, Calendars settings pane appears.

3. Tap Add Account. The Add Account options, shown in **Figure 21-8**, appear.

4. Tap an email choice, such as Outlook.com, Gmail, or Yahoo!. (Turn on Calendars for other accounts by tapping Other.)

5. In the screen that appears (see **Figure 21-9**), enter your email address and email account password.

Figure 21-8   **Figure 21-9**

6. Tap Next. iPhone verifies your address.

7. On the following screen (see **Figure 21-10**), tap the On/ Off switch for the Calendars field; your iPhone retrieves data from your calendar at the interval you have set to fetch data. Tap the back arrow in the top-left corner. To review these settings, tap the Fetch New Data option in the Mail, Contacts, Calendars dialog.

Set this to On, as it is here

Figure 21-10

8. In the Fetch New Data dialog that appears, be sure that the Push option's On/Off switch reads *On* and then scroll down to choose the option you prefer for how frequently data is pushed to your iPhone: every 15 minutes; every 30 minutes; hourly; or manually.

If you store birthdays for people in the Contacts app, by default the Calendar app then displays these when the day comes around so that you won't forget to pass on your congratulations! You can turn off this feature by tapping Calendars in the Calendar app and deselecting Birthdays.

 Though you can have calendar events pushed to you or synced from multiple email accounts, remember that having data pushed to your iPhone may drain your battery more quickly.

Use a Family Calendar

1. If you set up the new Family Sharing feature (see Chapter 12 for how to do this), you create a Family calendar that you can use to share family events with up to five other people. After you set up Family Sharing, you have to make sure that the Calendar Sharing feature is on. Tap Settings on the Home screen.

2. Tap iCloud and check that Family Sharing is set up in the second line of the dialog (see **Figure 21-11**) (it will say Family rather than Set Up Family Sharing if it has been set up).

3. Tap the switch for Calendars to turn it on if it's not already on.

4. Now tap the Home button and then tap Calendars. Tap the Calendars button at the bottom of the screen. Scroll down, and in the Calendars dialog that appears, make sure that Family is selected. Tap Done.

5. Now when you create a new event in the New Event dialog, tap Calendar and choose Family or Show All Calendars. The details of events contain a notation that an event is from the Family calendar.

Family Sharing is already set up

Figure 21-11

Delete an Event

1. When an upcoming luncheon or meeting is canceled, you should delete the appointment. With Calendar open, tap an event and then tap the Edit button in the dialog that appears (see **Figure 21-12**). The Edit dialog opens.

2. In the Edit dialog, tap the Delete Event button at the bottom (see **Figure 21-13**).

Tap this button

●●●○○ Verizon 🛜 11:28 AM 🖊 ⚭ 🔋	●●●○○ Verizon 🛜 11:28 AM 🖊 ⚭ 🔋
❮ Jul 28　**Event Details**　Edit	Cancel　**Edit Event**　Done
Mo and Mark 1945 White Pt. Rd.	Show As　Busy ❯
Monday, Jul 28, 2014 from 3 PM to 4 PM	Private　⬤
Calendar　● My Calendar ❯	URL
Alert　12 hours before ❯	Notes
Delete Event	Delete Event

Tap this button

Figure 21-12　　　　　　　**Figure 21-13**

3. If this is a repeating event, you have the option to delete this instance of the event or this and all future instances of the event (see **Figure 21-14**). Tap the button for the option you prefer. The event is deleted, and you return to Calendar view.

 If an event is moved but not canceled, you don't have to delete the old one and create a new one. Simply edit the existing event to change the day and time in the Event dialog.

Figure 21-14

Display Clock

1. Clock is a preinstalled app that resides on the Home screen along with other preinstalled apps such as Videos and Camera. Tap the Clock app to open it. Preset locations are displayed (see **Figure 21-15**).

2. You can add a clock for many (but not all) locations around the world. With Clock displayed, tap the Add button.

3. Tap a city on the list or tap a letter on the right side to display locations that begin with that letter (see **Figure 21-16**) and then tap a city. You can also tap in the Search field and begin to type a city name to find and tap a city. The clock appears in the last slot at the bottom.

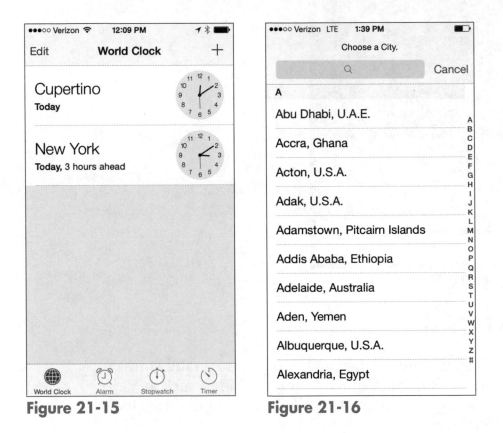

Figure 21-15   **Figure 21-16**

Delete a Clock

1. To remove a location, tap the Edit button in the top-left corner of the World Clock screen.

2. Tap the minus symbol next to a location and then tap Delete (see **Figure 21-17**).

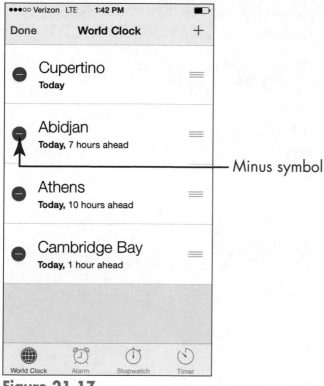

Minus symbol

Figure 21-17

Set an Alarm

1. With the Clock app displayed, tap the Alarm tab.

2. Tap the Add button. In the Add Alarm dialog shown in **Figure 21-18,** take any of the following actions, tapping Back after you make each setting to return to the Add Alarm dialog:

- Tap Repeat if you want the alarm to repeat at a regular interval, such as every Monday or every Sunday.

- Tap Sound to choose the tune the alarm will play.

- Tap the On/Off switch for Snooze if you want to use the Snooze feature.

- Tap Label if you want to name the alarm with a name such as "Take Pill" or "Call Helen."

●●●○○ Verizon LTE   1:43 PM   ■□

Cancel   **Add Alarm**   Save

10	40	
11	41	
12	42	AM
1	**43**	**PM**
2	44	
3	45	
4	46	

Repeat   Never >

Label   Alarm >

Sound   Marimba >

Snooze   ⬤

Figure 21-18

3. Place your finger on any of the three columns of sliding numbers at the top of the dialog and scroll to set the time you want the alarm to occur; then tap Save. The alarm appears on the calendar on the Alarm tab.

To delete an alarm, tap the Alarm tab and tap Edit. All alarms appear. Tap the red circle with a minus in it and then tap the Delete button.

Use Stopwatch and Timer

Sometimes life seems like a countdown or a ticking clock counting the minutes you've spent on a certain activity. You can use the Timer and Stopwatch tabs of the Clock app to do a countdown to a specific time, such as the moment when your chocolate chip cookies are done cooking or to time an activity such as a walk.

These two work very similarly: Tap the Stopwatch or Timer tab from Clock's World Clock screen and then tap the Start button. When you set the Timer, iPhone uses a sound to notify you when time's up. When you start the Stopwatch, you have to tap the Stop button when the activity is done (see **Figure 21-19**).

Tap this button

Figure 21-19

Stopwatch allows you to log intermediate timings, such as a lap in the pool or the periods of a timed game. With Stopwatch running, just tap the Lap button and the first interval of time is recorded. Tap Lap again to record a second interval, and so forth.

Working with Reminders and Notifications

Chapter 22

The Reminders app and the Notification Center features warm the hearts of those who need help remembering all the details of their lives.

Reminders is a kind of to-do list that lets you create tasks and set reminders so that you don't forget important commitments.

You can even be reminded to do things when you arrive at or leave a location. For example, you can set a reminder so that when your iPhone detects that you've left the location of your golf game, an alert reminds you to pick up your grandchildren, or when you arrive at your cabin, iPhone reminds you to turn on the water . . . you get the idea. Notifications allows you to review all the things you should be aware of in one place, such as mail messages, text messages, calendar appointments, and alerts.

If you occasionally need to escape all your obligations, try the Do Not Disturb feature. Turn this feature on, and you won't be bothered with alerts until you turn it off again.

In this chapter, you discover how to set up and view tasks in Reminders and how the Notification Center can centralize all your alerts in one easy-to-find place.

Create a Task in Reminders

1. Creating a task in Reminders is pretty darn simple. Tap Reminders on the Home screen.

2. On the screen that appears, tap a blank slot in the displayed list to add a task (see **Figure 22-1**). The onscreen keyboard appears.

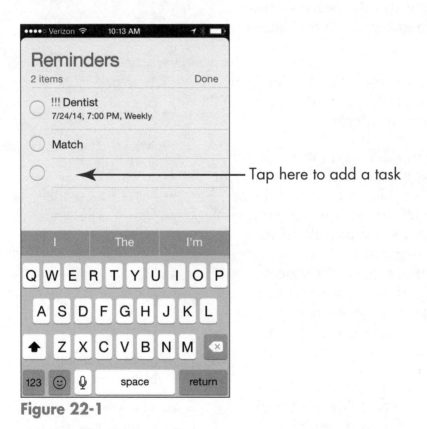

Figure 22-1

3. Enter a task name or description using the onscreen keyboard and then tap Done.

See the next task to discover how to add more specifics about an event for which you've created a reminder.

Edit Task Details

1. Tap a task and then tap the Details button (an *i* in a circle) that appears to the right of it to open the Details dialog shown in **Figure 22-2.** (Note that I deal with reminder settings in the following task.)

2. Tap a Priority: None, Low (!), Medium (!!), or High (!!!) from the choices that appear.

3. Tap Notes and enter any notes about the event (see **Figure 22-3**).

Enter notes here

Figure 22-2

Figure 22-3

4. Tap List and then tap which list you want the reminder saved to, such as your calendar, iCloud, Exchange, or a category of reminders that you've created. Tap Details to return to the Details screen.

5. Tap Done to save the task.

 With this version of the app, priority settings now display the associated number of exclamation points on a task in a list to remind you of its importance.

Schedule a Reminder by Time or Location

1. One of the major features of Reminders is to remind you of upcoming tasks. To set a reminder, tap a task and then tap the Details button that appears to the right of the task.

2. In the dialog that appears (refer to **Figure 22-2**), tap Remind Me on a Day to turn the feature on.

3. Tap the Alarm field that appears below this setting (see **Figure 22-4**) to display date settings.

4. Tap and flick the day, hour, and minutes fields to scroll to the date and time for the reminder.

5. Tap Remind Me at a Location and then tap the Location field. If prompted, tap OK to let Reminders use your current location.

6. Use the field labeled Search or Enter Address to find or enter a location. Tap Details to return to the task detail screen.

7. Tap Done to save the settings for the reminder.

Details   Done

Dentist

Remind me on a day ⬤

Alarm   Thu, 8/15/13, 11:00 AM ←— Tap here

Repeat   Never >

Remind me at a location ⬤

Priority   None   !   !!   !!!

List   Reminders >

Notes

Figure 22-4

If you want a task to repeat with associated reminders, tap the Repeat field in the Details dialog, and from the dialog that appears, tap Every Day, Week, 2 Weeks, Month, or Year (for those annual meetings or great holiday get-togethers with the gang). Tap Done to save the setting. To stop the task from repeating, tap the End Repeat field, tap End Repeat Date, and select a date from the scrolling calendar.

You have to be in range of a GPS signal for the location reminder to work properly.

Create a List

1. You can create your own lists of tasks to help you keep different parts of your life organized and even edit the tasks on the list in List view. Tap Reminders on the Home screen to open it. If a particular list other than Reminders is open, tap its name to return to the List view.

2. Tap New List (the + symbol) to display the New List form shown in **Figure 22-5**.

Enter a name for the list here

Figure 22-5

3. Enter a name for the list and tap a color; the list name will appear in that color in List view.

4. Tap Done to save the list. Tap a blank line to enter a task, or tap the list name to return to the List view.

Sync with Other Devices and Calendars

 Note that to make all these settings work, you should set up your default Calendar in the Mail, Contacts, Calendar settings and set up your iCloud account under Accounts to enable Reminders. (Your default Calendar account is also your default Reminders account.)

1. To determine which tasks are brought over from other calendars such as Outlook, tap the Settings button on the Home screen.

2. Tap iCloud. In the dialog that appears, be sure that Reminders is set to On.

3. Tap Settings to return to the main settings list, and then tap Reminders.

4. Tap the Sync button and then choose how far back to sync Reminders.

Mark as Complete or Delete a Reminder

1. You may want to mark a task as completed or just delete it entirely. With Reminders open and a list of tasks displayed, tap the check box to the left of a task to mark it as complete. When you tap Show Completed, the task now appears as completed and is removed from the Reminders category.

2. To delete more than one reminder, with the list of tasks displayed, tap Edit, and in the screen shown in **Figure 22-6**, tap the red minus icon to the left of any task.

Red minus icon

Figure 22-6

3. Tap Done. On the confirming dialog, tap Delete again.

Set Notification Types

Notification Center is a list of various alerts and scheduled events; it even provides information such as stock quotes that you can display by swiping down from the top of your iPhone screen. Notification Center is on by default, but you don't have to include every type of notification there if you don't want to; for example, you may never want to be notified of incoming messages but always want to have reminders listed here — it's up to you. Some Notification Center settings let you control what types of notifications are included:

1. Tap Settings and then tap Notifications.

2. In the settings that appear (see **Figure 22-7**), you see a list of items to be included in Notification Center and a list of items to not be included. For example, Messages and Reminders may be included, but alerts in game apps may not.

3. Tap any item, and in the settings that appear, set an item's switch (see **Figure 22-8**) to On or Off, to include or exclude it from Notification Center.

Items in Notification Center

Include in/Exclude from Notification Center

Figure 22-7

Figure 22-8

4. Tap an Alert Style to choose to have no alert, view a banner across the top of the screen, or have a boxed alert appear. If you choose Banner, it will appear and then disappear automatically. If you choose Alert, you have to take an action to dismiss the alert when it appears.

5. If you want to be able to view alerts when the Lock screen is displayed, turn on the Access on Lock Screen setting for Notifications view or Today view (if you want to see only today's notifications there).

6. Tap the Notifications button to return to the main Notifications settings screen. When you've finished making settings, press the Home button.

 You can drag across or tap an alert displayed in Notification Center to go to its source, such as the Reminders app, to see more details about it.

View Notification Center

After you've made settings for what should appear in Notification Center, you'll regularly want to take a look at those alerts and reminders.

1. From any screen, tap and hold the black Status bar on top and drag down to display Notification Center (see **Figure 22-9**).

2. Note that items are divided into lists by type — for example, you see items categorized as Reminders, Mail, Calendar, and so on.

3. To close Notification Center, swipe upward from the bottom of the screen.

 To determine what is displayed in Notification Center, see the previous task.

Today	Notifications

Stocks

DOW J	17,058.55	− 41.63
NASDAQ	4,426.64	− 5.51
S&P 500	1,973.41	− 4.81
AAPL	94.09	− 0.34
GOOG	589.76	− 5.32
YHOO	33.24	− 0.09

Show All…

Reminders

Groomer   11:00 AM

Figure 22-9

 You can display Stocks in Notification Center by tapping Settings from the Home screen, tapping Notifications, and making sure that Stocks is set to On.

View Notifications from the Lock Screen

You will receive notifications on your Lock screen when a message has been received or you've missed a phone call, for example. You have two possible ways to respond to notifications:

⟶ You don't have to unlock your phone; just tap and drag down from the Status bar to view Notification Center.

➡ Tap an item, and you're taken to the originating app, where you can take the appropriate action: Create and send a return message, initiate a phone call, or whatever.

Check Out Today and Notifications Tabs

iOS 8 provides two tabs in Notification Center for you to play with: Today and Notifications.

1. Swipe down from the top of the screen to display Notifications.

2. Tap Today to show all information about today, such as Reminders, weather, stock prices, Calendar items, and other items you've selected to display in Notification Center (see the previous task).

 You select what appears in the Today tab by tapping the Edit button at the bottom of the Today screen and then selecting which items you want to see: Today Summary, Traffic Conditions, Calendar, Stocks, Reminders, or Tomorrow Summary. Tap Done to return to the Notifications screen.

3. Tap the Notifications tab to see all notifications that you set up in the Settings app for Notification Center. You'll see only notifications that you haven't responded to or deleted in the Notifications tab or that you haven't viewed in their originating app.

Go to an App from Notification Center

You can easily jump from Notification Center to any app that caused an alert or reminder to appear.

1. Swipe down from the top of the screen to display Notification Center.

2. Tap any item category such as Reminders or Stocks; it opens in its originating app. If you tap a message such as an email, you can then reply to the message using the procedure described in Chapter 11.

Get Some Rest with Do Not Disturb

1. Do Not Disturb is a simple but useful setting you can use to stop any alerts, phone calls, text messages, and FaceTime calls from appearing or making a sound. You can make settings to allow calls from certain people or several repeat calls from the same person in a short time period to come through. (The assumption here is that such repeat calls may signal an emergency situation or urgent need to get through to you.) Tap Settings and then tap Do Not Disturb.

2. Set the Manual switch to On to turn the feature on.

3. In the other settings shown in **Figure 22-10,** do any of the following:

- Tap Scheduled to allow alerts during a specified time period to appear.

- Tap Allow Calls From and then from the next screen select Everyone, No One, Favorites, or Groups such as All Contacts.

- Tap Repeated Calls to allow a second call from the same person in a three-minute time period to come through.

4. Press the Home button to return to the Home screen.

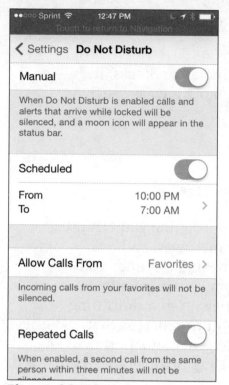

Figure 22-10

Making Notes

*N*otes is the included app that you can use to do everything from jotting down notes at meetings to keeping to-do lists. It isn't a robust word processor (such as Apple Pages or Microsoft Word) by any means, but for taking notes on the fly, jotting down shopping lists, or writing a few pages of your novel-in-progress while you sit and sip a cup of tea on your deck, it's a useful option.

In this chapter, you see how to enter and edit text in Notes and how to manage those notes by navigating among them, searching for content, or sharing or deleting them.

Open a Blank Note

1. To get started with Notes, tap the Notes app icon on the Home screen. If you've never used Notes, it opens with a blank notes list displayed. (If you have used Notes, it opens to the last note you were working on. If that's the case, you might want to jump to the next task to display a new, blank note.) You see the view shown in **Figure 23-1**.

2. Tap New. The onscreen keyboard, shown in **Figure 23-2**, appears.

Figure 23-1   **Figure 23-2**

3. Tap keys on the keyboard to enter text or, with Siri enabled, tap the Dictation key (the one with the microphone on it) to speak your text. If you want to enter numbers or symbols, tap the key labeled *123* on the keyboard (refer to **Figure 23-2**). The numeric keyboard, shown in **Figure 23-3**, appears. Whenever you want to return to the alphabetic keyboard, tap the key labeled *ABC*.

4. To capitalize a letter, tap the Shift key that looks like a bold, upward-facing arrow (refer to **Figure 23-2**) and then tap the letter. You can activate the Enable Caps Lock feature in the General Keyboard Settings so that you can then turn Caps Lock on by double-tapping the Shift key (this upward-pointing arrow is available only in the letter keyboard); tap the Shift key once again to turn the feature off.

Figure 23-3

5. When you want to start a new paragraph or a new item in a list, tap the Return key (refer to **Figure 23-2**).

6. To edit text, tap to the right of the text you want to edit and either use the Delete key (refer to **Figure 23-2**) to delete text to the left of the cursor or enter new text.

When you have the numerical keyboard displayed (refer to **Figure 23-3**), you can tap the key labeled #+= to access more symbols, such as the percentage sign or the euro symbol, or additional bracket styles.

No need to save a note — it's kept automatically until you delete it.

Create a New Note

1. With one note open, to create a new note, tap the Done button (refer to **Figure 23-3**) and then tap New.

2. A new, blank note appears (refer to **Figure 23-1**). Enter and edit text as described in the previous task.

Tap an individual note to display it. When you're displaying a note, you can tap the Back button to see a list of all notes you've created.

You can press on a spot on your Note and from the menu that appears, choose Select or Select All. Then you can tap the button labeled BIU to apply bold, italic, or underlined formatting.

Use Copy and Paste

1. The Notes app includes two essential editing tools that you're probably familiar with from using word processors: Copy and Paste. With a note displayed, press and hold your finger on a word. The toolbar shown in **Figure 23-4** appears.

2. Tap the Copy button.

Tap this button

Figure 23-4

3. Tap in the document where you want the text to go and then press and hold your finger on the screen.

4. On the toolbar that appears (see **Figure 23-5**), tap the Paste button. The copied text appears (see **Figure 23-6**).

If you want to select all text in a note to either delete or copy it, tap the Select All button on the toolbar shown in **Figure 23-4**. All text is selected, and then you use the Copy command on the toolbar shown previously in **Figure 23-4** to copy the selected text.

To extend a selection to adjacent words, press one of the little handles that extend from the selection and drag to the left, right, up, or down.

Tap this   Copied text

Figure 23-5   **Figure 23-6**

 To delete text, you can also choose text using the Select or Select All command and then tap the Delete key on the onscreen keyboard.

 To insert a photo into a note, tap and hold within the note until a menu appears. Tap Insert Photo and then select a photo from the Photos app to insert. Tap Choose.

Display the Notes List

1. Tap the Notes app icon on the Home screen to open Notes.

2. The notes list appears, as shown in **Figure 23-7.** This list is organized chronologically (the date isn't indicated if you created the note today). If an individual note is displayed, tap the Back button to go to the notes list.

●●●○○ Verizon 📶   2:23 PM   ❊ 🔋

New

Vacation To-do List	2:20 PM	>
Vacation To-do List: Jo...	8/17/13	>
Bread	11/11/12	>
Agenda	10/7/12	>
Special meeting	9/8/12	>
Party	9/8/12	>

Figure 23-7

3. Tap any note on the list to display it.

 Notes names your note, using the first line of text. If you want to rename a note, first display the note, tap at the start of the first line of text, and then enter a new title and press Return on the keyboard; the new first line is now reflected as the name of your note in the notes list.

Move Among Notes

1. Tap the Notes app icon on the Home screen to open Notes.

2. With the notes list displayed (see the previous task), tap a note to open it.

3. To move among notes, tap the Back button and tap another note in the list to open it.

 Because Notes lets you enter multiple notes with the same title — which can cause confusion — name your notes uniquely!

Search for a Note

1. You can search to locate a note that contains certain text. The Search feature lists only the notes that contain your search criteria, and it highlights only the first instance of the word or words you enter when you open a note. Tap the Notes app icon on the Home screen to open Notes.

2. Tap the Back button in the top-left corner to display the notes list if it isn't already displayed.

3. Press your finger on the middle of the screen and swipe down. The Search field appears above the notes list, as shown in **Figure 23-8**.

4. Tap in the Search field. The onscreen keyboard appears (see **Figure 23-9**).

Search field

Figure 23-8

Figure 23-9

5. Begin to enter the search term. All notes that contain matching words appear on the list, as shown in **Figure 23-10.**

6. Tap a note to display it with the first instance of the search term highlighted; locate other instances of the matching word the old-fashioned way — by skimming to find it.

Figure 23-10

Share a Note

1. If you want to share what you wrote with a friend or colleague, you can easily use AirDrop (iPhone 5 or later), Mail, or Message to send the contents of a note. With a note displayed, tap the Share button at the bottom of the screen and a popover appears, as shown in **Figure 23-11**.

2. Tap Mail or Message. In the email or message form that appears (see **Figure 23-12**), type one or more addresses in the appropriate fields. At least one address must appear in the To field.

3. If you need to make changes to the subject or message, tap in either area and make the changes.

Figure 23-11

Figure 23-12

4. Tap the Send button, and your email is sent.

5. To send via AirDrop to an AirDrop-enabled device (including Macs running OS X Yosemite with an AirDrop Finder window open) nearby, tap AirDrop in Step 2 and then tap the detected device to which you want to send the note.

 If you want to print a note, in Step 2, choose Print rather than Mail. Complete the Printer Options dialog by designating an AirPrint-enabled wireless printer (or shared printer on a network that you can access using AirPrint) and how many copies to print; then tap Print.

To cancel an email message and return to Notes without sending it, tap the Cancel button in the email form and then tap Delete Draft on the menu that appears. To leave a message but save a draft so that you can finish and send it later, tap Cancel and then tap Save Draft. The next time you tap the email button with the same note displayed in Notes, your draft appears.

Delete a Note

1. There's no sense in letting your notes list get cluttered, making it harder to find the ones you need. When you're done with a note, it's time to delete it. Tap Notes on the Home screen to open Notes.

2. Tap a note in the notes list to open it.

3. Tap the Trash Can button, shown in **Figure 23-13**.

4. Tap the Delete Note button that appears (see **Figure 23-14**). The note is deleted.

 An alternative method to delete a note is to swipe to the left on a note in the Notes list and then tap the Delete button that appears.

 Notes is a nice little application, but it's limited. It offers no formatting tools beyond Bold, Italic, and Underline, for example. So if you've made some notes and want to graduate to building a more robust document in a word processor, you have a couple of options. One way is to buy the Pages word-processor app for iPad, which costs about $10.00 and is free with a new iOS device, and copy your note (using the copy-and-paste feature discussed earlier in this chapter).

Alternatively, you can send the note to yourself in an email message or sync it to your computer. Open the email or note and copy and paste its text into a full-fledged word processor, and you're good to go.

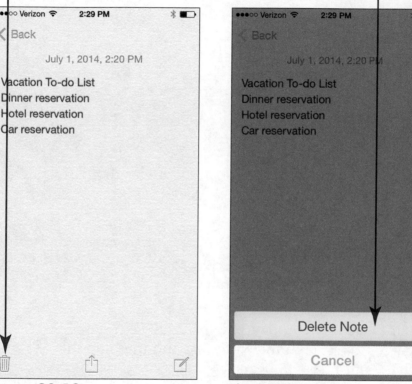

Figure 23-13

Figure 23-14

Troubleshooting and Maintaining Your iPhone

*i*Phones don't grow on trees — they cost a pretty penny. That's why you should learn how to take care of your iPhone and troubleshoot any problems it might have so that you get the most out of it.

In this chapter, I provide some advice about the care and maintenance of your iPhone, as well as tips about how to solve common problems, update iPhone system software, and even reset the iPhone if something goes seriously wrong. In case you lose your iPhone, I even tell you about a feature that helps you find it, activate it remotely, or even disable it if it has fallen into the wrong hands. Finally, you get information about backing up your iPhone settings and content using iCloud and the new fingerprint reader feature, Touch ID.

Keep the iPhone Screen Clean

If you've been playing with your iPhone, you know (despite Apple's claim that the iPhone has a fingerprint-resistant screen) that it's a fingerprint magnet. Here are some tips for cleaning your iPhone screen:

➤ **Use a dry, soft cloth.** You can get most fingerprints off with a dry, soft cloth such as the one you use to clean your eyeglasses or a cleaning tissue that's lint and chemical free. Or try products used to clean lenses in labs, such as Kimwipes or Kaydry, which you can get from several major retailers such as Amazon.

➤ **Use a slightly dampened soft cloth.** To get the surface even cleaner, very slightly dampen the soft cloth. Again, make sure that whatever cloth material you use is free of lint.

➤ **Remove the cables.** Turn off your iPhone and unplug any cables from it before cleaning the screen with a moistened cloth.

➤ **Avoid too much moisture.** Avoid getting too much moisture around the edges of the screen, where it can seep into the unit.

➤ **Don't use your fingers!** That's right, by using a stylus rather than your finger, you entirely avoid smearing oil from your skin or cheese from your pizza on the screen.

➤ **Never use household cleaners.** They can degrade the coating that keeps the iPhone screen from absorbing oil from your fingers.

 Do *not* use premoistened lens-cleaning tissues to clean your iPhone screen. Most brands of wipe contain alcohol, which can damage the screen's coating.

Protect Your Gadget with a Case

Your screen isn't the only element on the iPhone that can be damaged, so consider getting a case for it so that you can carry it around the house or around town safely. Besides providing a bit of padding if you drop the device, a case makes the iPhone less slippery in your hands, offering a better grip when working with it.

Several types of cases are available, but be sure to get one that will fit your model of iPhone. iPhone 5, 5s, and 5c have a 4" screen, which is larger than previous models, but iPhone 6 is 4.7" and iPhone 6 Plus is 5.5", and some models have slightly different thicknesses. You can choose covers from manufacturers such as Griffin (www.griffintechnology.com) that come in materials ranging from leather to silicone.

Cases range from a few dollars to $70 or more for leather (with some outrageously expensive designer cases costing upward of $500). Some provide a cover for the screen and back, and others protect only the back and sides. If you carry your iPhone around much, consider a case with a screen cover to provide better protection for the screen or use a screen overlay, such as InvisibleShield from Zagg (www.zagg.com). If you're the literary type, try the BookBook case that looks like a well-worn leather book.

Extend Your iPhone's Battery Life

The much-touted battery life of the iPhone is a wonderful feature (and much improved with iPhone 6 and 6 Plus), but you can do some things to extend it even further. Here are a few tips to consider:

⇒ **Keep tabs on remaining battery life.** You can estimate the amount of remaining battery life by looking at the Battery icon on the far-right end of the Status bar, at the top of your screen.

➡ **Use standard accessories to charge your iPhone most effectively.** When connected to a recent-model Mac or Windows computer for charging, the iPhone can slowly charge; however, the most effective way to charge your iPhone is to plug it into a wall outlet using the Lightning to USB Cable and the 10W USB power adapter that come with your iPhone.

➡ **Use a case with an external battery pack.** These cases are very handy when you're traveling or unable to reach an electrical outlet easily.

➡ **The fastest way to charge iPhone is to turn it off while charging it.**

➡ **The Battery icon on the Status bar indicates when the charging is complete.**

Your iPhone battery is sealed in the unit, so you can't replace it yourself the way you can with many laptops or other cellphones. If the battery is out of warranty, you have to fork over about $79 to have Apple install a new one. See the "Get Support" task, later in this chapter, to find out where to get a replacement battery.

Apple has introduced AppleCare+. For $99, you get two years of coverage, which even covers you if you drop or spill liquids on your iPhone (Apple covers up to two incidents of accidental damage). If your iPhone has to be replaced, it will cost you only $49, rather than the $250 it used to cost with garden-variety AppleCare. You can purchase AppleCare+ when you buy your iPhone or within 60 days of the date of purchase. See www.apple.com/support/products/iphone.html for more details.

Find Out What to Do with a Nonresponsive iPhone

If your iPhone goes dead on you, it's most likely a power issue, so the first thing to do is to plug the Lightning to USB Cable into the 10W USB power adapter, plug the 10W USB power adapter into a wall outlet, plug the other end of the cable into your iPhone, and charge the battery.

Another thing to try — if you believe that an app is hanging up the iPhone — is to press the Sleep/Wake button for a couple of seconds, and then press and hold the Home button. The app you were using should close.

You can always try the tried-and-true reboot procedure: On the iPhone, you press the Sleep/Wake button on top until the red slider appears. Drag the slider to the right to turn off your iPhone. After a few moments, press the Sleep/Wake button to boot up the little guy again.

If the situation seems drastic and none of these ideas works, try to reset your iPhone. To do this, press the Sleep/Wake button and the Home button at the same time until the Apple logo appears onscreen.

 If your phone has this problem often, try closing out some active apps that may be running in the background and using up too much memory. To do this, press the Home button twice and then from the screen showing active apps, tap and drag an app upward. Also check to see that you haven't loaded up your phone with too much content, such as videos, which could be slowing down the phone's performance.

Update the iOS Software

1. Apple occasionally updates the iPhone system software to fix problems or offer enhanced features. You should occasionally check for an updated version (say, every month). You can do so by hooking up your iPhone to a recognized computer (that is, a computer that you've used to sign into your Apple account before) with iTunes installed, but it's even easier to just update from your iPhone Settings, though it's a tad slower. Tap Settings from the Home screen.

2. Tap General and then tap Software Update (see Figure 24-1).

3. A message tells you whether your software is up-to-date; if it's not, the phone is updated to the latest software version.

●●●○○ Sprint 📶	6:15 AM	◢ ✳ ▬
❮ Settings	**General**	

About	❯
Software Update	❯	← Tap this option

Siri	❯
Spotlight Search	❯
Text Size	❯
Accessibility	❯

Usage	❯
Background App Refresh	❯

Figure 24-1

If you're having problems with your iPhone, you can use the Update feature to try to restore the current version of the software. Follow the preceding set of steps and then click the Restore button instead of the Update button in Step 3.

Restore the Sound

On the morning I wrote this chapter, as my husband puttered with our iPhone, its sound suddenly (and ironically) stopped working. We gave ourselves a quick course in sound recovery, so now I can share some tips with you. Make sure that

➡ **You haven't touched the volume control buttons on the side of your iPhone.** They're on the left side of the phone. Be sure not to touch the volume decrease button and inadvertently lower the sound to a point where you can't hear it.

➡ **You haven't flipped the Silent switch.** Moving the switch located on the left side above the volume buttons mutes sound on the iPhone.

➡ **The speaker isn't covered up.** It may be covered in a way that muffles the sound.

➡ **A headset isn't plugged in.** Sound doesn't play over the speaker and the headset at the same time.

➡ **The volume limit is set to Off.** You can set up the volume limit for the Music app to control how loudly your music can play (which is useful if you have teenagers around). Tap Settings on the Home screen and then, on the screen that displays, tap Music and then tap Volume Limit and use the slider that appears (see **Figure 24-2**) to set the volume limit.

When all else fails, reboot. This strategy worked for us — just press the Sleep/Wake button until the red slider appears. Press and drag the slider to the right. After the iPhone turns off, press the Sleep/Wake button again until the Apple logo appears, and you may find yourself back in business, sound-wise.

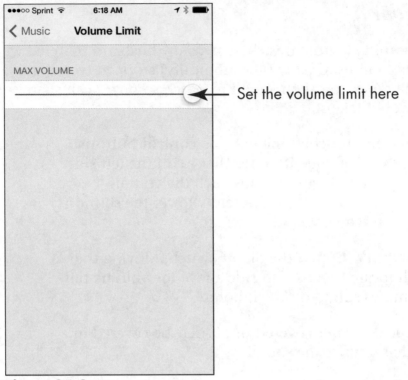

Set the volume limit here

Figure 24-2

Get Support

Every single new iPhone comes with a year's coverage for repair of the hardware and 90 days of free technical support. Apple is known for its helpful customer support, so if you're stuck, I definitely recommend that you try it. Here are a few options that you can explore for getting help:

→ **The Apple Store:** Go to your local Apple Store (if one is handy) to see what the folks there might know about your problem. Call first and make an appointment at the Genius Bar to be sure to get prompt service.

→ **The Apple support website:** It's at www.apple.com/support/iphone. You can find online manuals, discussion forums, and downloads, and you can use the Apple Expert feature to contact a live support person by phone.

⟹ **The *iPhone User Guide:*** You can download the free manual that is available through iBooks from the iBookstore.

⟹ **The Apple battery replacement service:** If you need repair or service for your battery, visit `www.apple.com/batteries/replacements.html`. Note that your warranty provides free battery replacement if the battery level dips below 50 percent and won't go any higher during the first year you own it. If you purchase the AppleCare+ service agreement, this is extended to two years.

 Apple recommends that you have your iPhone battery replaced only by an Apple Authorized Service Provider.

Find a Missing iPhone

You can take advantage of the Find My iPhone feature to pinpoint the location of your iPhone. This feature is extremely handy if you forget where you left your iPhone or someone steals it. Find My iPhone not only lets you track down the critter but also lets you wipe out the data contained in it if you have no way to get the iPhone back.

 If you're using Family Sharing, someone in your family can find your device and play a sound. This works even if the ringer on the iPhone is turned off. See Chapter 12 for more about Family Sharing.

Follow these steps to set up the Find My iPhone feature:

1. Tap Settings on the Home screen.

2. In Settings, in the left pane tap iCloud.

3. In the iCloud settings, tap Find My iPhone and then tap the On/Off switch for Find My iPhone to turn the feature on (see **Figure 24-3**).

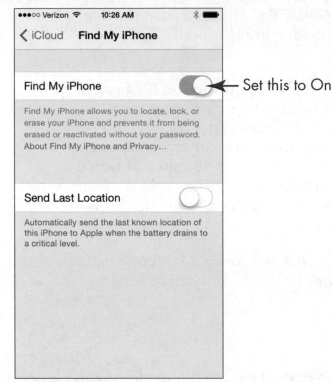

Figure 24-3

4. From now on, if your iPhone is lost or stolen, you can go to https://www.iCloud.com from your computer, iPad, or another iPhone and enter your ID and password.

5. In your computer's browser, the iCloud screen appears. Click the Find My iPhone button to display a map of its location and some helpful tools (see **Figure 24-4**).

6. Click the circle representing your phone, and then click the Information button (the small *i*). In the toolbar that appears, to wipe information from the iPhone, click the Erase iPhone button. To lock the iPhone from access by others, click the Lost Mode button. Tap Play Sound to have your phone play a sound that might help you locate it if you're in its vicinity.

Figure 24-4

 Erase iPhone will delete all data from your iPhone, including contact information and content such as music. However, even after you've erased your iPhone, it will display your phone number on the Lock screen along with a message so that any good Samaritan who finds it can contact you. If you've created an iTunes or iCloud backup, you can restore your phone's contents from those sources.

The Lost Mode feature allows you to send whomever has your iPhone a note saying how to return it to you. If you choose to play a sound, it plays for two minutes, helping you track down your phone in case you left it on top of the refrigerator or somebody holding your iPhone is within earshot.

Back Up to iCloud

You used to be able to back up your iPhone content using only iTunes, but since Apple's introduction of iCloud with iOS 5, you can back up via a Wi-Fi network to your iCloud storage. You get 5GB of storage (not including iTunes-bought music, iTunes Match and Photo Sharing content, video, apps, and e-books) for free or you can pay for increased storage (an additional 10GB for $20 per year, 20GB for $40 per year, or 50GB for $100 per year).

1. To perform a backup to iCloud, first set up an iCloud account (see Chapter 3 for details on creating an iCloud account) and then tap Settings from the Home screen.

2. In Settings, tap iCloud and then tap Backup (see **Figure 24-5**).

3. In the pane that appears (see **Figure 24-6**), tap the iCloud Backup switch to enable automatic backups. To perform a manual backup, tap Back Up Now. A progress bar shows how your backup is moving along.

 If you get your iPhone back after it wanders and you've erased it, just enter your Apple ID and password and you can reactivate it.

 You can also back up your iPhone using iTunes. This method actually saves more types of content than an iCloud backup, and if you have encryption turned on in iTunes, it can save your passwords as well. However, this method does require that you connect to a computer to perform the backup. Unfortunately, you can't back up to both iTunes and iCloud.

Tap this option

Set this to On

Figure 24-5

Figure 24-6

Checking Out iPhone 6 Plus Horizontally

The new iPhone 6 Plus has such a large, lovely screen that it can fit a lot of information, especially when you hold it horizontally. Several preinstalled apps take advantage of this. In this appendix, I run down how the Home screen and several preinstalled apps change when held horizontally on your iPhone 6 Plus.

Appendix A

Get ready to . . .

Get a New Slant on the Home Screen

The Home screen shifts to put the dock to the right side (see **Figure A-1**).

Figure A-1

See Messages Differently

Now you can see the Search screen and message threads together (see **Figure A-2**).

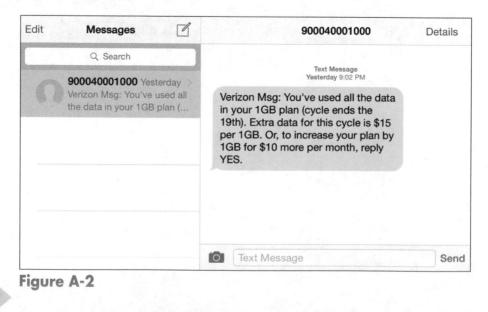

Figure A-2

Make a Date with Calendar

Get an event list side by side with your Day or Month calendar (see **Figure A-3**).

Figure A-3

See Weather Expand

Weather can now appear sideways, fitting loads of data on that single wide screen (see **Figure A-4**).

Figure A-4

Scope Out Clock

More clocks can fit across the iPhone 6 Plus horizontal screen (see **Figure A-5**.

Figure A-5

Make Notes

Both a notes list and the selected note's contents show here; note the expanded keyboard (see **Figure A-6**).

Figure A-6

Keep Reminders Visible

Reminders now turns sideways and shows both Search, categories, and individual reminders on one screen (see **Figure A-7**).

Figure A-7

Check Stocks Plus

Now you can view both a graph of trends and the latest prices together in horizontal orientation (see **Figure A-8**).

Figure A-8

Handle Settings

Now you can see both the main categories of settings and subsettings on one screen (see **Figure A-9**).

Settings		General	
✈ Airplane Mode	⬭		
📶 Wi-Fi	Not Connected	About	>
❋ Bluetooth	On	Software Update	>
⦿ Cellular			
◉ Personal Hotspot	Off	Siri	>
		Spotlight Search	>
▣ Notifications		Handoff & Suggested Apps	>
▤ Control Center			
☾ Do Not Disturb		Accessibility	>

Figure A-9

Index

• K •

• L •

About the Author

Nancy Muir is the author of over 100 books on technology and business topics. In addition to her writing work, Nancy runs a companion website for her iPad books in the For Dummies series at www.iPadMadeClear.com. She holds a certificate from The University of Washington in Distance Learning, and is Senior Editor for the website UnderstandingNano.com. Prior to her writing career, Nancy was a manager at several publishing companies and a training manager at Symantec.

Dedication

To Dennis Cohen, who helped me for many years on this book and who is very much missed.

Author's Acknowledgments

Thanks to Susan Christophersen, who led the team on this book and did a stellar job. Thanks also to Galen Gruman for his able work as technical editor. Last but never least, thanks to Kyle Looper, Acquisitions Editor, for giving me the opportunity to write this book.

Publisher's Acknowledgments

Acquisitions Editor: Kyle Looper

Project and Copy Editor: Susan Christophersen

Technical Editor: Galen Gruman

Editorial Assistant: Claire Johnson

Sr. Editorial Assistant: Cherie Case

Project Coordinator: Patrick Redmond

Cover Image: ©iStock.com/PamelaJoeMacFarlane

& Mac

or Dummies,
dition
-118-72306-7

e For Dummies,
dition
-118-69083-3

All-in-One
ummies, 4th Edition
-118-82210-4

Mavericks
ummies
-118-69188-5

ing & Social Media

ook For Dummies,
dition
-118-63312-0

Media Engagement
ummies
-118-53019-1

Press For Dummies,
dition
-118-79161-5

ess

Investing
ummies, 4th Edition
-118-37678-2

ting For Dummies,
dition
-470-90545-6

Personal Finance
For Dummies, 7th Edition
978-1-118-11785-9

QuickBooks 2014
For Dummies
978-1-118-72005-9

Small Business Marketing
Kit For Dummies,
3rd Edition
978-1-118-31183-7

Careers

Job Interviews
For Dummies, 4th Edition
978-1-118-11290-8

Job Searching with Social
Media For Dummies,
2nd Edition
978-1-118-67856-5

Personal Branding
For Dummies
978-1-118-11792-7

Resumes For Dummies,
6th Edition
978-0-470-87361-8

Starting an Etsy Business
For Dummies, 2nd Edition
978-1-118-59024-9

Diet & Nutrition

Belly Fat Diet For Dummies
978-1-118-34585-6

Mediterranean Diet
For Dummies
978-1-118-71525-3

Nutrition For Dummies,
5th Edition
978-0-470-93231-5

Digital Photography

Digital SLR Photography
All-in-One For Dummies,
2nd Edition
978-1-118-59082-9

Digital SLR Video &
Filmmaking For Dummies
978-1-118-36598-4

Photoshop Elements 12
For Dummies
978-1-118-72714-0

Gardening

Herb Gardening
For Dummies, 2nd Edition
978-0-470-61778-6

Gardening with Free-Range
Chickens For Dummies
978-1-118-54754-0

Health

Boosting Your Immunity
For Dummies
978-1-118-40200-9

Diabetes For Dummies,
4th Edition
978-1-118-29447-5

Living Paleo For Dummies
978-1-118-29405-5

Big Data

Big Data For Dummies
978-1-118-50422-2

Data Visualization
For Dummies
978-1-118-50289-1

Hadoop For Dummies
978-1-118-60755-8

**Language &
Foreign Language**

500 Spanish Verbs
For Dummies
978-1-118-02382-2

English Grammar
For Dummies, 2nd Edition
978-0-470-54664-2

French All-in-One
For Dummies
978-1-118-22815-9

German Essentials
For Dummies
978-1-118-18422-6

Italian For Dummies,
2nd Edition
978-1-118-00465-4

e Available in print and e-book formats.

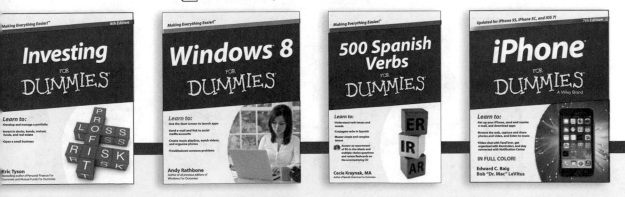

Available wherever books are sold. **For more information or to order direct visit www.dummies.com**

Math & Science

Algebra I For Dummies,
2nd Edition
978-0-470-55964-2

Anatomy and Physiology
For Dummies, 2nd Edition
978-0-470-92326-9

Astronomy For Dummies,
3rd Edition
978-1-118-37697-3

Biology For Dummies,
2nd Edition
978-0-470-59875-7

Chemistry For Dummies,
2nd Edition
978-1-118-00730-3

1001 Algebra II Practice
Problems For Dummies
978-1-118-44662-1

Microsoft Office

Excel 2013 For Dummies
978-1-118-51012-4

Office 2013 All-in-One
For Dummies
978-1-118-51636-2

PowerPoint 2013
For Dummies
978-1-118-50253-2

Word 2013 For Dummies
978-1-118-49123-2

Music

Blues Harmonica
For Dummies
978-1-118-25269-7

Guitar For Dummies,
3rd Edition
978-1-118-11554-1

iPod & iTunes
For Dummies, 10th Edition
978-1-118-50864-0

Programming

Beginning Programming
with C For Dummies
978-1-118-73763-7

Excel VBA Programming
For Dummies, 3rd Edition
978-1-118-49037-2

Java For Dummies,
6th Edition
978-1-118-40780-6

Religion & Inspiration

The Bible For Dummies
978-0-7645-5296-0

Buddhism For Dummies,
2nd Edition
978-1-118-02379-2

Catholicism For Dummies,
2nd Edition
978-1-118-07778-8

Self-Help & Relationships

Beating Sugar Addiction
For Dummies
978-1-118-54645-1

Meditation For Dummies,
3rd Edition
978-1-118-29144-3

Seniors

Laptops For Seniors
For Dummies, 3rd Edition
978-1-118-71105-7

Computers For Seniors
For Dummies, 3rd Edition
978-1-118-11553-4

iPad For Seniors
For Dummies, 6th Edition
978-1-118-72826-0

Social Security
For Dummies
978-1-118-20573-0

Smartphones & Tablets

Android Phones
For Dummies, 2nd Edition
978-1-118-72030-1

Nexus Tablets
For Dummies
978-1-118-77243-0

Samsung Galaxy S 4
For Dummies
978-1-118-64222-1

Samsung Galaxy Tabs
For Dummies
978-1-118-77294-2

Test Prep

ACT For Dummies,
5th Edition
978-1-118-01259-8

ASVAB For Dummies,
3rd Edition
978-0-470-63760-9

GRE For Dummies,
7th Edition
978-0-470-88921-3

Officer Candidate Test
For Dummies
978-0-470-59876-4

Physician's Assistant E
For Dummies
978-1-118-11556-5

Series 7 Exam For Dum
978-0-470-09932-2

Windows 8

Windows 8.1 All-in-On
For Dummies
978-1-118-82087-2

Windows 8.1 For Dum
978-1-118-82121-3

Windows 8.1 For Dum
Book + DVD Bundle
978-1-118-82107-7

e **Available in print and e-book formats.**

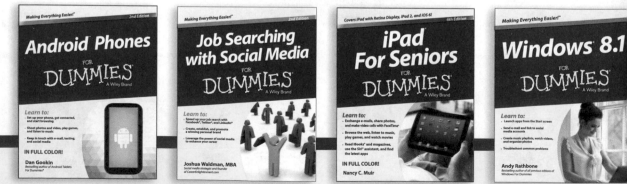

Available wherever books are sold. **For more information or to order direct visit www.dummies.com**

Take Dummies with you everywhere you go!

Whether you are excited about e-books, want more from the web, must have your mobile apps, or are swept up in social media, Dummies makes everything easier.

Visit Us

bit.ly/JE0O

Like Us

on.fb.me/1f1ThNu

Follow Us

bit.ly/ZDytkR

Watch Us

bit.ly/gbOQHn

Join Us

kd.in/1gurkMm

Pin Us

bit.ly/16caOLd

Circle Us

bit.ly/1aQTuDQ

Shop Us

bit.ly/4dEp9

Leverage the Power

For Dummies is the global leader in the reference category and one of the most trusted and highly regarded brands in the world. No longer just focused on books, customers now have access to the For Dummies content they need in the format they want. Let us help you develop a solution that will fit your brand and help you connect with your customers.

Advertising & Sponsorships

Connect with an engaged audience on a powerful multimedia site, and position your message alongside expert how-to content.

Targeted ads • Video • Email marketing • Microsites • Sweepstakes sponsorship

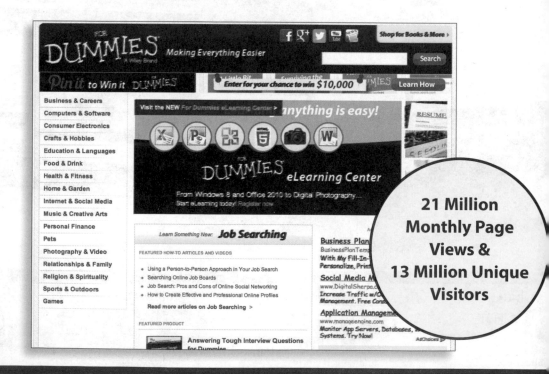